INFORMATION
COMPUTER
COMMUNICATIONS
POLICY

12 INFORMATION TECHNOLOGY AND ECONOMIC PROSPECTS

ORGANISATION FOR ECONOMIC CO-OPERATION AND DEVELOPMENT   PARIS 1987

Pursuant to article 1 of the Convention signed in Paris on 14th December, 1960, and which came into force on 30th September, 1961, the Organisation for Economic Co-operation and Development (OECD) shall promote policies designed:

- to achieve the highest sustainable economic growth and employment and a rising standard of living in Member countries, while maintaining financial stability, and thus to contribute to the development of the world economy;
- to contribute to sound economic expansion in Member as well as non-member countries in the process of economic development; and
- to contribute to the expansion of world trade on a multilateral, non-discriminatory basis in accordance with international obligations.

The original Member countries of the OECD are Austria, Belgium, Canada, Denmark, France, the Federal Republic of Germany, Greece, Iceland, Ireland, Italy, Luxembourg, the Netherlands, Norway, Portugal, Spain, Sweden, Switzerland, Turkey, the United Kingdom and the United States. The following countries acceded subsequently through accession at the dates hereafter: Japan (28th April, 1964), Finland (28th January, 1969), Australia (7th June, 1971) and New Zealand (29th May, 1973).

The Socialist Federal Republic of Yugoslavia takes part in some of the work of the OECD (agreement of 28th October, 1961).

Publié en français sous le titre:

TECHNOLOGIES DE L'INFORMATION
ET PERSPECTIVES ÉCONOMIQUES

© OECD, 1987
Application for permission to reproduce or translate
all or part of this publication should be made to:
Head of Publications Service, OECD
2, rue André-Pascal, 75775 PARIS CEDEX 16, France.

The effects of information technologies (IT) including micro-electronics, computers and robots are increasingly important in public debate. Opinions on these effects vary considerably, ranging from pessimism that robots and computers will cause technological mass unemployment, to sheer optimism that the market can handle the broader production and use of IT-based goods, systems and services, thus providing opportunities for economic and social progress.

The OECD's Committee for Information, Computer and Communications Policy has undertaken a broad work programme to assess these effects in a more objective way. This report is the result of this effort.

The report confirms the increasing importance of information technologies and its relevance for most economic parameters including output, international trade and employment. With regard to employment, this investigation shows that the vision of mass-unemployment resulting from office automation and computer/robot controlled factories is unrealistic. In fact, it seems most likely that past employment trends can be expected to continue with a rising share of employment in the service sector and a declining share of employment in manufacturing. This does not mean a de-industrialisation of OECD economies. It rather indicates that the firm of the future is an organism which increasingly processes, collects and transmits information rather than materials in the past.

Further production and use of IT do yield opportunities for quantitative and qualitative output growth and new employment opportunities. If these opportunities are to be fully exploited and are to contribute to maximal economic performance in OECD economies, there may well be a role for governments to play in the process of IT-induced change, both in facilitating the production and use of the new technologies and in creating a regulatory and market framework within which to reap their benefits to the fullest extent.

The report is in three parts -- Part I: Findings and Conclusions; Part II: Analytical Summary, and Part III: Supporting Research Papers. Those papers not included in this publication in their full version and the case studies listed in the ANNEX on page 221 are available on request as free documents from the OECD Secretariat.

This report is published under the responsibility of the Secretary General; the opinions expressed are those of the authors and do not necessarily reflect those of the Committee for Information, Computers and Communication Policy nor of the Organisation.

Also available

ICCP "INFORMATION, COMPUTER AND COMMUNICATION POLICY" Series

VENTURE CAPITAL IN INFORMATION TECHNOLOGY (March 1985)
(93 85 02 1) ISBN 92-64-12696-1   54 pages   £5.50   US$11.00   F55.00   DM25.00

No. 11 – TRENDS IN THE INFORMATION ECONOMY (September 1986)
(93 86 03 1) ISBN 92-64-12861-1   42 pages   £4.00   US$8.00   F40.00   DM19.00

No. 10 – COMPUTER RELATED CRIME: ANALYSIS OF LEGAL POLICY (August 1986)
(93 86 01 1) ISBN 92-64-12852-2   72 pages   £4.00   US$8.00   F40.00   DM20.00

No. 9 – SOFTWARE. An Emerging Industry (September 1985)
(93 85 04 1) ISBN 92-64-12755-0   204 pages   £12.00   US$24.00   F120.00   DM53.00

No. 8 – AN EXPLORATION OF LEGAL ISSUES IN INFORMATION AND COMMUNICATION TECHNOLOGIES (January 1984)
(93 83 03 1) ISBN 92-64-12527-2   136 pages   £7.00   US$14.00   F70.00   DM31.00

No. 7 – MICRO-ELECTRONICS, ROBOTICS AND JOBS (May 1983)
(93 82 02 1) ISBN 92-64-12384-9   266 pages   £12.50   US$25.00   F125.00   DM62.00

TELECOMMUNICATIONS. Pressures and Policies for Change (April 1983)
(93 83 02 1) ISBN 92-64-12428-4   142 pages   £6.90   US$14.00   F69.00   DM34.00

GUIDELINES ON THE PROTECTION OF PRIVACY AND TRANSBORDER FLOWS OF PERSONAL DATA (February 1981)
(93 81 01 1) ISBN 92-64-12155-0   42 pages   £1.60   US$4.00   F16.00   DM8.00

Prices charged at the OECD Bookshop.

THE OECD CATALOGUE OF PUBLICATIONS and supplements will be sent free of charge on request addressed either to OECD Publications Service, Sales and Distribution Division, 2, rue André-Pascal, 75775 PARIS CEDEX 16, or to the OECD Sales Agent in your country.

Published by North-Holland Publishing Co., Netherlands on behalf of the OECD:

CHANGING MARKET STRUCTURES IN TELECOMMUNICATIONS
ISBN 0-444-85327-3   276 pages   US$67.50 DFL.180.00

TRANSBORDER DATA FLOWS – PROCEEDINGS OF AN OECD CONFERENCE
ISBN 0-444-87700-2   US$74.00 DFL.200.00

Both publications available from: and in the USA and Canada from:

Elsevier Science Publishers   Elsevier Science Publishing Inc.
P.O. Box 211   P.O. Box 1663
1000 AE Amsterdam   Grand Central Station
The Netherlands   New York. New york
                                           United States 10163

TABLE OF CONTENTS

Part I

FINDINGS AND CONCLUSIONS

I.	OBJECTIVES	12
	1. Definition and Economic Scope of Information Technology	12
	2. The Analytical Framework	13
II.	THE RESULTS	14
	1. The Historical Approach	14
	2. The Biases	14
	3. On Substitution Possibilities	14
	4. IT and Demand	14
	5. The Case Studies	15
	6. Micro/Macro Issues	16
III.	POLICY ISSUES	19
	1. Use of IT	19
	2. Production of IT	20
	3. Institutional Flexibility	21
	4. Market Flexibility	21
IV.	LONGER TERM PROSPECTS	22
V.	IMPLICATIONS FOR FUTURE RESEARCH	24

Part II

ANALYTICAL SUMMARY

INTRODUCTION 26

I. AN HISTORICAL OVERVIEW 28

II. CASE STUDIES 36

    1. Engineering 36
    2. Office-Based Services 38
    3. Banking 39
    4. Clothing 40

    Conclusion 41

III. MICRO/MACRO ISSUES 43

IV. ALTERNATIVE CONCEPTUAL FRAMEWORKS 53

V. SOME POLICY ISSUES 55

    1. Diffusion Policy 56
    2. Education and Training 60
    3. Trade Policy 61
    4. Domestic Production Capabilities 62
    5. Institutional and Market Flexibility 64
    6. Market Power and Anti-Trust Policy 66

CONCLUSIONS 67

NOTES AND REFERENCES 67

Part III

RESEARCH PAPERS

I. INTRODUCTION 70

    An Analytical Framework for Analysing the Impact of Information
    Technologies on Economic Perspectives
    by Paul Stoneman, University of Warwick (<u>United Kingdom</u>) 70

	1. The Project	70
	2. Introduction	70
	3. A Neo-Classical Approach to the Impact of New Technology on Factor Demands	74
	4. Micro-Macro Issues	81
	5. The Speed of Diffusion	83
	6. A Guide to other Contributions	83
	7. Conclusion	84
	Notes and References	85
	Bibliography	86
	Annex: The Responsiveness of Labour Demand to Technological Change	88
II.	GENERAL STUDIES	94
	1. Information Technologies and the Rate and Direction of Technical Change by Pari Patel and Luc Soete (United Kingdom) -- Summary	94
	2. Information Technology, Capital Structure and the Nature of Technical Change in the Firm by Gunnar Eliasson (Sweden)	97
	Abstract	97
	I. From a Process Towards a Product-Based Industrial Technology	98
	II. The Modern Manufacturing Firm -- A Knowledge-Using and Information Processing Entity	99
	III. Finance and Organisation	103
	IV. Technical Change in a Modern Firm	108
	V. Why is Technical Change Shifting in a Capital Saving Direction?	117
	VI. Summing Up	120
	Notes and References	121
	Bibliography	122
III.	PRODUCTION AND DEMAND: ESTIMATION OF ELASTICITIES	125
	1. Evidence from Econometric Studies of Production Functions by R.A. Wilson (United Kingdom) -- Summary	125
	2. Prices, Costs and Elasticity of Demand by Derek Bosworth (United Kingdom)	127
	Summary	127
	I. Introduction	133
	II. Elasticities of Demand	136

	III.	Price Elasticities of Demand in International Trade .	142
	IV.	Technical Characteristics, Prices, Output and Employment	147
	V.	Quality and International Trade	152
	VI.	Monopoly Power	157
	VII.	Summary of Results: With Special Reference to Employment Effects	161
	VIII.	Conclusions and Suggestions for Future Research	166

Notes 167
Bibliography 168

IV. MICRO-MACRO ANALYSIS 174

1. Dynamic Micro-Macro Market Co-ordination and Technical Change
by Gunnar Eliasson (Sweden) -- Summary 174

2. Quantifying the Impact of Information Technology on Employment Using a Macroeconometric Model of the United Kingdom Economy
by J.D. Whitley and R.A. Wilson (United Kingdom) 176

I.	Introduction	176
II.	The Main Elements of the Debate	177
III.	A Macroeconomic Framework	181
IV.	The Macroeconomic Model	184
V.	The Base Run Simulation: Background Assumptions	186
VI.	The Base Run Simulation: Results	193
VII.	Alternative Simulations	204

Conclusions 211
Notes and References 214
Appendix -- Tables A1-3 215
Bibliography 219

ANNEX LIST OF CASE STUDIES 221

This report was prepared and directed by Dieter Kimbel of the Secretariat and by Paul Stoneman, Professor of Economics of Technical Change, Warwick University, United Kingdom.

The following researchers contributed individual research papers on which the content of Part I and II is based:

Richard Barras, Technical Change Centre, London, United Kingdom;
Derek Bosworth, Polytechnic of Central London, United Kingdom;
Gunnar Eliasson, The Industrial Institute for Economic and Social Research, Stockholm, Sweden;
Pari Patel and Luc Soete, SPRU, Sussex University, United Kingdom;
Pascal Petit, CEPREMAP, Paris, France;
Howard Rush and Kurt Hoffman, Brighton Polytechnic, Brighton, and SPRU, University of Sussex, respectively, United Kingdom;
Robert W. Wilson, University of Warwick, Warwick, United Kingdom.

Alf Modvar from the Norwegian Ministry of Cultural and Scientific Affairs chaired the expert meetings and provided the liaison between the experts and the ICCP Committee.

Friedrich Klau from the OECD Department of Economics and Statistics also provided advice and participated in the various stages of this project.

Part I

FINDINGS AND CONCLUSIONS

I. OBJECTIVES

This project investigates the relationships between information technology (IT) and IT-based innovations on the one hand and, on the other hand, industry and economy wide patterns of output, employment and trade in the medium term future (5-10 years).

Specific questions addressed include:

1. Which are the industries or sectors which will grow, or at least which factors distinguish growth sectors from declining sectors?

2. What will happen to factor demands, especially the demand for labour?

3. To what extent will IT affect the international division of labour?

4. What barriers exist that affect the use of IT based systems and techniques?

In addition, a number of policy issues are discussed.

1. Definition and Economic Scope of Information Technology (IT)

The term "information technology" is used throughout this study to cover technologies used in the collection, processing and transmission of information. It includes micro-electronic and opto-electronic based technologies incorporated in many products and production processes and increasingly affecting the service sector. It covers inter alia, computers, electronic office equipment, telecommunications, industrial robots and computer controlled machines, electronic components and software products. Three particular characteristics of IT innovations in the recent past are noteworthy:

-- miniaturisation;

-- expanded capabilities;

-- reduced costs.

It is argued by some experts that some 80 per cent of today's (and medium-term future) technological advances are IT-based. Industry estimates also indicate that to date, diffusion of recent IT based innovations has been limited (perhaps to 10 to 20 per cent of potential), which suggests that there will be a much larger impact of IT based innovations in the future.

2. The Analytical Framework

Over the last 10 years, there has been a dramatic outpouring of work on the impact of new technologies (a recent bibliography indicates in excess of 2 500 publications on this topic since 1977). Much of this work has been case study based. Such analyses can however often be considered anecdotal rather than capable of generalisation. In the project therefore, a more general analytical framework is adopted. This approach has the advantage of highlighting crucial aspects of a firm's, industry's, market's or technology's character that affect the impact of a technological advance and at the same time enables one to provide a consistent interpretation of case study evidence prior to making generalisations. The limitations of the particular framework adopted are discussed and to the extent that it is possible, overcome by ad-hoc supplementation.

In particular, the framework stresses as important:

a) the extent to which technological advance saves one factor at the expense of another (capital or labour saving bias);

b) the extent to which one factor can be substituted for another (capital/labour substitution);

c) the rate of technological advance (evolutionary/revolutionary);

d) the impact of IT, and price and quality changes on demand (the elasticity of demand).

Considerations of differences in these factors across industries, for example, can indicate whether an industry is likely to grow or decline and whether its employment is likely to rise or fall. This approach is supplemented -- to consider economy-wide factors -- with work at the macro-economic level.

The project proceeds by considering estimates of the above characteristics taken from (historical) econometric studies. To provide a more forward looking input this is supplemented by case studies loosely guided by the analytical framework. The macro-economic issues are then approached by the use of large scale macro-economic models. A number of measurement problems had to be faced in these exercises prior to the drawing of conclusions.

II. THE RESULTS

1. The Historical Approach

The investigations start with an examination of some post war movements in output and capital and labour inputs at a high level of aggregation. The results generated for the years 1955-1982 report increasing labour productivity (increased output per unit of labour input), declining capital productivity (decreased output per unit of capital input), and increased capital/labour ratios. Suggestions that these trends could be used to support an argument that much of the currently high level of unemployment could be attributed to technical change or that capital shortage problems may inhibit a move back to full employment were considered unduly speculative.

2. The Biases

The interpretation of these figures as indicating that recent technical advances have been of a labour saving nature is not considered to be appropriate (or eventually important), especially in the light of the results of Eliasson (cf. Part III.II.2. of this volume). There it is argued that the increasing intensity of "soft-capital", i.e. information processing, R&D and marketing in the modern firm, makes studies like the above based on "hard-capital", misleading. Consideration of this new dimension suggests a capital saving and not labour saving bias.

3. On Substitution Possibilities

Further evidence on biases, substitution possibilities and rates of technical change is provided by a survey of past econometric work on production functions. This extensive work leads to the suggestion that the impact of technical change is independent of its bias, but depends crucially on whether the elasticity of demand for the products of the industry into which the new technology is being introduced is sufficiently large.

4. IT and Demand

As new technology is introduced, production costs will fall or product quality will be enhanced. If demand is sufficiently responsive to improved quality, or prices fall as costs fall, and demand is sufficiently responsive to price, output will increase. If this output increase is sufficiently great when costs fall, it can more than offset reduced input requirements per unit of output and thus increase total input demand. If demand increases when product quality increases, this can also offset any changes in input per unit of output. The survey of demand elasticities (Part III. III.) reveals that little is known about reactions to quality changes and one can therefore say very little about their impact. This is a reflection of one weakness of the project -- it has not been possible to adequately deal with issues of product innovation. There are, however, good grounds for arguing that if IT enhances the quality of a product (by for example adding "intelligence") then at a given price demand for that product would increase. This is supported by market research findings showing that electronics in general increases consumer appeal.

There is more extensive evidence on the effect of price change, and the work suggests that, although some industries have elasticities of demand that are low compared to what is necessary to indicate increased employment, others, especially in consumer durables manufacturing and perhaps in services, do exceed the necessary limits. These estimates, as is appropriate, take account of the international nature of most OECD economies and thus some of the "compensation" being generated in one economy could be at the expense of another non-innovating economy. It is further argued that as the elasticity estimates are presented at an industry level, changes at the industry level might hide changes in the opposite direction at the level of the firm or at some sub-sectoral level. It has not been possible to answer the question, whether world demand as a whole will increase sufficiently to compensate for the increase in productivity (see also Part III.I. of this volume).

It is also argued that for these price effects to operate, it is necessary that prices fall as costs fall, but monopolisation in production and/or trade barriers may inhibit this process. With this reservation, it is considered that industries with low elasticities will tend to show low output growth and reduced demand for inputs as technology advances. This applies to, for example, food, drink, tobacco and clothing. Industries with high elasticities tend to be in manufacturing -- especially durables -- and services. These will tend to show the higher growth rates of output and employment. In addition, the responsiveness of industrial demands to income growth in the economy as a whole is expected to reinforce these effects (in particular a high income responsiveness of demand for services is found).

5. The Case Studies

Four case studies are reported upon in this project (see ANNEX, page 221), two in manufacturing in engineering and clothing and two in the service industries on office-based services in general and banking in particular. Although guided by the analytical framework, this analysis did not exclude the exploration of other analytical approaches. Each of these studies details the kinds of technologies that will be introduced into these industries over the next ten years discussing their associated biases, etc. A common theme running through each of the studies is that the actual diffusion of the technologies will be slow rather than fast. The reasons for this tend to be related to factors such as:

-- skill and/or training issues;

-- information and awareness problems;

-- technical incompatibilities;

-- regulation barriers;

-- profitability factors.

Largely on account of this, these industries will tend to be subject to slow, evolutionary rather than revolutionary change.

An advantage of case studies is that product innovation can be considered more explicitly than in the historical analysis of time series. In all the industries product innovation is considered to be important, but perhaps in services more than in any other industry the generation and marketing of new products is seen as essential if the new IT technologies are to realise their full potential.

Each study raises its own important issues. In the study of clothing for example, the question is raised as to whether technological advance is a better way to maintain employment and output than protection. In engineering, the complex nature, or systems-based nature of new information technology is highlighted as a factor behind the expected slow diffusion of the technology. In addition, the study stresses the differential expected impact from product as opposed to process innovation.

Overall, the studies suggest that the future for each of these industries is likely to reflect a continuation, rather than reversal or reinforcement, of past trends. One might thus expect to see employment share decreasing in the manufacturing sector and increasing in the service sector. The growth in the service sector will namely be based on services for the production, use and marketing of IT based goods and processes (high-tech services). This suggests the appearance of many new products in the market in every sector. Perhaps the major difference between manufacturing and services is that the manufacturing sector tends to be traded more intensively than the products in the service sector (although there are tendencies towards greater trade in services). This suggests that in the manufacturing sector to a greater extent than in services, it is rates of advance relative to international competitors that will determine an individual country's output and employment level. However, this consideration will also be relevant to those service industries that are particularly intensively traded.

6. Micro/Macro Issues

Modern economies are complex; there are many intersectoral connections and numerous linkages between markets. These interconnections are in fact subject to change as new technology is introduced. However, the existence of these linkages means that industry-level analyses can only give part of the answer to the questions posed above. To reinforce the earlier analysis, two large scale macro-econometric models were subject to a number of simulation exercises to produce answers to a number of distinct questions:

i) What is the "most likely" path for industry and economy wide levels of output and employment as new information technology is introduced?

ii) Does the bias in technological change matter?

iii) How important is wage and price flexibility?

iv) What impacts would an increase in the diffusion speed in one country generate?

No IT Based Mass Unemployment

On the first of these questions the results reflected optimism. There seems to be little indication that the spectre of mass unemployment resulting from the broad production and application of IT is a realistic forecast. In fact, the continuation of past trends with a rising service sector share of employment and a declining manufacturing share seem most likely. The results generated do not give any indication that on the most likely path new IT will dramatically reduce the current high levels of unemployment in OECD economies.

No Bias

On the second question, the general irrelevance for employment of the bias in technical change is confirmed, although it is argued that a different capital saving bias will mean a different size for capital producing relative to capital using sectors.

"Intermediate" Flexibility

The wage/price flexibility issue is pursued, for it is often argued that if wages and prices are sufficiently flexible there will never be unemployment. This is confirmed to some extent in the models, but the finding is not that perfect flexibility is required -- the work suggests that too much flexibility can mean overshooting -- the conclusion is that some intermediate flexibility is best.

Faster Diffusion and Product Innovation

On the final issue of diffusion speeds, it is often argued that faster diffusion in one country can generate gains in international competitiveness that lead to increased employment and thus faster diffusion is to be encouraged. The results generated in the models suggest that this argument is largely correct when manufacturing is discussed -- although one should note that the extra jobs generated by the diffusion tend to be located in the service sector. When faster diffusion in the service sector is modelled, the results are less optimistic. As the service sector does not trade as extensively as manufacturing it has limited potential for increasing output in reaction to improvements in competitiveness. In fact, the simulation exercises reveal greater unemployment -- across all sectors of the economy -- as diffusion speeds increase in services. To counteract this, it is argued that the effect could be overcome if the faster diffusion generates faster product innovation which will in turn stimulate demand, output and employment.

IT based innovations enable many product and process improvements to be made. The potential of IT to impact on the standard of living of a country and its people is enormous. It has however been feared that as the potential is realised, society will bear heavy transition costs. Of course, any dynamic process involves some transition costs. The changes likely to be induced by IT or made possible by the diffusion of IT involve adjustments which, though they may be costly, are part of the price that society pays for the benefits of technological innovations, that is, higher real incomes and increasing standards of living. In the case of information technology based innovations, it has often been argued that these costs may be unacceptably high. The results of this project allay many, but not all, of these fears while at the same time confirming the gains to be made. Economies are always changing, but the underlying theme in the results is that although IT advances are perhaps different from what has been experienced in the past, their impact is likely to be evolutionary rather than revolutionary. Partly this is due to the expected slow diffusion of these new technologies, but largely it is precisely because economies are large and complex, adaptable, flexible institutions that are able to accommodate extensive shocks. This is not to argue that economies will not change. This shows that in the OECD economies, some industries such as food, drink, tobacco or clothing will decline in terms of employment if not output. Other industries such as services and consumer durables are likely to experience increases in employment and output. These and other similar results show a future experiencing change of a kind that reflects a continuation of past trends rather than a dramatic change in direction.

III. POLICY ISSUES

A number of important policy issues are identified. Six particular issues are singled out for consideration:

-- diffusion policies;

-- training and education;

-- trade policy;

-- domestic production capabilities, including R&D policy;

-- institutional and market flexibility;

-- anti-trust and/or competition policy.

Although the design of particular policy instruments is not discussed, the rationale behind and objectives of the different policy initiatives in the light of the findings of this report are explored. Basically, there are two main underlying themes:

-- The first theme refers to the production and use of IT and IT based advances. It covers issues such as R&D policy and diffusion policy.

-- The second theme refers to improved arrangements for ensuring that the largest benefit from the use of IT is realised and covers issues (such as institutional and market flexibility and anti-trust policy) which influence allocation mechanisms in product and factor markets.

1. Use of IT

Two aspects of diffusion policy are considered, the first being when will faster diffusion be beneficial and thus when might policy initiatives be appropriate. It is argued that faster diffusion might not always be desirable, although it is difficult to be precise as to whether any of the OECD economies are currently in a position where diffusion cannot usefully be speeded up. The second issue concerns the barriers to faster diffusion and thus indicates areas where policy eventually can be targeted. Information deficiencies are considered a valid target of policies. Appropriate regulatory and institutional environments are seen in a similar light. There is an underlying line of argument, however, that policies aimed at making IT more attractive through subsidy might not be an appropriate course to pursue largely because this may extend the use of technology into areas where the benefits from use are less than the costs. Perhaps more than any of these other issues, the barriers to faster diffusion through skill shortage is considered to be important but difficult to overcome, basically because forecasting future skill and education requirements is fraught with problems. The prime objective of any policy in this area should be aimed at providing a labour force with maximum skill and educational flexibility. An appropriate policy may also help minimise the transition costs of introducing IT (see above, Chapter II).

One advantage from faster diffusion may come through improvements in international competitiveness. Trade policy may be an adjunct to diffusion policies.

Diffusion of new technology is often talked of as purely a demand based phenomenon. It does, however, have a supply side, too. The supply side, or domestic production capability, is also a legitimate target of policy, for such domestic capability can both encourage diffusion and internalise compensation effects in an economy.

2. Production of IT

Encouragement of the supply side is very much the target of R&D policy. The discussion of R&D policy is couched in terms of opportunity costs -- what alternatives are foregone by an economy in stimulating the supply side. The skill and capital resources of an economy are limited and greatest benefit from their use may arise from allocations that do not involve domestic production capabilities in all IT based systems and techniques. It is argued that:

   i) no economy can afford to ignore the potential gains from the use of IT based processes and the incorporation of IT into consumer products;

  ii) the manufacture of IT based capital goods, such as computers and industrial robots and NC-machine-tools, are skill intensive and expensive operations and economies of scale suggest that not all countries may be able to operate effectively in this area on a large scale;

 iii) the third level is the design and manufacture of electronic components or chips. It is suggested that these two activities can be separated, but the low wage economies may have some advantage in certain aspects of chips manufacture. Design, again, is very skill intensive and may therefore not be appropriate for all economies.

This tiered approach would suggest that whether an economy engages in i) and/or ii) and/or iii), is very much related to its available pool of technological skills and thus the design of appropriate R&D policies should be considered in the light of this. What is appropriate however, may well change as technology makes further advances. However, as there are externalities that may derive from domestic production capabilities, the possibility of maintaining technology monitoring and information units that can help provide the externalities in the absence of production is raised.

3. Institutional Flexibility

Two aspects of flexibility are discussed -- market and institutional flexibility. The latter refers to, inter alia, the regulatory environment. It is considered that an inappropriate environment may limit both the introduction of new IT based technology and/or the realisation of the benefits that the new technology can generate, and thus a review of regulations in the light of technological possibilities is proposed. Of course the appropriate regulatory environment is conditioned by numerous factors, but two examples of how technological change may condition the choice of appropriate regulations are:

- a) Telecommunications: the full potential of cabling, network or satellite technology to increase the production of new equipment and the proliferation of new services may only be fulfilled under some regulatory regimes.

- b) Vehicle emissions: the possibility of realising the potential that IT based systems provide to reduce vehicle emissions, with their consequent social benefits, may only occur if sufficiently stringent standards are set.

The point to be made is that the state of technology is a factor to be considered in the setting of the regulatory environment.

4. Market Flexibility

Market flexibility covers such issues as price and wage flexibility, entry and exit of firms, monopolisation, etc. Price and wage flexibility rather than rigidity enables an economy to adjust automatically to new technology, the incentives being created by the flexibility encouraging output and employment. Yet monopolisation may hinder this process which provides a rationale for anti-trust policy (although anti-monopoly policy may not always be favourable to innovation per se). The arguments on entry and exit are that new technology often is introduced by new firms and such new firms are an important part of an economy's dynamic development. The existence of significant entry barriers cannot be conducive to innovation or obtaining the maximum benefit from innovations.

The overview of these arguments is that the appropriate role of government is not always passive or always active. There are, however, many situations where policy initiatives can either beneficially influence the production and use of technology, or where the government can help to generate the desired flexibility in an economy to allow the new technologies to yield their maximum benefit.

IV. LONGER TERM PROSPECTS

Although this report is directed towards a medium term horizon, there are a number of hints in the studies as to some longer term implications of advances in IT.

One contribution (Eliasson, Part III.II.2) discusses the growing importance of information processing as "soft capital" within the firm. The firm of the future is perceived to be much more of an organism processing, collecting and transmitting information rather than materials as in the past. This implies, in the longer term, a very different mix of skills and activities for the firm. How the new structure might behave is unknown. Information in this view is being regarded as a direct input to the production process, which is foreign to most current modes of analysis. It raises issues, for example, that will concern accountants and stock market analysts in the valuation of information in the firm.

Much of the discussion looking at the short and medium term (Stoneman, Part III.I.) assumed that diffusion will be slow and thus the impacts will be realised slowly. As diffusion proceeds, however, much new IT is of a kind that when some critical mass eventually appears, synergistic gains may generate more dramatic impacts. Two examples may illustrate this:

i) The full benefits from word processors may only be realised when networking of stand alone processors occurs. At that stage, the maximum benefits of these machines with electronic data transfer can be realised.

ii) The spread of FAX (facsimile machines) will be slow until a user has a significant number of recipients with such machines. When this stage is reached, diffusion may be fast.

It is worth noting that such synergistic effects may be considerably delayed by inconsistent industry standards (nationally, internationally, firm standards) and this has obvious policy implications.

In addition to ignoring synergistic effects, shorter term analysis holds as constant a number of factors that may change in the long term, e.g. in the short term one might not expect the "buildings"-component of the capital stock to change by much. In the longer term, it might. As such fixed factors do change, their replacements are likely to be more appropriate to the new technology and thus further indirect benefits from the use of that technology might arise. In fact, such changes may even encourage further use of the new technology. An example of the sort of effect considered in this context might be that as current management is replaced by the next generation, there may arise new attitudes to IT and its use in the firm.

A second example is slightly different; at the moment much transfer of data and graphical material is limited in speed due to the capacity of the telephone lines; as the infrastructure including telecommunications is updated, so these constraints are lifted and the full potential of IT can be realised.

In the longer term also, as more information technology is introduced, intelligent reprogrammable machines may become the norm rather than the exception. This may imply changes in the production process that cannot adequately be treated as capital or labour saving. More use of these technologies will generate more just in time systems, automated warehousing, CAD/CAM systems, etc., that have major impacts on required levels of inventories and work in progress. They will also mean greater flexibility in manufacturing and the possibilities of more high quality, custom-tailored, small batch production at economic cost.

This underlines that in the longer term, the economy may be very different in its structure and thereby in its reaction to change. One possible way to illustrate this is to ask how, in the face of expanding demand, the IT intensive economy may react. In the 50/60/early 70s, demand growth was accompanied by production expansion largely based on large firms reaping the benefits of scale economies in producing large quantities of standardized products. In the future, a different scenario may emerge -- the new technology makes more customisation possible, smaller batches and greater production flexibility. The scale benefits are no longer so important, smaller scale industry is economically viable and perhaps more dynamic. The capital saving bias of IT reported on earlier, might indeed support such trends to "smallness" and the productivity gains to be forthcoming with such trends. Associated with this might be less centralisation, more decentralisation, perhaps even a general relocation of industry in the very long term. This relocation may even involve international relocation on a broad scale.

When discussing the international division of labour, it should not be forgotten that in addition to historical, technological and other influences, there exist in the world today a whole panoply of subsidies, tariff walls and protective barriers. The impact of medium or long-term changes in these latter factors may have considerably more influence on the international location of production than just technological change.

V. IMPLICATIONS FOR FUTURE RESEARCH

This project has yielded a number of well supported insights and conclusions. It does however have its limitations and cannot pretend to answer all questions. It is expected that work in this general area will continue in academia, government and international organisations. Some of the major lessons and implications of the present work for such future study are that:

    i) The discipline and cohesiveness provided by a particular analytical framework is important in a field of study where normally speculation and value judgement are dominant. It is suggested therefore that future work ought to be conditioned by similar use of a framework. This work selected a particular framework, there are advantages to alternative paradigms.

    ii) This project was constrained by the limited availability of data with consistent aggregative structures. If further work within this paradigm is to proceed, more work on such data problems is a prerequisite.

    iii) This project is weak on the product innovation aspect of technological change, both because of a lack of quantitative information and because of the restrictions of the paradigm adopted. This represents a fruitful line for future enquiry.

    iv) The project's conclusions and policy recommendations indicate that there is still much to learn about diffusion processes and their control and stimulation. In a world where technology policy is often taken to mean R&D policy, further investigation of diffusion issues and diffusion policies represents a major avenue for future study.

Part II

ANALYTICAL SUMMARY

INTRODUCTION

The objectives of this study are to investigate the potential impacts of information technology in the medium-term and future and the investigative methods are centred on the use of a neoclassical approach. This Analytical Summary has two main tasks. The first is to critically draw together the various contributions to this project to see what we can say about both the impact and the determinants of the impact of new information technology. The second is to pursue, to some degree, the policy implications arising from these findings.

To provide a background on the following discussions it is worth briefly summarising the approach that has arisen from the theoretical discussion (Part III.I.). We considered an industry level of analysis initially, and investigated what would happen to output, employment, etc., in that industry as new technology is introduced. First, as the technology is introduced productivity is increased and costs are reduced which enables prices to fall. This fall in prices will lead to an increase in demand and output according to the size of the elasticity of demand. If the elasticity of demand is large the increase in output may be sufficiently great that although input per unit of output has decreased the demand for inputs might increase. Second, the technology being introduced may change the relative productivity of labour and capital in the production process, which may change the desired mix of these two inputs. This "bias" in technological change may thus lead to an increase in the demand for one factor at the expense of another. Thus to predict movements in factor demands we need to have information on the bias in technical change and the extent to which one factor can be substituted for another (the elasticity of substitution). Third, if we are to quantify the size of any impacts we need to know the rate at which technology is improving in an industry -- we measure this as a weighted sum of the rate of improvement of labour and capital productivity, called the rate of growth of total factor productivity.

These three arguments clarify why we discuss demand and substitution elasticities, biases and the rate of technological change. As we shall make clear however, our work extends beyond this simple framework in order to overcome limitations and objections, and thus although the above guides us, it does not constrain us.

In drawing together our findings on impacts we have essentially four types of contributions. The first set we can call general findings -- these centre on the studies by Patel and Soete, Eliasson, Wilson and Bosworth -- where published statistical data has been investigated in order to get some feel for the sizes of the crucial parameters identified, i.e. the bias and rate of technical change, elasticities of substitution and elasticities of demand. Our first aim is to bring together these findings to see what contribution they can make to predicting likely movements in factor demands and outputs.

This initial investigation has numerous limitations, as we have seen and shall see, not the least of which being that it is backward looking. We thus have a second set of studies, the case studies, which are more forward looking, less dependent on published data and also less tied by the neo-classical structure. Our second purpose is to try to summarise these findings.

Our third contribution is the section on micro/macro issues discussed in the papers by Eliasson and Whitley and Wilson. The importance of taking a macro-economic perspective has been stressed in Part III (Analytical Framework, Stoneman) and the implications thus must be discussed if a full picture is to be presented.

Also, scattered throughout the various contributions are numerous comments upon the basic underlying modelling framework proposed for this study and the suggestion of various alternatives.

Once these tasks have been completed we can move to consider the general policy issues that arise from the findings.

I. AN HISTORICAL OVERVIEW

In the contribution by Patel and Soete two main objectives are pursued. The first is to investigate the extent to which recent changes in the level of unemployment are the result of structural factors as opposed to demand deficiency, the second is to tabulate recent changes in output, capital and labour inputs and their ratios. The authors then proceed to provide an interpretation of their findings relating employment to technology. The majority of this work is carried on at a high level of aggregation, the manufacturing sector as a whole being the principal unit of observation.

Using an analysis based on Okun's curve which relates capacity utilisation to the unemployment rate, the authors suggest that, post-1975, a significant proportion of unemployment in various OECD economies can be attributed to structural factors. (Their figures suggest more than a half in France and Japan, more than a third in Germany, and less than a third in Canada, the United States and the United Kingdom.) The authors see technological change with its impact on skill requirements, demand mixes and capital obsolescence as a major contributor to this structural unemployment.

These results are, the authors agree, rather preliminary and should not be overemphasized. In particular one might note:

a) that the Okun relationship used takes very little, if any, account of labour supply factors;

b) the economics profession as a whole has suggested many reasons why the employment/output relationship post-1973 has changed, most of which have nothing to say about technical change;

c) perhaps most importantly, the preliminary investigations reported take no account of all those factors discussed in the analytical framework as influencing factor demand, and as such should be treated cautiously.

Thus with respect to this first contribution, we should note the implications of the analysis, but reserve judgement on the validity of the findings. The second contribution of this piece is the generation of new estimates of productivity and capital intensities for the 1955 to 1982 period. The figures on best practice productivity are reproduced in the following Table 1. The methods of calculation of these figures led to a heated debate in the meeting of experts largely relating to the quality of the capital stock data. However, the general findings of measured increasing labour productivity, declining capital productivity and increasing capital/labour ratios are probably not too divorced from reality. Patel and Soete also show that, for the United Kingdom at least, most industries (except electronics) have shown a similar pattern to the aggregate.

The figures produced by this exercise are then used by Patel and Soete to argue that:

a) much of the structural unemployment is the result of capital mismatching; and

b) employment prospects in the immediate and medium-term future will be limited by capital shortage.

Unfortunately the first part of this argument is not made at all clear whereas the second part relies upon a limited degree of substitution in the product relationship.

If there are extensive substitution possibilities between capital and labour, such a result does not necessarily follow. We consider (see below) that the evidence tends to support a view that such substitution possibilities do exist, and as such we do not lay much emphasis on this capital shortage problem.

The work of Patel and Soete may be taken to imply that the nature of technological change has been labour saving/capital using. It is not definite on this point and there are arguments to the contrary, but we proceed for a while with this result.

At this point it is particularly informative to consider the first contribution by Eliasson (Part III.II.2) on the nature of technical change, for in a very innovative piece he is suggesting some particular divergencies between the past and the future. In particular he argues that the growing importance of information processing in the activities of the firm, and the concentration of technical change on such functions, suggests that the future pattern of changes may be different from the past, e.g. a change from capital using to capital saving technological change. He also notes how, if this is the case, the standard models used for analysing technical change may no longer be appropriate.

To the extent that the changes stressed by Eliasson are already of importance, this would suggest that we have some conflict in our results as to whether technical change has a capital using or capital savings bias. However we have isolated the bias of technical change, (with rates of augmentation, elasticities of substitution and elasticities of demand) as one of the crucial parameters in our analysis. We thus turn to Wilson's first contribution (Part III.III.1.) where he considers in detail the problems of trying to estimate biases, and other parameters in a rigorous way. His analysis clearly illustrates that any parameter estimates must be handled with great care. It is very difficult given the objections that Wilson raises to be at all definitive about the parameters we wish to estimate. However, to get to this point and to avoid conclusions completely is to deny the validity of our exercise.

Wilson, although cautious, suggests that a value for the elasticity of

Table 1

TRENDS IN BEST-PRACTICE LABOUR AND CAPITAL PRODUCTIVITY AND
CAPITAL INTENSITY (1955 to 1982)

(Capital stock corrected for long-term underutilised capital)

	Best Practice O/L	Best Practice O/K	Best Practice K/L
UNITED STATES			
1955 to 1982	2.28	-2.54	4.81
1955 to 1973	2.44	-1.63	4.06
1973 to 1982	1.97	-4.36	6.34
CANADA			
1955 to 1982	3.17	-1.78	4.95
1955 to 1973	3.33	-1.05	4.39
1973 to 1982	2.84	-3.23	6.09
JAPAN			
1965 to 1982	6.28	0.30	6.00
1965 to 1973	5.76	0.80	4.98
1973 to 1982	6.74	-0.15	6.88
FRANCE			
1955 to 1982	3.79	-1.72	5.51
1955 to 1973	4.10	-1.36	5.46
1973 to 1982	3.17	-2.43	5.60
GERMANY			
1960 to 1982	3.35	-1.63	4.99
1960 to 1973	3.43	-1.90	5.34
1973 to 1982	3.24	-1.25	4.48
UNITED KINGDOM			
1955 to 1982	3.30	-2.20	5.99
1955 to 1983	3.09	-1.99	5.17
1973 to 1982	3.72	-4.13	7.84

substitution close to unity may be reasonable. He argues that there is no systmatic evidence to refute this, but neither any systematic evidence to support it. It does seem however to be a reasonable and extremely useful basis for a working hypothesis. The reason for this is that, by inspection of Table 1 of this report, it is clear that if the elasticity of substitution is unity, then the sign of movements in factor demands depends solely on the elasticity of demand and not the bias in technical change (given factor prices). Thus acceptance of this unit elasticity of substitution assumption implies that we do not have to resolve conflicts over the actual bias in technological change. The bias is no longer of great importance. We may note at this early stage that the macro analysis discussed below reinforces this view.

This leads us to the question: how can one take this position when we see that capital/labour ratios have actually increased? Response: such an increase is perfectly consistent with a unit elasticity of substitution if labour has become more expensive relative to capital over time. This is a line of reasoning we would accept, and thus feel on reasonably firm ground in accepting the unit elasticity of substitution as a working hypothesis.

Once we have taken this position we can state that within the context of our neo-classical analysis the direction and extent of movement of output and employment in a sector will depend on the rate of technological change (the rate of total factor productivity growth) and the elasticity of demand for the output of the sector.

In Table 2 we present some inter-industry estimates of increases in total factor productivity for US industries to indicate those showing the fastest and slowest rates of technological advance. These were estimated with a unit elasticity of substitution assumption.

Our earlier work has shown that if the elasticity of substitution is unity, then given a positive rate of growth of total factor productivity, employment under given factor prices will increase if the elasticity of demand is greater than one and decrease if it is less than one.

Let us turn then to consider demand elasticities. Bosworth discusses in detail the available estimates of demand elasticities and their limitations. His contribution has two main parts, the estimates of domestic demand elasticities and the estimates of import and export elasticities. In the domestic case most studies provide elasticity estimates that are particularly low. However, at a general level, it is possible to class goods (products) into high and low elastiticy groups. Thus he finds for example that basic necessities (food, drink, housing and perhaps clothing) and habit-forming goods (tobacco) have low price elasticities whereas other goods (durables and services) have high price elasticities, although as an exception to the rule recreation has a low own price elasticity of demand. Because increases in output in reaction to price reduction are the main forces that counteract direct reductions in labour demand through technological change, knowledge of such rankings can indicate to us which industries are most likely to experience offsetting employment effects for a given technological change. A high price elasticity in the case of services is particularly important, for it is often argued that the main impact of the information revolution will be in the service sector.

Table 2

ESTIMATES OF TOTAL FACTOR PRODUCTIVITY 1974/1985
IN US INDUSTRIES

Industry Code and Name		Index (a)
1000	Agriculture, Forestry, Fisheries	1.018783
2000	Metal Mining	1.060745
3000	Coal Mining	1.307544
4000	Crude Petroleum and Natural Gas	.810343
5000	Nonmetal Mining & Quarry	1.025700
6000	Construction	1.124264
7000	Food and Kindred Products	.999716
8000	Tobacco Manufacturing	1.137350
9000	Textile Mill Products	1.107542
10000	Apparel Fab. Textile Products	1.128511
11000	Lumber and Wood Products	1.217859
12000	Furniture and Fixtures	.967096
13000	Paper and Allied Products	1.253802
14000	Printing and Publishing	1.145649
15000	Chemical and Allied Products	1.197169
16000	Petroleum Refining	1.140607
17000	Rubber and Plastic Products	1.222271
18000	Leather Products	.852346
19000	Stone Glass Clay Products	1.195253
20000	Primary Metals	1.204778
21000	Fabricated Metal Products	1.031909
22000	Machinery excluding Electrical	1.096017
23000	Electrical Machinery	1.298730
24000	Motor Vehicles and Equipment	1.217665
25000	Transport Equipment Ordnance	.970699
26000	Instruments	1.423852
27000	Miscellaneous Manufacturing	1.230469
28000	Transport and Warehousing	1.328222
29000	Communications	1.297131
30000	Electrical Utilities	1.102859
31000	Gas Utilities	1.081230
32000	Wholesale and Retail Trade	1.298792
33000	Finance, Insurance, Real Estate	.937380
34000	Other Services	1.044576

(a)   Tornqvist chain-linked index.

Source: H. Furchtgott-Roth (2).

However, as we have seen above, not only the ranking of the elasticity of demand is important, its size is too. Here we face a problem. Theory tells us that not all demand elasticities can be less than unity, but in many of the estimates Bosworth reports this is exactly what is found. He argues however that this may be the result of poor models or excessive concentration on short-run analysis. In his Table 6 however, where some longer-run results are produced, although some elasticities are less than unity, many, e.g. cars and durable goods, are greater than one (services has an elasticity of 0.9).

In a trading world, the use of domestic elasticities is not sufficient. One must also consider import and export elasticities. In his report on estimates of these Bosworth finds differences across countries and across product groups. The elasticity estimates are however much larger than the domestic elasticities found. He concludes that the majority of countries have relatively price elastic trade on either the import or export side. This suggests that it is through the trading nexus that many of the compensating effects on factor demand are going to depend.

In terms of product grouping the results in his Table 12 are perhaps most informative. In general, food, beverages and tobacco have low elasticities; materials, oils and fats, medium; and manufactured goods high elasticities (services are not generally traded).

In the most general terms, these results indicate that ceteris paribus, those industries most likely to benefit from compensation through demand are in manufacturing (durables in particular) and services. The least likely are in materials, and food, drink and tobacco. In manufacturing the compensation will largely arise through the trading nexus, in services through the domestic market. This also implies that if price reductions are made by other countries and are not matched in domestic markets, it is manufacturing that will suffer most. A failure to innovate at home in a product line that has low trade elasticities or is not traded may not be as harmful to factor demand as a failure to innovate in a market where there is a high trade elasticity.

At this point, it would of course be most informative to match the demand elasticity estimates to the factor productivity estimates found in Table 2, thereby predicting movements in output and employment by sector. We have expended some considerable effort on this exercise to little avail. The basic problem is that as the estimates are all derived from secondary sources the aggregative structure of the productivity estimates does not match the structure of the estimates of demand elasticities. Matters are further complicated by the macro issues that we discuss further below. We have decided therefore that as an approximate matching of the two aggregative structures may be more misleading than helpful, to not proceed to report on this exercise. However what we do below is to consider the information on demand elasticities when discussing individual case studies, and also when discussing the macro level results to take account of what has been found here. Two particular points are however of note and we emphasize them at this time.

    i)   basic necessities have low demand elasticities, luxury items have high elasticities.

    ii)   despite cross country differences in trading elasticities, the majority of countries have relatively price elastic trade on either the export or import side. Most countries thus have the potential to compensate job losses through faster technological change. However, such elasticities differ across product groups (see Bosworth's Table 12) and thus some industries will be more capable of compensation through trade than others. Of course, by the same token, they will be more susceptible to job losses through faster innovation abroad.

We have come to the point where we have laid particular emphasis on demand elasticities. It seems appropriate at this point to raise three relevant issues. First, we must realise that compensation through demand will only arise if prices fall when costs fall. Bosworth suggests that high levels of market power may affect this process. He also shows that in many OECD markets there are high concentration ratios, and this may be of particular importance for any compensation conclusions already drawn. It is not possible at this time to be precise as to the extent of this market power, but theory suggests it may be important.

Second, we have talked above of price elasticities in terms of the effect on demand of a price change. Bosworth also raises the issue that demand is responsive to product quality. This raises two points:

a) much of our discussion has considered technological change implicitly as process orientated. This is somewhat offset in the case studies, but it must be admitted, product innovation is probably not given sufficient emphasis in the neo-classical paradigm;

b) we do not have any reliable extensive estimates of demand responsiveness to product innovation.

Overall, even if we were to give more emphasis to product innovation, it is unlikely that we could be at all specific about its impact.

Finally, to a large extent, the results we have are derived at a very high level of aggregation. It is generally recognised that as the level of aggregation gets lower, demand elasticities increase (e.g. the elasticity of demand for any particular food will be greater than that for food as a whole). Thus although technological change may reduce factor demand in a whole sector (e.g. food, drink and tobacco), demand may well increase in some of its sub-sectors at the expense of others.

Despite these reservations the thrust of our argument should not be unduly affected. There is however one further issue to discuss, the size of income elasticities of demand. As we argued in the Introduction, an industry with a high income demand elasticity faces the prospect of a growing market. A low elasticity implies a declining market. In his Table 1, Bosworth presents some income demand elasticity estimates again suggesting a particularly poor prospect for the industries providing basic necessities. Sifting through his other tables, of particular interest is the high income demand elasticities in services, the one industry we have discussed before as a key target of current technological advance. Such a high income elasticity may suggest that output and employment prospects for this sector are not particularly poor.

To conclude this Chapter, we can make a few relevant comments:

i) Wilson observes that in many studies the relationship between capital and labour (the elasticity of substitution) differs across labour types: productive labour being a complement to capital, non-productive labour a substitute. Thus as technological change proceeds the mix of types and skills in the labour force will change.

ii) The results we have been discussing refer to the industry level of aggregation. We must also make some comments on the individual firm: first just as when we decrease the level of aggregation so the elasticity of demand increases, so as we look at the firm rather than the industry so does its own price elasticity of demand increase. Thus a single innovating firm may be able to compensate direct reductions in factor demand at the expense of non-innovators. Thus although the analysis may suggest industry reductions in factor demand, this may hide increases in some firms and reductions in others.

iii) We should also be clear as to how technological change is being considered in the general approach. To a large extent it is treated as exogenous and disembodied. The production function estimation approach gives us some estimates of an average rate of technological improvement and its direction. There is no real issue of diffusion speeds, the kinds of technologies being introduced or the cost of introducing them. That is why we consider specific case studies.

iv) We should also realise that the estimates we have been discussing in this chapter are essentially backward looking. They contribute an answer to the question: "If past patterns are repeated in the future what will happen?". The case study analysis perhaps helps us to be more precise about the future.

II. CASE STUDIES

In the following we have attempted to highlight the conclusions of the individual case studies (see ANNEX, page 221). Their full richness cannot be summarised in a few paragraphs. We have tried, however, to see what can be learnt from those studies themselves and from the interaction of this contribution with the other contributions to this work.

1. Engineering

The engineering sector is at the centre of the microelectronics revolution. Not only is it expected that its processes of production will be changed but so will its products. And, moreover, it is largely by the use of these new products in other industries that the microelectronic revolution will proceed. In this sense the engineering industry will be the major recipient of any compensation effects that arise in capital goods production as the new technology is used more extensively.

Engineering, covering mechanical, electrical and electronic and instrument engineering, transport equipment and miscellaneous metal goods accounts for about 40 per cent of all manufacturing employment. Compared to other sectors it exhibits much greater scope for IT based product innovation than other sectors. These products represent the basis for process innovations in both the other sectors and within itself.

Within products, the incorporation of microelectronics within existing products -- through the replacement of mechanical and electrical components by electronic components -- has already started and is expected to continue, e.g. watches, calculators, etc. New products are also being generated. In general the new and improved products require low levels of productive labour, and it is suggested that demand (especially on the consumer side) is not sufficiently responsive to the improvement in product quality and price to offset this reduction. When producer goods are being so changed, it is the speed of diffusion that will determine whether demand increases sufficiently to offset the reduced labour intensity of production.

It is argued that the use of microelectronics in products yields better quality and greater customer appeal. However, production cost does not seem to be ranked as an important benefit. Demand increases must therefore be related to these product improvements not price and on this issue we have very limited information.

Within engineering processes, we see many examples of what IT may be capable one day. Discussion of CAD/CAM, FMS, IMS, robots and their potential are frequent. One of the key characteristics of these new technologies is the way they make production more of an integrated system than it is at present. However, Wilson (cf. his study "IT in the Engineering Industry") argues that at least in the near future, it is mainly extensions of CCMT (including robots), rather than the more complex systems, that will be the pattern. He also argues that given the integrated nature of many production processes, of which only part will be enhanced by IT, the cost reductions effected by IT will be limited. Moreover, although IT will be basically increasing labour productivity, the systems effect plus limited diffusion will mean small rather than large impacts on employment. The rate at which the new technologies are likely to be incorporated, despite their financial advantages, is slow. Numerous reasons are proposed for this, which may provide a guide for policies on diffusion, but we shall discuss this below. Wilson calculates that, although some dramatic developments are to be expected,

"... in the short and medium term, it seems unlikely that future patterns of technical change will be very different from the past in terms of their impact on employment."

In his work on econometric production studies, Wilson's evidence suggests that in manufacturing, an hypothesis of a unity elasticity of substitution is not too unreasonable. Bosworth's estimates of price elasticities suggest that in the area of manufactured goods, (e.g. automobiles) demand elasticities are quite high. Taken together this would suggest that compensation of direct factor demand reduction through process innovation is possible in the engineering sector. However, Bosworth's results also suggest that import elasticities are high in this sector. This could reinforce Wilson's argument that innovation may not affect employment dramatically but a failure to innovate could have much greater (deleterious effects) and innovation faster than others could yield employment gains.

However, Bosworth's results also show one other important point. The engineering industries tend to have high levels of concentration, which may in fact throw some doubt on the automaticity of price reductions following cost reductions. If this is so, then the higher price elasticities may not in fact come into play. We should also note that in many cases, it is product quality that is being affected, not price per se, and we do not really have any feelings for the size of demand elasticities with respect to quality. Finally, Bosworth's data suggests a high income demand elasticity for the products of this sector which may suggest growth potential.

Overall, therefore, we have a sector where potential for technical change is great, but the realisation of this potential will be slow. As the potential is realised many changes will come about, but in the important area of factor demands the results suggest that process innovations are not to be too greatly feared. The impact of product innovations is more problematical, past examples -- calculators and watches -- suggest dramatic impacts on labour demand. However, more than anything else, especially with product innovations, it seems to be rates of change relative to competitors that is the big issue.

The stress in this study on the importance of relative (to other countries) rates of diffusion suggests that if output and employment are to be maintained or increased then a country cannot afford to lag behind either in product or process innovation. We discuss below the policy issues surrounding diffusion, but this work on engineering suggests that skills, standardization and the need for organisational adaptation are important, and if policy is to be directed towards faster diffusion speeds these are significant issues to consider.

2.   Office-Based Services

We have two contributions on the service sector. The first is by Petit specifically on banking. The second is by Barras on office-based services in general, including banking. Much of the discussion in this area centres on how the service sector will be affected by new technology. As Barras shows, the service sector has been a major source of new jobs in the past thirty years, but it is argued by some that increasing automation in this sector will change the trend, making the sector a net loser of jobs. It is to this sort of issue we now turn.

Barras observes how in all of his selected OECD countries, the service sector has increased its employment share, in both the 1962 to 1970 and 1970 to 1979 periods. To a certain extent this reflects the increased size of the government sector, but not totally, for private services and financial/business services have also increased their share of employment. The growth has been associated with generally low rates of labour, capital and total factor productivity growth, particularly with rates lower than manufacturing. The growth of employment in such circumstances would imply either a positive price elasticity of demand (which is unlikely) and/or a high income elasticity of demand, for which there is some support in Bosworth's study.

Barras points out that in the service industries the major changes have been increased capital intensities (which he realistically ascribes to cheaper improved capital goods coming from the computer and related industries), a shift from buildings to physical capital investment, small increases in labour productivity and declines in capital productivity. Although, it is difficult to translate this into estimates of factor augmentation, without knowledge of the substitution elasticity, Barras argues that the elasticity of substitution between labour and capital is greater than unity, which implies that capital is being augmented faster than labour.

Using Table 1 in Chapter I, this puts us in the penultimate columns where a positive impact of these changes on the inputs of K and L are very much dependent on having a higher value for the demand elasticity than the substitution elasticity (which considering Bosworth's estimates is not impossible). Moreover Barras observes that as new technology has been introduced, improved service quality has been a stimulus to demand.

For the future, which is more important here, Barras argues:

a) that the rate of improvement in the price/performance ratio of information technology will slow initially and then perhaps increase;

b) that the new technologies may have a changed factor saving bias;

c) the elasticity of substitution will increase in the longer term;

d) after a medium term increase, capital's share in total costs will settle at a new higher level;

e) labour productivity growth will increase;

f) capital productivity growth will increase but still be negative;

g) total factor productivity growth will become positive but still be less than in manufacturing.

This is a very comprehensive list of possibilities. Barras considers that the net effect of these changes may be a decline in employment prospects in the 0-5 year horizon with a possible reversal of this trend in the 5-10 year horizon. These results do not seem inconsistent with our framework. Moreover if the argument and Bosworth's data supporting an income elasticity in excess of unity are correct, there is no reason to disbelieve that as the OECD economies come out of recession, there will also be an upward trend of employment in the 0-5 year period. However, we should not ignore Barras's comments that the skill composition of the labour force may be required to change considerably.

3. <u>Banking</u>

In his contribution on banking Petit reflects a number of issues similar to those raised by Barras, e.g. the problems of output measurement. Petit however stresses also how new technology changes not only the production process, but perhaps more importantly the quality and nature of products being offered by the banking sector. The introduction of computerised technology has led to the sector offering a whole new range of services. The other main emphasis in the work of Petit is on the importance of regulatory and institutional environment in the determination of both the rate of introduction of new technology and its impact. This regulatory issue we raise again below. Petit considers, however, that the particular nature of banking and the service sector in general makes the neo-classical framework with its bias towards the analysis of the manufacturing sector more than usually inappropriate.

Petit views the automation of banking as having two distinct phases. The first was the computerisation and resulting centralisation of back-office operations. The second phase, based on remote access data processing systems, is enabling a return to decentralised operations. This second stage is marked also by automatic cash dispensers and seems likely to lead to further use of electronic fund transfers, given the right external environment. These more distributed systems are also the basis of the more intense competition from non-bank financial institutions.

Petit views the transition to a more highly automated banking sector with lower levels of over-the-counter staff as basically slow. To quote,

"... what inhibits such a trend is the sluggishness of demand. Major firms have installed their own computerised networks to manage their financial activities. Smaller firms are interested in the new banking products, but are fearful ... of having to bear the costs of changing the payment system. The reluctance of households is still more evident ...".

On employment, Petit considers that all the evidence argues against extrapolating trends of the 1960s and 1970s into the 1980s, which may throw doubt on views propounding stabilisation or job reduction in the sector. As an overall picture we have a sector where the extended use of networks is leading to changes in products offered, the competitive environment, job contents and to some extent pressures on institutional and regulatory frameworks. The exact outcome from these changes is, in the circumstances, difficult to predict.

These two contributions on office based services and banking represent the non-manufacturing part of our case studies. Whitley and Wilson in their macro-economic contribution (discussed below) also looked at the service sector and has discussed the impact of a faster diffusion of technology into this sector. Each of these authors lays particular emphasis on the role of new products in maintaining or improving employment and output in the sector, and if these new services do appear then the prospects for the sector are good. However, although one might not completely agree with Barras' view that the service sector can be a new "engine of growth", the points he raises as to the need for government policy to encourage technological advance in this sector do not fall on completely barren ground. A need for more skilled personnel, standards and a favourable environment to encourage infrastructural investment all merit consideration. The actual mechanics of this process are outside our remit here, but the issues are relevant to our policy discussion below.

4. Clothing

Rush and Hoffman (cf. their study "Microelectronics in the Clothing Industry") give us a number of detailed insights into the clothing industry, illustrating the role of competition from NICs, the decline in OECD employment in the industry and future (and current) technological changes. In particular, they oppose to each other protection and technological changes as ways of job preservation in the future.

In Table 3 of their contribution they present some estimates of the impact of trade, demand and technology on jobs, suggesting that productivity gains have led to reduced employment. To some degree this may suggest that the job impact question is settled for this industry. To argue this would be misleading. Although no details are presented on how these figures are produced it seems most unlikely that all the ramifications of productivity change have been taken into account. For example, it is unlikely that the relationship between rates of productivity change, and demand and trading have been accounted for. We cannot therefore consider our question answered.

Rush and Hoffman argue that although CAD/CAM systems are playing a larger role in the industry, their impact on overall factor productivity to date has been limited. However, capital intensities are beginning to increase in reaction to new technologies and this is tending to shift competitive advantage towards developed countries. Moreover CAD/CAM like a number of other technologies, although somewhat labour-saving, mainly has a material-saving bias. However CAD/CAM is largely acting on the pre-assembly stage. At the assembly stage although microelectronics has potential, to date, the potential has not been realised to any degree, although this may be reversed as time proceeds. At this stage new technology is considered to be labour-saving.

Bosworth's estimates of demand elasticities tend to indicate (from admittedly a mixed set of observations) domestic elasticities for clothing close to unity but high import and export elasticities. Following our discussions above this tends to suggest that it is relative rates of cost reduction (through technology in the OECD versus wage rates in NICs and LDCs) that will primarily bear on employment trends. These elasticities suggest (given an elasticity of substitution not far from one) that employment can be preserved in the developed countries if a relatively faster rate of take up of new technology can overcome the wage differential (whether such reversals of international labour demand movements is considered desirable is another matter).

Rush and Hoffman, although not discussing demand elasticities, argue that, given the slow rate of take up of new technologies expected, in the medium term, the future is unlikely to be much different from the past. The OECD countries will continue to see reductions in employment, declines in their share of world trade, and deteriorating trade balances in clothing. They do however argue that a trend towards increased concentration may stimulate faster technological innovation (although the impact of this on employment will depend on the impact of the increased concentration on the relationship between cost and prices). They also see the possibility of major, government funded, research projects making more dramatic new technologies available. However the effect that these might have is very speculative, not the least reason for this being that even if the technologies are there, it is their diffusion that will generate the impact, and on that we know very little.

Overall however their judgement is that the potential gains in productivity that new technology presents, are unlikely to be realised particularly quickly and as such their impact is unlikely to reverse (or strongly reinforce) past trends. To this we might add that Bosworth's income elasticity estimates suggest that clothing is not a sector with major growth prospects.

The major policy issue raised in this case study is that of protectionism. Is it necessary or desirable and if so when? We return to this below.

Conclusion

At this point we have reached a stage where the several contributions most closely tied to the analytical framework have been discussed. Although we still have the important micro/macro contribution to consider, this is probably a good stage to draw a few preliminary conclusions. From the case study analyses we obtain a picture of a medium-term future where a number of information technologies are going to be used more widely in products and processes. Such technologies as CAD/CAM systems, robots, networks, microprocessor control, etc., are all predicted to gain much wider diffusion.

Each of the case study authors view the effect of these changes as significant but not dramatic or draconian. The predictions, where they are made, tend to centre on a continuation of, rather than reversal of past trends. This is not to say that the expected changes are to be played down, or that products, job contents, skills or demand patterns are not going to change. The view is very much one that the slowness of transition will produce gradual rather than dramatic change.

The more widely based work on econometric estimates of elasticities and rates of growth is both promising and disappointing. The potential is there to predict at a reasonably high level of aggregations future patterns of output growth and factor demand. However problems of industry matching have prevented us from taking this exercise too far. Moreover, the macro issues to be discussed below would impinge on any results we derive and perhaps the matter is best postponed to that section.

The final observations that arise from the work so far are issues that have policy implications, e.g. the factors influencing diffusion speeds. These we consider in Chapter IV in some detail.

III. MICRO-MACRO ISSUES

This far our analysis has concentrated on the industry level of aggregation. However, the full richness of the impact of new technology on an economy cannot be fully explored without extending the analysis to the macro-economy (1). Two major contributions by Eliasson and Whitley and Wilson that look at the macro-economy are included in this study. Only by going to this macro level is it possible to consider:

a) that as one industry changes in reaction to new technology other industries may be affected by this change;

b) that as an economy experiences changes in technology resultant changes in factor incomes (wages and profits) may have further repercussions on output and employment levels in the economy;

c) that excess demand or supply in factor markets, -- e.g. the labour market -- may react to induced factor price change that can only be adequately considered at the macro level;

d) that we can adequately deal with the foreign trade aspects of the issues under discussion only at the macro level.

The two contributions are in one sense similar and in another quite different. Both contributions detail the results of simulation exercises on large scale macro-econometric models. However these models are very different in their structures and are applied to very different economies -- the United Kingdom (Whitley and Wilson) and Sweden (Eliasson). Given this, the apparent lack of conflict in the results generated is perhaps indicative of the robustness of the findings.

First of all it is best to give some detail of how the models are constructed, beginning with Eliasson's micro-macro model (cf. "Dynamic Micro-Macro Market Co-ordination and Technical Change").

The theoretical base here is a Schumpeterian type economic process with individual -- real -- firms forming their own decisions as to prices, production, hiring of labour, wages, investment and how fast to grow in an endogenised market framework. The model is oriented mainly towards analysing industrial growth. Therefore, the manufacturing sector is the most detailed in the model. Manufacturing is divided into four industries (raw material processing, semi-manufactures, durable goods manufacturing, and manufacture of consumer non durables). Each industry consists of a number of firms, some of which are real (with data supplied mainly through an annual survey) and some of which are synthetic. The rest of the economy is a ten sector Keynesian-Leontief model.

Firms in the model constitute short and long-run planning systems for production and investment. Each quarter they decided on their desired production, employment and investment. Armed with these plans they go into the labour market where their employment plans confront those of other firms as well as labour supply. The labour force is treated as homogeneous in the model, i.e. labour is recruited from a common "pool". However, labour can also be recruited from other firms. This process determines the wage level, which is thus endogeneous in the model. Even though the labour market is homogeneous, wages vary among both firms and industries without any tendency to converge.

Domestic product prices and the production volume in the four product markets are determined through a similar process. The export volume is also determined endogenously.

The exogenous variables (besides government policies) which drive the model are the rate of technical change (which is specific to each sector and raises the labour productivity associated with new, best practice equipment in each firm) the rate of change of prices in the export markets, and the labour supply.

There is also a capital market in the model where firms compete for investment resources and where the rate of interest is determined. It is in this component of the model that we are most interested and where the Schumpeterian flavour is most noticeable. Basically as new technologies are exogenously developed profit opportunities are generated for firms. These opportunities lead to investment in the latest technologies, i.e. diffusion begins. As the new technology is diffused the profits being realised by non innovating firms change because the use of the new technology impacts on prices in product and factor markets. Non-innovators must then either eventually exit or change to the new technologies. It is as firms adopt the new technologies that productivity in the economy increases.

The model is constructed so that by varying the assumptions about the characteristics of new technologies one can explore the impact of more or less labour saving types of technological change. One may also consider variations in the rates at which markets adjust to disequilibria, and also the impact of varying the elasticities of exports to domestic prices to investigate the importance of "rigidities" and "trade impacts" in the determination of the impact of new technologies.

Before moving to detailed results let us briefly describe the Wilson model (Cambridge Growth Model). It has a Keynesian structure incorporating an input-output system and concentrating on the determination of changes in the real sector of the economy. The level of disaggregation of commodities and industries is considerable. The model is a large one and comprises over 1 400 behavioural and technical relationships (excluding accounting identities). Its main components are equations explaining consumption, investment, employment, exports, imports, prices and an input-output sector which deals with the flows of goods and services between industries and determines total industrial outputs. These equations are all solved together so that the final results are consistent with the various identities required by the national accounts. There are 49 employing activities distinguished, with 16 aggregate groups normally used for the presentation of results. The model includes a monetary sector, which endogenises the exchange rate, and a wage model as well as sub-models to disaggregate employment by occupation and region.

Productivity in the model is treated as follows. An exogenously determined rate of 'optimal' productivity growth is generated for each sector, growing discontinuously and at different rates in each sector. Employment levels adjust slowly to those appropriate to this "optimal" productivity. This adjustment process in conjunction with endogeously determined output levels determines actual productivity levels and growth. Adjustment to the assumptions on "optimal productivity" are used to model changes (acceleration of) the rate of technical change.

The exogenous variables in the model can be classified into five groups:

i) the world environment;

ii) public expenditure;

iii) taxation;

iv) optimal productivity;

v) institutional characteristics of the labour market.

Wilson argues that the endogeneity of particular variables in this model makes it particularly appropriate for considering how any possible direct reductions in employment due to higher optimal productivity may be offset by:

i) increased domestic demand resulting from higher real incomes;

ii) increased foreign demand resulting from improved price and non-price competitiveness;

iii) increased demand for investment goods in order to implement the new technology;

iv) dynamic effects such as the multiplier effects on real incomes following increases in autonomous expenditures;

v) equilibrating effects in the labour market.

It is now time to consider the results.

The starting point is the paper by Wilson who in previous work has illustrated that when certain compensation effects are incorporated in his model then simulations suggest that faster technological change can increase employment levels. It is worth noting here that Eliasson argues that these effects are weakened in times of slack demand. In his present contribution, however, Wilson's initial step is to generate a "most likely" path for employment in the United Kingdom given all the knowledge we have on the likely effect of technology on production processes in different industries (cf. "Quantifying the Impact of Information Technology on Employment Using a Macroeconomic Model" by Whitley and Wilson).

Although this "most likely" projection contains a considerable margin for error, the results indicate that even with the introduction of new IT based technologies into the economy, the projected path of economic aggregates differs little from their past trends. Output and productivity at the macro level are projected to maintain growth at about two per cent per annum to 1995, and unemployment is also expected to stay around the three million. These results are summarised in more detail in Wilson's tables. Thus at the macro-level, the most likely path is not one that seems to indicate any revolutionary impact on the United Kingdom macro economy. Similar sorts of outcomes at the macro level can be found in a number of large scale econometric models. Eliasson for example states that in his past work, technological change, whether local or universal only generates minor, local unemployment situations that disappear after a two to five year period. Eliasson attributes this robustness of the economy to the ability of real wages to adjust to remove unemployment in the system. Whitley and Wilson's results however illustrate that the other compensatory factors are of more importance in his world and thus the results are not purely dependent on an assumption of price and wage flexibility that is perhaps unacceptable to many.

Macro-economic stability could hide micro-economic instability, thus the simulation results at the industry level are as important as the macro results. Now, one may recall that prior to moving to this section on micro-macro issues, we had been discussing industry level analysis where we concentrated on price and income elasticities of demand, substitution possibilities and the bias in technological change. Each of these macro models incorporates assumptions on each of these for each industry but in addition takes account of inter-industry connections and macro-economic feedback. The latter aspect is new to our work, and it is thus worth considering the forecasts in some detail. In Tables 3 and 4, we reproduce two of Wilson's tables. Firstly at the sectoral level of aggregation we see in the forecasts how past trends are predicted to continue. Primary and Manufacturing shares of employment are forecast to continue their decline whereas the transport, communication and other service sectors continue their expansion in shares. The figures do not really indicate even any acceleration of trends. At the level of individual industries, we see a number of points, and we quote directly from Whitley and Wilson:

> "One of the main features in the projection, as far as employment is concerned, is the continued decline in primary and manufacturing industries despite quite substantial output growth. In these sectors productivity advances continue to offset any rise in output. Agriculture and mining are together projected to lose over 200 000 jobs by 1995. Within manufacturing, employment is expected to continue its long-run trend decline in most sectors. Productivity gains are quite rapid in many industries compared with long-run trends. Nevertheless, despite the beneficial effects this has on the United Kingdom's international competitiveness, the consequent growth in demand for domestic output is insufficient to prevent a fall in employment. One hundred thousand jobs are projected to go in food, drink and tobacco. In engineering as a whole, over 450 000 jobs are projected to be lost between 1985 and 1995, of which more than 150 000 are in mechanical engineering. Textiles and clothing are also expected to see a continuation of the decline in both output and employment levels observed in recent years. In contrast, employment in certain service

Table 3

OUTPUT, PRODUCTIVITY AND EMPLOYMENT IN GREATER DETAIL
FOR THE UNITED KINGDOM 1985-1995

(average per cent per year)

Employing activity	Output	Growth 1985-1995 Productivity	Employment	Net change in employment 1985-1995 000s
Agriculture	1.5	3.7	-2.3	-126
Mining	-1.2	2.9	-4.0	-103
Food, drink and tobacco	1.5	3.2	-1.7	-96
Chemicals	3.3	4.3	-0.8	-32
Metals	2.0	3.8	-1.8	-44
Engineering	1.7	3.6	-1.8	-467
of which:				
Mechanical engineering	1.0	3.3	-2.4	-166
Electrical engineering	3.6	5.0	-1.4	-90
Motor vehicles	-0.2	2.5	-2.8	-76
Textiles and clothing	-0.9	3.0	-4.2	-205
Other manufacturing	2.3	2.9	-0.4	-44
Construction	1.5	1.0	0.6	91
Public utilities	2.1	4.4	-2.4	-71
Transport and communication	3.9	3.3	0.4	53
Distribution	2.3	2.0	0.2	85
Professional services	3.7	1.5	2.4	669
Miscellaneous services	2.8	0.5	2.3	904
Manufacturing	2.0	-1.7	-1.7	-887
Services	3.1	1.9	1.5	1 713
Public services	-	-	-0.0	-10
Whole economy	2.4	2.3	0.2	604

Table 4

EMPLOYMENT BY BROAD INDUSTRY SECTOR -- United Kingdom 1954-1995

	Share of Total Employment (%)					
	1954	1975	1980	1985	1990	1995
Primary	8.7	4.0	4.0	3.6	3.1	2.6
Manufacturing	33.9	30.2	27.5	23.5	21.4	19.3
Construction and Public Utilities	7.8	8.2	8.2	7.6	7.5	7.5
Transport, Communication and Distribution	19.7	19.1	19.2	20.7	20.8	20.8
Professional and Miscellaneous Services	12.4	17.0	19.6	23.0	25.8	28.8
Total	82.5	78.5	78.5	78.4	78.6	79.0
Social Services and Public Administration	17.5	21.5	21.5	21.6	21.3	21.0
Whole Economy	100.0	100.0	100.0	100.0	100.0	100.0

	1954-75	1975-80	1980-85	1985-90	1990-95	1985-95
Primary	-1 085	1	-152	-120	-109	-229
Manufacturing	-505	659	-1 306	-464	-403	-887
Construction and Public Utilities	200	-6	-249	-4	24	20
Transport, Communication and Distribution	104	57	114	58	80	138
Professional and Miscellaneous Services	1 320	674	567	702	871	1 573
Total	33	68	-1 026	150	463	615
Social Services and Public Administration	1 211	35	-256	-48	38	-10
Whole Economy	1 244	104	-1 284	102	502	604

industries is projected to increase as a consequence of strong output growth coupled with relatively modest increases in productivity. Professional and business services and miscellaneous services fall into this category, with over a million and a half jobs being created in these two sectors between 1985 and 1995. Other more mature service industries, such as transport, communications and distribution, as well as the public utilities are expected to experience changes more like those in the manufacturing sector, with productivity gains largely offsetting any growth in output levels, and total employment in these three sectors showing only a very slight increase over the projection period. Finally the public sector, in contrast to the experience of the 1950s, 1960s and 1970s, is not expected to provide any significant employment growth over the 1985 to 1995 period, given current government plans. In the United Kingdom, this latter sector includes the vast bulk of both education and health services which are of course provided by the State."

Although the aggregative structure of these results is again different from that in our earlier results we can perhaps look at how these results compare to those found in our earlier analysis. Our earlier analysis suggested that the food, drink and tobacco sector because of low price and income elasticities was likely to see reductions in employment. This is reflected in these results. Similarly textiles and clothing were predicted to continue past trends of reductions in employment in the developed country, a result here particularly stressed. In engineering the results here are perhaps more pessimistic than our earlier analysis would suggest, although in services the results are more optimistic than our earlier analysis indicated. However despite these minor differences the major impression one gets from all these results is that the "most likely" outcome is a continuation of rather than reversal of trends.

Despite our concentration so far on "most likely" outcomes, the two micro-macro papers contain much more of interest to us. The papers contain the results of a number of simulation exercises that are designed to illustrate particular issues often raised in the discussions of the impact of new technology. We start with Eliasson's contribution as to whether the "bias" in technological change matters.

The popular notion would be that labour saving technological change creates unemployment while capital saving technical change of the same "size" does not. Although our earlier work does dispute the validity of this popular notion, it is worth seeing what results are produced in the macro models as the labour saving nature of the technological change is varied.

When a capital saving scenario is compared to a labour saving scenario in Eliasson's work, and the foreign trade setting is such that a firm's exports are determined exogenously, in the longer run (30 years), differences are not that large. Less people work in manufacturing and manufacturing output is lower, but terminal labour productivity in manufacturing is roughly the same in both scenarios, although investment is somewhat higher in the capital saving scenario. In the shorter term, total unemployment comes out roughly the same under both scenarios, though in the long run, unemployment is somewhat higher under the capital savings scenario.

When these scenarios are combined with export demand endogenised, the long run unemployment generated is largely eradicated through export expansion, with higher output and less slack in the economy. The comparison of the scenarios shows that after ten years aggregate manufacturing output is the same even though it follows different cycles. In the capital saving case, by the fifteenth year there is a strong export boom. Towards the end of the simulation (30 years), the difference between the cases is again being reduced.

The interpretation we can put on these results are that:

i) The bias in the technological advance in this model is not of any great significance. The bias towards the saving of any particular factor is not the only determinant of the demand for the factor. We have argued this before in partial analysis, it is reconfirmed in macro-analysis.

ii) The difference in the results between the endogenous/exogenous export demand regimes reflects the view that success in foreign markets is an important factor in determining the impact of technological change.

This second result is also stressed in Wilson's analysis.

The next exercise that is simulated refers to the impact of an increase in the speed at which new technology is introduced into an economy -- an increase in the diffusion speed. Wilson's initial results, looking at the faster introduction of new technology in manufacturing stimulating investment, trade performance, etc., suggest the existence of a "virtuous circle". The faster take up in manufacturing generates higher productivity, faster growth in exports, output and consumption and higher employment. At the industry level, the engineering industry and those industries facing strong competition from overseas particularly benefit, but employment rises in all industries, including services. The results of a related simulation exercise whereby new technology is introduced more quickly into the service sector yields quite an opposite result, with substantial job loss in both the service and manufacturing sectors. As Wilson states, this result arises because:

i) the number of jobs at risk is large;

ii) there are only modest compensation effects in capital equipment supply;

iii) much of the impact falls on non-traded goods and thus no offset is derived from gains in international competitiveness; and

iv) the simulation is unable to account for product innovation in the sector.

This latter point is perhaps one we ought to stress, for the work of Barras and Petit, especially on the service sector, is much more optimistic than these results, largely because they consider the product innovation side of technological advance in the sector. Wilson's results do however indicate to us that bold statements that faster diffusion means more jobs must be treated with caution; the location of the faster change is also important.

Wilson's simulation results although making some allowance for the endogeneity of wages, and the possibility that wage and price flexibility might remove unemployment from an economic system, do not incorporate complete flexibility. It is often argued in the economics literature however, that if we do have complete wage and price flexibility, this will mean we will never suffer unemployment. The result is usually established in a neo-classical Walrasian general equilibrium framework. There are opponents to this view both on the grounds of using wage and price flexibility models to describe actual economies and opponents to the result itself. However, as we are particularly concerned with economies reactions to shocks it seemed important that we investigate the impact of wage and price flexibility on output and employment paths as new technology is introduced. Eliasson has undertaken simulations in his model to illustrate the impact of such flexibility. We may note that this model is not neoclassical, and thus the neoclassical result may not hold. In fact he shows that the speed of price and quantity adjustment in reaction to a disequilibrium can be crucial to the development of the economy in the long term. With some wage and price flexibility long term technological unemployment is not feasible, although some short term unemployment can exist. Perhaps of particular note is Eliasson's result that one can have market adjustment regimes that are too fast: thus a medium rate of adjustment seems optimal. Basically, if adjustment of prices is too fast, the signals it generates in the economy lead to overshooting. In the "market regime" that best fits historical experience, technological changes create only minor unemployment situations that disappear after a two to five year period.

It is important to be clear here. This is not saying that wage cuts cure unemployment, it is saying that if the market mechanism operates in such a way that wages and prices do adjust to disequilibria within the market, at some not too fast or too slow a rate, then long term unemployment can be avoided.

To summarise this work in the light of our earlier results, what conclusions can we reach? First, the impact of IT is unlikely to be of a revolutionary nature, the impact is more likely to be evolutionary. Past trends are likely to continue. There seem to be no major macroeconomic upheavals in the projections although micro-economic change is going to occur. Some industries will do better than others. To some degree the extent of gains and losses depend on the rate at which the new technology is introduced. For some industries, a fast introduction is beneficial; for others less so. In particular we might note that faster than expected diffusion in services may in the absence of significant product innovation be to the detriment of employment in that and other sectors. The degree of flexibility in the economy in terms of the prevailing "market process" is relevant to the outcome. The results suggest that continuation of past characteristics would not imply a heavy unemployment burden from technological innovation. Finally, it is suggested that, in line with earlier results, the bias in technological change towards saving labour or capital although relevant in determining the time path of the economy, is not relevant when discussing employment impacts.

In terms of "most likely" impacts our results suggest the following paths for different industries:

> a) Engineering: A sector where international competitiveness is important and where faster technological advance can have beneficial effects on output and employment. In the long run however, employment is likely to continue to decline, although electrical engineering may decline more slowly than mechanical engineering.

b) Textiles and clothing: Again a sector continuing past trends with employment reduction although new technology represents an opportunity to partly, at least, reverse these trends.

c) Office based services and banking: A sector likely to expand its share of employment especially given a high income demand elasticity. Possible dangers arise from a very fast rate of new technology introduction in the absence of product innovation.

d) Others: Our work suggests little change of expansion in food, drink and tobacco employment; agriculture and mining will also continue to lose employment share. The most buoyant industrial sector is chemicals, otherwise employment growth is to be located in the services sector.

IV. ALTERNATIVE CONCEPTUAL FRAMEWORKS

The principal theme of this project has been closely tied to a simple neoclassical model of technical change. As we have stated earlier, there has not been any slavish adherence to the principles of this approach throughout the contributions, for it was considered that by enforcing rigidity one would lose a number of potentially valuable insights. In fact we did, earlier on, consider some of the failings of the neoclassical approach. Given this relaxed approach to methodology, the various authors of commissioned research papers (Part III) have taken the opportunity to express views and opinions on and in other methodological frameworks. It seems to be worth spending a short time considering these different frameworks, their advantages/disadvantages and extra insight each provides. We do not expect to add much to our above discussion from this consideration, for we have been sufficiently flexible to have already taken account of the implications arising from the alternatives for the main theme of our work.

In contrast to the simple neo-classical framework, three other approaches have been used or discussed:

-- The vintage model approach.

-- The macro-economic multi-sector approach.

-- The Schumpeterian approach.

We will discuss these in order.

The vintage approach is used principally in the contributions by Soete and Barras. The basic distinguishing characteristic of the vintage approach is that it considers that at any moment in time the existing capital stock is made up of machines of different "vintages" and thus productive capabilities. New technology is embodied in new machines and thus a technological advance is not costlessly introduced into the system, but only slowly as new machines replace old. In many ways the performance of these vintage models is not very different from that of the standard model. However as we have seen in Soete's contribution, the use of such a model can have dramatic implications for one's estimates of rates of capital and labour productivity growth.

There is no doubt that the vintage approach has the edge on the simple model in terms of realism. The use of such a model is however much more complicated. The main addition we get from a vintage model is that new technology is not instantaneously diffused. However, in our use of the standard model we have grafted this on, implicitly and explicitly. Such an ad hoc meshing of the standard model with a diffusion concept may in fact be preferable to the use of the more difficult vintage approach, not only on the grounds of simplicity but also on the grounds of realism. The argument behind this is that the vintage model considers only one aspect of the forces behind the diffusion phenomenon, whereas many forces act to influence the diffusion path. The ad hoc grafting may be a better way to incorporate these elements.

The macro-econometric multi-sector approach is used by Eliasson and Wilson. The great advantage of this approach is that it stresses inter-sectoral linkages and macro-economic phenomena. It is for this reason that this material has been included. However, it would be unwise to rely solely upon this approach, for in obtaining a usable macro-economic analysis one must necessarily be less detailed at the micro-economic level. Such a macro approach thus ideally goes hand-in-hand with a less aggregative analysis.

Finally, we have had presented by Barras and Soete, some of the advantages of using a Schumpeterian framework. The micro-macro model of Eliasson is also very Schumpeterian. These contributions have been useful in generating extra insights into our project, particularly at the micro-macro level. We do not consider however that a Schumpeterian approach invalidates insights based on the neoclassical approach, that demand elasticities, biases etc., are relevant and need consideration.

Overall, we consider the various approaches to be complementary to each other. Our eclectic approach enables a variety of observations to be made, each paradigm giving its own insights and assistance to the common goal.

V. SOME POLICY ISSUES

The discussion of policy in this area is generally labelled technology policy. An agreed definition for this term does not really exist, however most of the material published or produced under this heading is mainly concerned with research and development spending and the attitudes of government to this. Although we will have some points to make regarding R&D spending, the main thrust of our discussion lies elsewhere. When considered in context this is reasonable. Our objectives concern the costs and benefits arising from the use of new technology, and the use of new technology is not synonymous with research and development spending. R&D is expenditures incurred in generating new technologies rather than their use. We cannot ignore R&D -- it is a vital input into the generation of new products embodying IT advances -- but it is definitely not the whole issue.

Our concern with the introduction of new technology and how it impacts on the national economy implies that we must consider the factors that affect introduction, and just as important, consider the points at which policy may come to bear in order to ensure that the market mechanism either does not hinder or is aided in generating the compensation and other effects that are necessary for the economy to fully benefit from introduction. We may also raise the often ignored issue of whether there really is a need to improve upon the outcome that economies would produce unaided, i.e. we must ask what is better?

Technology policy is obviously not a new field, neither is it a field ignored in previous OECD discussions. One particular publication, Innovation Policy -- Trends and Perspectives (OECD, Paris, 1982), provides a useful reference point. In that volume the policies of a number of OECD countries are presented with a "Note by the Secretariat" summarising (pp. 150-161) and raising major questions. The majority of this summary concerns the content of innovation policies, i.e. the nuts and bolts issues (mainly relating to R&D policy). It is clear that in this particular area there are more questions than answers. The report avoids the design of actual policies, or the content of policy. Our analysis has given us little insight into this. We are more concerned with the wider general issues of the need for policies rather than the design of policies.

Even within this limited purview there are a number of policy issues that arise. We are going to concentrate on the six major ones, although no doubt further issues could be identified. The six are:

1. Diffusion policy.

2. Training and education.

3. Trade policy.

4. Domestic technological product capability.

5. Institutional and market flexibility.

6. Market power and anti-trust policy.

Each of these issues has been referred to above, but at the risk of repetition, in the discussion below we will illustrate now the relevance arises.

1. Diffusion Policy

Technological diffusion is the process by which new technology is introduced into an economy. The diffusion process really has two sides -- diffusion in supply, i.e. the growth of an industry supplying technologically new products, and diffusion in demand relating to the actual use or ownership of the new technology. It is only as new technology is diffused throughout an economy that the benefits will be realised and the costs be incurred. We have argued above that faster diffusion can (although not always will) yield trading and employment benefits mainly through improvements in international competitiveness. Thus it might seem that faster diffusion speeds can expedite the generation of the gains from the technology and also have wider economic advantages. We have also argued above that the factors affecting the speed of take up on new technology are numerous, varying from shortages of skilled manpower, information deficiencies, systems effects, economic viability, etc.

The implication of these two observations seems at first sight to be clear: policies that speed up diffusion will help to maintain if not increase employment at home. Secondly, policies to speed up diffusion can be designed, having their effect by overcoming skill shortages, etc.

Again, however, the issue is not really this simple. In fact to discuss the issue at all one has to have some greater understanding of the literature on diffusion and then consider policy issues in the light of that literature. At the risk of over simplification the diffusion theory literature splits into two main approaches:

i) The diffusion of technology can and has been viewed as a process that is based on imperfect information flows and uncertain environments. Diffusion is not instantaneous because information is limited and adopting new technology involves risks and uncertainty. A basic proposition in this approach is that the characteristics of the new technology are given and do not change over time.

ii) The second approach assumes complete information, but considers that the basic character of new technology changes over time. At each moment in time, technology is used by those for whom it is profitable, and as time proceeds changes in the technology lead to changes in the level of use.

These two approaches are not only very different in their conceptions of the technological change and diffusion process but have very different policy implications. It would of course be advantageous if one could a priori consider that one approach is more valid than the other. Unfortunately, that is not at present possible, and much more research is needed in this area. Moreover, the policy implications that result from either approach are also, at the present time, not completely clear. Only in the last couple of years has the second approach really been subjected to policy analysis and the results are still in an early stage.

However, a few policy alternatives can be discussed. In doing this we must make one further observation. An observed diffusion path will be the result of interaction between those demanding the technology and those supplying the technology, and policies that concentrate on the demand side must be evaluated taking into account the supply side reactions. Our discussion here will include such reactions, but we will not be discussing supply side orientated policies per se.

We can conceive of three basic types of policies. The first is policies aimed at improving information flows, the second financial incentives and the third training and education policies.

Two examples of information policies are the MAP programme in the United Kingdom and, for a different technology, the Agricultural Extension Service in the United States. The basic principle behind these programmes is that they either:

a) extend the knowledge of the existence of new technology to potential users;

b) aid potential users in discovering exactly what the new technology can do for them; or

c) reduce search costs for potential users;

and, in doing so, will speed up diffusion (the basic principle being that lack of knowledge is limiting usage). If information deficiencies are the barrier slowing diffusion, then such policies would seem to be appropriate. However, it is not certain that the desired effect will always result. We can suggest two reasons why this might be:

a) to a certain extent the incentive to use a new technology is the advantage one gains over competitors. The longer this advantage is expected to exist, the greater is the incentive. The whole intention of these information-based policies is to make emulation speedier, thereby implying a lower incentive to early users. This may slow their adoption process, if they foresee such stimulating policies;

b) secondly, these policies are designed to increase the demand for new technology at early dates in the diffusion process. Before one can predict the actual impact of this on usage, one must take account of the role played by the suppliers of the new technology. An increase in demand, firstly, will only result in increased usage if supply responds. If capacity is constrained, the supply need not be forthcoming, and if prices rise in response to the increased demand this may partly, or even wholly, offset the increased demand. The ability of the supplying industry to internalise the benefits of information stimulation programmes may well depend on its market structure. It is possible to conceive however, when new technology is imported, that the only effect of a government policy is to increase the prices of products embodying the new technology and increase the profits of overseas suppliers.

The next set of policies we can consider are financial incentives. In essence these incentives are designed to make new technology more attractive (profitable) to potential users and thereby increase usage. An example of such policies is investment incentives. These policies are relevant when it is the second approach to diffusion that is a fair reflection of the world. One should recall that in this approach users have adopted the new technology if it is profitable, have not adopted it if it is not, and new technology is changing (improving) over time.

In such a world, the use of incentives to stimulate use, will, if effective, lead to use of the technology by firms for whom it was not previously profitable. This implies that the use of these incentives will generate use of the technology by firms for whom private costs exceed private benefits. Unless private and social costs and benefits differ for some reason, the use of these incentives must thus make economy wide resource use less efficient, which cannot be an aid to international competitiveness. Justification for incentives in such a situation must thus rest on arguments showing that private and social costs and benefits differ. In particular as the policies are used to stimulate greater use, they must be justified on the grounds that private benefits are exceeded by social benefits and/or private costs exceed social costs. The social costs and benefits that arise from technological advance are by no means clear and thus it would be misleading to be definitive; but the sorts of issues that we can consider are as follows:

i) if a firm changing technology does not bear the costs of retraining deskilled workers, social costs may exceed private costs;

ii) if the example set by innovating firms is of value to others, social benefits may exceed private benefits;

iii) if markets are imperfect and do not clear instantaneously, the prices used in evaluating the profitability of a technology may be very different from those that would reflect resource scarcity;

iv) if success on foreign markets is valued more highly by decision makers (for whatever reason) than is reflected in exchange rates, private and social costs and benefits may differ;

v) if the cost of purchasing products embodying new technology is determined by a supplying industry with monopoly power, users private valuations may not reflect social valuations;

vi) in a world where technology is changing, incentives may induce firms to adopt a technology today, whereas it might be better for them to wait until tomorrow when either the technology is improved or could be produced at a lower resource cost.

Such propositions as these are really only the starting point in an area where a great deal more work is needed. However rather than pursue these tentative propositions, let us turn to quite a separate issue. Will the incentives actually speed up diffusion? Here we can proceed by stating the reservations that form part of the case against:

a) if there is a monopoly power in the supplying industry, the incentive may just be appropriated by the supplier in higher prices and profits and diffusion need not be affected;

b) if expectations play a role in the diffusion process, the expectation of a subsidy to come may slow down early adoption. On the other hand, expectations of a declining subsidy may speed up adoption;

c) finally, if a subsidy speeds up adoption, this may reduce the expected period of market advantage to be enjoyed by an earlier adopter and thus slow his take up rate.

Even at this point the diffusion policy discussion is not complete. There are still numerous questions that require answering before that point is reached. Unfortunately it is not possible to give definitive answers to these questions. Consider for example two such questions:

a) should technology policy be directed towards production or use, i.e. what is the appropriate mix of R&D subsidies and diffusion subsidies? Should diffusion be subsidised with a spin-off to suppliers of new technology products which will stimulate R&D, or should R&D be subsidised to generate better (or cheaper) products that may lead to faster diffusion? Conflicts between these two types of subsidies have been apparent in UK government policy over the last two decades;

b) should governments subsidise particular technologies or spread subsidies more widely to all investment and allow potential users to select their appropriate technology? Many OECD governments have offered investment incentives in the post-war era. One can raise the question of whether concentration on particular technologies would be more appropriate.

Both questions are neither simple to analyse or answer, but if a full appreciation of technology policy is to be made, they require answers.

The discussion, although incomplete, has been particularly lengthy, for three main reasons. Firstly, because it is not generally recognised that such issues as those discussed above are important. Secondly because international differences in diffusion rates are usually isolated as particularly important in determining the international distribution of employment, and thirdly because it illustrates to an extent our level of ignorance. The conclusions we can draw from the discussion are limited but the following seem relevant:

- i) we need more understanding of the forces behind the diffusion process before we can proceed to detailed policy making;

- ii) we need more understanding of diffusion before we can appreciate the impacts of policies; and

- iii) we cannot even fully accept that policies generating a faster diffusion rate will improve employment through increased competitiveness until we can show that the policies lead to improved resource utilisation efficiencies, implying of course that it is either information imperfections that slow the take up of new technology or more generally that private and social costs and benefits from innovation differ.

2. Education and Training

The relevance of education and training policies is twofold. Firstly it is argued that the lack of suitably qualified personnel will slow diffusion. Secondly it is argued that as the economy reacts to the new technology the jobs created and destroyed will have different skill requirements, and only by retraining and re-education can the labour market be made to clear more quickly.

There seems to be little doubt that a lack of suitably qualified personnel can slow the development and diffusion of new technology. However it is also clear that new technology often changes as it matures, and the skill requirements become lower, the use of the technology becoming more routine. In later stages skill requirements may well be less.

The question that arises is whether it is appropriate for government policies to be formulated to improve skill levels to speed up the diffusion process. It is probably reasonable to argue that in most countries the supply of labour of different skills is not primarily market determined. This raises the possibility for differences between private and social costs and benefits that are the main justification for government involvement. Exactly how the education and training policies should be directed is another matter. For there seems to be a particular controversy over the expected future development of labour demand (the issue, moreover, is relevant not only to the diffusion issue but also the labour market clearing issue). The two main competing hypotheses on likely movements in the labour market are that:

- i) higher education and skill levels will be required at all points on the skill spectrum;

- ii) the labour market will be polarised, with increased demands for low and high skill categories but reductions in the middle.

We are not in a position to judge between the two outcomes, but we can make observations on three related points:

- i) there is a tendency among commentators on technical change to consider that the skill demands of new technology have their own momentum. However, if it is the case that severe skill shortages affect the take up of new technology it is reasonable to expect the design of new versions of products that will, at least in part, alleviate these shortages (consider for example the development of software aids);

ii) it is clear that as new technology is introduced that certain skills will become redundant. A need thus arises for retraining. This leads to the third point;

iii) perhaps the overriding concern of training and education policies should be to provide a labour force that is adaptable and flexible. Flexibility will be the key to retraining, but more importantly, if one cannot predict future movements in the skill composition of labour demand, having the ability to respond quickly to realised outcomes will be the most valuable asset. With IT as the dominant technology, this must suggest the need for widespread general training in computing abilities and understanding.

3. Trade Policy

We have argued above that to a large extent, the compensation for direct employment reduction from new technology will come from increased international competitiveness, but also that losses in employment may come from losses in markets following a failure to innovate. To an extent, exchange rate flexibility is of importance in these conclusions. However, there are some further issues to discuss. The first is whether we are discussing a zero-sum game, i.e. is it the case that one economy can only maintain employment levels after changes in technology at the expense of another? This is equivalent to asking whether demand in the world as a whole would increase sufficiently to compensate for increased productiveness. Such world-wide questions are rarely asked, let alone answered. As an opinion, however, it certainly seems possible for certain goods that demand would increase sufficiently. One is getting into very difficult questions, but it would seem that there is certainly sufficient notional if not effective demand in the world for food, shelter and even less basic goods to fully utilise our most productive technologies.

However, even if there is an increase in world demand, there is still the whole issue of relocations of jobs either as a result of the introduction of new technologies at different rates in different countries, or because of the preferred location of productive units with different technologies.

On the latter issue first -- the location of production -- it has often been observed that the new chip technologies have been assembled in NICs rather than in the more highly developed Western countries (e.g. the United States). It is suggested that the new technologies make low wage countries particularly favourable production centres. This is only one possible outcome of the appearance of these new technologies. However, the neo-technology theories of trade suggest quite a different pattern. High technology industries arise and initially grow in developed economies and only as they mature and their demand for specialised inputs decline do they shift to other nations. In such a scenario continued advance is both the progenitor and transferor of employment in developed countries. The static theory of comparative advantage has little role to play in a world of rapid technological advance.

However, the main issue we wish to confront here is one of government policy in the face of international competition: in essence, protectionism in a world of fast technological change. This issue is discussed at some length in the paper by Rush and Hoffman (cf. "Microelectronics in the Clothing Industry"). One may argue that the case for or against protection for an industry challenged by innovators overseas essentially reduces to answering why the domestic industry cannot meet that challenge without protection. With an answer to this question, one can then proceed to consider the relative resource costs of meeting the challenge through different policies of which protection will be only one, and perhaps even questioning whether meeting the challenge will be the best use of resources or whether the resources could best be employed in an alternative area.

As should be obvious, this raises very difficult and often politically charged issues. However, rather than become too involved in these, we note firstly that the "infant-industry" and "senile-industry" arguments are usually the only arguments accepted for protection, and secondly we can think of a number of cases where protection would not be a suitable policy, e.g. where diffusion is slow because of monopoly power, or where information oriented policies could provide a quick response to new technological opportunities.

4. Domestic Production Capabilities

Many developed nations who do not already have domestic production capabilities in the area of IT, are actively pursuing, in one way or another, the objective of acquiring them. To discuss the merits of this it is worth breaking IT into three parts:

i) the production of components (chips);

ii) the production of producer goods incorporating the components; and

iii) the production of consumer goods, either using the new producer goods or incorporating new components.

We have already considered iii) in some detail above. Here we are concerned mainly with i) and ii). In discussing the issue of domestic production capability it is important to realise that we are discussing not a once and for all technological change, but a process of technological change that has been and is expected to continue at a fast rate.

The main argument in favour of domestic production capabilities are as follows:

i) in order to capture many of the compensation effects it is necessary to supply the new technology from domestic sources;

ii) domestic production capabilities generate a closer relationship between user and producer, making technology more relevant to local circumstances and diffusion faster; it may also help in generating local skills;

iii) IT is so basic to the expected development of the world economy over the next decade, that a failure to develop an IT capability will make many markets inaccessible;

iv) a domestic capability is necessary for national security and defence.

These benefits have to be offset by certain costs.

i) At the present stage of development, chip design and manufacture especially, and capital goods production to a lesser extent, are intensive in skills that are scarce in many economies. As the industry is dynamic there will be a continued demand for skilled electrical and software engineers, designers, etc., if domestic capability is to remain competitive.

ii) Besides the use of scarce human skills, the set up costs, especially of chip production are large.

It would seem that countries should approach domestic production capabilities in terms of an hierarchical approach, the stage at which the country settles in the hierarchy depending on the resources.

i) It would appear that to compete in world markets IT based production processes should be used where profitable and consumer products incorporating IT components should be developed.

ii) The manufacture of capital goods embodying IT technology is the next stage. The existence of a domestic capability in this area will enable compensation effects to be internalised and also create a domestic information environment conducive to the use of the technology. It seems undesirable however that this objective should be pursued at the expense of i), and it is also probably more intensive in scarce skilled labour than i). The option exists for creating this capability through licensing of domestic production for a foreign owned producer. As yet we know little of scale economies in this area and so it is impossible to say, in the final analysis, how many domestic industries of this type can exist in a free world market.

iii) The third level is component or chip manufacture. It is worth noting that in the United States most design and research is US based whereas production is farmed out to low wage economies. This suggests that most developed countries would not wish to enter, or could not compete in chip manufacture at this time. This leaves the possibility of developing a design/R&D capability in the area of components. Such activity is especially intensive in skilled personnel, and may not be the best use of resources for an economy without any background in this area.

We should note however that technologies have a tendency to change over time, to become less intensive in skills and other scarce resources. This may suggest that although now may not be the time for a country to enter the industry, the conclusion may be reversed at a later date. We would also note, that a major advantage arising from domestic production is in terms of improved information flows. If a domestic production capability is not encouraged, there would seem to be a role for domestic information agencies that can provide the externalities. We may further note that software provision is as important as hardware provision, and perhaps more labour intensive. A domestic software industry is not necessarily dependent on a domestic hardware industry.

It is in this area of domestic production capability that the major questions concerning R&D policy arise. The foundation or development of industries producing IT based products is intensive in R&D funds. The OECD report on Innovation Policy (referred to in the introduction to this Chapter) states many of the unanswered policy questions we face in this area. The following three are raised as examples.

a) What is the appropriate policy mix between supporting producers of IT goods through R&D support and supporting users through diffusion subsidies?

b) What is the best method of R&D support -- direct aid, tax incentives or another route?

c) Should R&D support be concentrated on particular technologies, firms or sectors, or generalised?

These issues are important yet as of now answers are extremely difficult to provide. They are not really issues on which this study throws much extra light. But the discussions of the service sector above raise the issue of infrastructure. The authors (Petit, Barras) view the provision of an infrastructure conducive to private sector innovativeness as a prime task for government technology policy. If the government policy provides this, the private sector will follow market incentives to generate technological advance.

5. Institutional and Market Flexibility

The topic of institutional and market flexibility is a large one, the implications of which extend in many directions. To make the topic manageable we will look at two aspects, the first being the impact of flexibility or rigidities on diffusion patterns, the second the impact of flexibility or rigidities on the realisation of compensation effects.

Consider then the impact of institutional rigidities on diffusion patterns. Often considered under the heading of "barriers to innovation", a recent study by Piatier (3)(p. 176) considers general legislation, bureaucracy, norms and standards as the most important and significant of the factors that have slowed innovation in the EEC member countries. The sort of examples one can consider might be:

a) the existence of public telecommunications monopolies as a factor preventing technological advance through new entry; or

b) controls on broadcasting as a barrier to cabling; or

c) the inability to gain patent protection for software.

Examples similar to these may be thought of, but the effect of such rigidities will be to significantly affect the use of new technology. Similarly, norms, standards or regulations may affect the extent to which compensation can be realised as new technology is introduced. Petit considers how the growth of services in the banking sector are affected by regulation and control. The nature of competition in financial markets that may be capable of change as new technology appears, could be significantly affected by regulation.

This is not the place to consider detailed changes in the regulatory environment. It is of course the case that regulations have been generated for particular purposes. The interface between such regulations and technical change is that appropriate regulations may well be technology dependent (e.g. emission control requirements have changed as technological possibilities have changed, which possibilities in turn have been stimulated by regulation). One may argue that new technology generates a need for regulation reviews, and that as a general policy statement, regulations should be appropriate to technology. Taking such a view regulations may be used to stimulate desirable technical change as well as to moderate its harmful effects. In particular one might consider that recent technology advances may enable greater environmental protection than was previously possible.

This argument also raises the further possibility that in the light of the potential presented by IT that institutional and regulatory change can be used to generate beneficial compensation effects in the market. Thus if IT makes new lower emission levels possible, then regulating for such lower levels could stimulate the motor industry. Regulatory change in telecommunications or cabling could also generate expansions in consumer demand and thus output and employment. The possibilities are there.

Turning from institutional to market flexibility, we may consider two issues. The first concerns general wage and price flexibility in an economy. The second concerns the extent to which parts of the economy are protected from many market forces and thus may not respond to economic incentives. This latter includes the question of market power and anti-trust policy which merits separate treatment below.

Turning first to wage and price flexibility, we have argued above that some intermediate extent of such flexibility is most appropriate to overcoming unemployment. Too much or too little are equally undesirable. Exactly how one is to gauge what amount is right is an open question.

The second issue of market flexibility concerns, as well as monopoly power, those elements of demand that are government controlled, e.g. health and education. In the absence of reaction to market forces one may find that such sectors are either backward in adopting new technology or slow in responding to cost changes, thereby limiting their contribution to the compensation of job reductions. The design of flexible bureaucracies is perhaps what is needed, but this is easier to state than institute. One must however state that a fast changing world is inconsistent with an educational system that is slow to change or a health system that does not take advantage of major advances. The first would severely limit the extent of use of new techology while the second would represent many missed opportunities.

6. Market Power and Anti-Trust Policy

Bosworth suggests, and there is a certain amount of evidence to support the proposition, that the existence of market power and/or entry barriers tends to interfere with the compensation mechanism. Specifically market power enables a firm to appropriate more of the benefits from an innovation for itself, prices do not fall by the full extent of any cost reduction and thus demand does not increase to offset direct reductions in labour demand. Moreover, one could argue, the existence of monopoly power leads to a dynamic equivalent of monopoly welfare loss. Policies that lead to greater competition would thus seem to be desirable. However, we must be very careful over such simple policy prescriptions. For example:

i) it may be that the monopoly power observed is a reward for technological innovation and without this reward the incentives to innovate will be less, i.e. by being an innovator the firm builds up market power and it is by the use of this power that innovation is encouraged. Policies that remove the power also remove the incentive and may slow down technological innovation. This is in fact the basis of the model in Eliasson's contribution;

ii) even if market power is not the reward for innovativeness it may be that in a risky world, the existence of such power speeds up innovation. Although the empirical evidence is weak, the Schumpeterian hypothesis of a link between technological advance and bigness and fewness plays a leading role in the technological change literature;

iii) in a roundabout way, the greater gains an innovator can make because of his monopoly power, may induce beneficial behaviour on the part of the suppliers of new technology. The more profitable is the new technology to the user, the greater is the price (ceteris paribus) at which the supplier can sell. This may well induce beneficial effects in the supply of technology products.

It is possible to envisage therefore a conflict between having sufficient incentive to undertake innovation or the adoption of new technology and having a market that will generate the required compensation effects. Such conflicts as this are common in the anti-trust area. They are not, unfortunately, conflicts that empirical evidence has resolved.

Our view of the evidence is that existing monopoly positions are not unduly favourable to innovation and may also limit compensation. Anti-trust efforts at entrenched monopolies should be encouraged. However, monopoly power that arises through innovative behaviour is a way that provides incentives to innovation work, and to direct anti-trust policy here is probably harmful. On a more positive note, we may observe that innovation, i.e. the use of inventions, is not the prerogative of large firms -- the source of many innovations are new firms. Barriers to entry or predatory pricing to keep out or drive out new entrants cannot be conducive to innovation and are legitimate targets for anti-trust policy.

VI. CONCLUSIONS

In this Part, we have attempted to bring together the several contributions made to this project. Our main conclusions are that the future development of OECD economies in light of the IT revolution are likely to be evolutionary rather than revolutionary, with little change from past trends. This suggests that some industries, largely those providing basic necessities will continue to decline, while others have better growth prospects. A continued growth of services at the expense of manufacturing is envisaged.

We do not see in IT any salvation for employment prospects, but we do not see IT as a mass destroyer of jobs. The introduction of IT will definitely change the skill and industrial composition of labour demand, but will not to any greater extent than we have seen in the past.

The IT revolution we see as requiring flexibility in institutions, markets and policies. Flexibility in education and training, in market behaviour and the setting of standards seem important policy issues. Such flexibility is necessary to encourage the introduction of IT and the effective realisation of its benefits and compensation impacts. It is clear that when any new technology is introduced some economic actors will gain and others will lose. On balance with IT we see the net effect to be positive, but only with appropriate policies will the costs to the losers be minimised while the gains to the winners are optimised.

NOTES AND REFERENCES

1. It is significant that one of the more widely reported recent studies on the impact of new technologies, by Leontief, takes a macro perspective on the issue.

2. H. Furchtgott-Roth, "Some Problems in the Use of Index Numbers to Measure Technical Change", a paper presented at the Warwick Summer Workshop on the Economics of Technical Change, 1984.

3. A. Piatier, Barriers to Innovation, Frances Pinter, London, 1984.

Part III

RESEARCH PAPERS

I. INTRODUCTION

AN ANALYTICAL FRAMEWORK FOR ANALYSING THE IMPACT OF
INFORMATION TECHNOLOGIES ON ECONOMIC PERSPECTIVES

by

Paul Stoneman
University of Warwick
United Kingdom

1. THE PROJECT

The aims of this project involve the evaluation and the analysis of the relationships between on the one hand, IT and IT-based innovations, and on the other hand, output growth, relative capital/labour costs, employment and the international division of labour in a macro-economic context. This also includes the analysis and design of IT promotion and procurement policies.

It should be realised at the outset that the analysis of the role of new technology in promoting economic growth and development involves a number of extremely complex economic and social issues. The means we have at hand for investigating the technological change phenomenon are limited and we are thus constrained in how far it is possible to pursue the main objective. Given these limitations, however, the papers in this part of the volume represent an attempt to bring together original work and material from numerous sources, in order to form a coherent view of the opportunities presented by and potential impacts arising from advances in information technology. In order to make such an exercise practical and meaningful, the project has been structured around a particular analytical framework that is used to provide a guide to individual investigations of separate industrial sectors and basic economic relationships. In the Introduction that follows, this framework is presented and discussed, and the relationship of the other contributions to this framework is also detailed.

2. INTRODUCTION

Information technology may be broadly defined as "products and processes concerned with the collection, transmission and manipulation of information". It covers, among other things, computers, telecommunications, robotics and micro-electronics. In our view, the majority of the future and near future technological advances can be labelled as advances in information technology, although certain recent changes in, for example, biotechnology and ceramics are also occurring. In case studies, the actual changes in technology that are expected or are already occuring are discussed in more detail.

For this analytical framework we may talk of "new technology" in more general terms without any loss of relevance, for the issues are similar, whatever the specific technology being discussed.

Technological change is not a simple phenomenon. It is even a term that is not simple to define. It is common to treat the phenomenon as made up of three (interrelated) stages. Invention (the generation of ideas), innovation (the development of ideas into marketable products) and diffusion (the spread of the new products across the potential market). Commonly known as the Schumpeter trilogy, this conceptual division is a useful tool for looking at technical change. In particular, one may argue that an economy is only materially affected by technological change once diffusion has begun, i.e. technologies invented but not diffused are irrelevant to the economic system.

In terms of time, new technologies are generally somewhat slow in both reaching the market and diffusing across a market. Time periods between invention and innovation of ten years would not be uncommon, and between innovation and extensive use, similar time scales are not out of the ordinary [see for example Mansfield (1968)]. If this is the case then any analysis of medium term prospects, i.e. a five to ten year horizon, can largely proceed independently of technologies that are not already in the market or close to being marketed. In fact, the medium term will largely be influenced by only those technologies that are currently being diffused, and thus the major part of our perspective may concern the impact of diffusion rather than R&D.

At a general level, as the use of new process technology proceeds or as a new product technology expands its market, we may observe a process of economic adjustment and change that, to many economists, is the true reflection of economic behaviour. As new technology is introduced, new firms are born, others die. Some firms expand and some decline. Industries rise and fall. The patterns of factor demand ebb and flow under the influence of new technologies, and the economy proceeds in an "evolutionary" way. In fact the influential work of Nelson and Winter (1974), following on that of Schumpeter (1934), describes such a process as an "evolutionary" process.

The set of questions that we wish to approach as this process occurs are as follows:

i) Which are the industries which will grow or at least what factors distinguish the industries that grow from those that decline?

ii) As the process of technological change occurs what will happen to factor demands, especially the demand for labour?

iii) To what extent can international competition in technology be used to reduce unemployment?

iv) What barriers exist to, and what policies are appropriate to stimulating, the use of new technologies?

The fourth of these questions merits a somewhat separate approach and is dealt with separately. The first three questions are interrelated and merit a common approach. There are a number of ways to go about this of which the empirical case study approach is most prevalent. Usually an individual firm is investigated and changes in its pattern of factor demands are related to changes in its technological base. The major problems with this approach are that:

a) knock-on effects outside the firm are generally ignored but these may be quite important;

b) case study, by its nature, only gives specific and not general results.

However, both these objections can be overcome and the analysis improved if a more general approach is used into which the results from case study analysis are introduced. In essence, this is one of the underlying rationales of this project: to set up a general analytic framework and to use this framework to relate the impact of technological change to the values of specific economic parameters, estimates of which can then be provided from case study results.

The choice of analytic framework is crucial to the results that one achieves, however the choice set is quite small. The number of alternative operational frameworks is limited. The dominant paradigm in economics is that labelled neo-classical. Without going into excessive detail, one can characterise the neo-classical approach to economics by three basic tenets:

i) that production relationships can be summarised by a production function exhibiting substitution possibilities and the arguments of that function (i.e. the inputs) can be defined and measured;

ii) that economic actors are rational and act to maximise their objective functions. The usual assumption is that firms maximise profits;

iii) that all markets clear through price adjustments implying an analysis that concentrates on equilibrium positions and the comparative statics properties of such equilibria.

Such an approach to economics is, of course, not without its critics. The objections rest on a number of levels, some of which can be dealt with, others which cannot.

a) There are a number of objections based on the measurement of inputs, in particular whether capital can be measured. These are so basic that they cannot be overcome. However, by working mainly at the firm or industry level rather than the aggregate, where the objections are strongest, we do minimize the problem.

b) There are problems concerning the acceptance of market clearing through price adjustments. In fact, the whole of modern

Keynesianism rejects such an hypothesis. However, this problem can be adequately considered by looking at relationships between prices and costs and be reflected perhaps in price elasticity estimates.

c) A third set of objections concerns the behaviour and objectives of economic actors. A lengthy, detailed discussion of the validity of assuming maximising behaviour cannot be provided here, suffice it to say that in the long run the alternative of satisfying behaviour may be adequately approximated by maximising behaviour.

d) Finally, when discussing issues within the economics of technological change it is often argued that neo-classical economics cannot adequately represent the "evolutionary" story and is thus an inappropriate tool for such analysis [see Stoneman (1983)]. This is a particularly difficult objection to overcome, and the only reply available is that unfortunately a rigorous analysis based on Schumpeterian principles does not seem feasible at the present time.

The neo-classical approach does also have advantages, not the least of these being that it is widely accepted. However, perhaps its greatest advantage is that it does enable one to be precise in detailing the crucial parameters that determine the impact of technology on factor demands, and moreover the parameters are in principle measureable. In fact the view we take of the neo-classical paradigm is perhaps best expressed by Nelson (1981), from whom we quote:

"The purpose of any theoretical formulation is to provide a particular focus and interpretation. Reality inevitably is much richer than any theory. Empirical scholars in economics recognize that theory is abstraction, and try to take into account important factors omitted by prevailing theory. Further, a simple theory, initially formulated, is amenable to later widening, deepening, and to modifications that deal with anomalies. The fruitfulness of a broad theoretical structure has to be judged in terms of the energy it lends to research, and the power of the knowledge won through that research. By these criteria the neo-classical art form clearly must be judged as having been very fruitful. It has given life, direction, and a considerable degree of coherency to research done by a large number of economists over a considerable period of time."

However, given the objections above, it would be particularly inappropriate to exclude other approaches from our work or to adhere too rigidly to the neo-classical structure. To quote Nelson (1981) again,

"But while sensible scholars treat formal theoretical frameworks pragmatically, still these frameworks constrain as well as focus, blind as well as illuminate, the empirical research endeavour. Prevailing formal theory influences profoundly what empirical data are ignored, and how attended empirical data are interpreted."

Thus, we tend to view the neo-classical paradigm as an organising and conceptual framework rather than a rigid structure and, especially as regards the Case Studies, although a contribution to the general neo-classical theme is always presented, individual authors have had the freedom and encouragement to present their analysis, using those paradigms that seem most appropriate to them. This makes for a much richer collection of contributions than could have been provided if a neo-classical straightjacket had been imposed.

In the next section, the neo-classical approach is used to discuss relationships between factor demands and outputs and technological change at the firm and industry level. There, "non basic" objections to the approach are dealt with as the analysis proceeds. Underlying the discussion of the results is the view that most economies engage in international trade and this must be taken into account. The majority of this analysis is conducted at the industry level. The macro-economic implications of the micro results are thus discussed further in Section 4. After this discussion, the speed of adoption of new technology is considered. Finally, conclusions are drawn and the relationship of the other papers that form part of this project to the analytical framework is considered.

3. A NEO-CLASSICAL APPROACH TO THE IMPACT OF NEW TECHNOLOGY ON FACTOR DEMANDS

The starting point for most neo-classical analysis studying the implications of technological change is usually the production relationship. Let Y, K and L represent output and the inputs of capital and labour services respectively. Use t to represent time or technology. The production function may then be written as

$$Y = F(K,L,t) \qquad (1)$$

and output is seen to be related to the inputs and time. The effect of technological advance is modelled by the inclusion of the t term in (1). The two important classifications that one must first consider are:

a) the disembodiment or embodiment of technological change;

b) the neutrality or bias of technological change.

Technical progress is embodied if it is put into effect by introducing new capital or labour. It is disembodied if it is not so introduced but falls like "manna from heaven" on all existing capacity. In analysing the effect of technological change we will be assuming disembodiment but will later discuss the implications of removing this assumption.

The bias of technological change in essence refers to whether the introduction of new technology changes the "balance between factor inputs in the production process". The "balance" is usually considered in terms of factor shares. Under certain assumptions about factor price paths and elasticities of substitution factor, shares can be translated into relative factor demands and thus bias can indicate the effect on relative factor intensities of specific technological changes.

The discussion of biases is directed towards obtaining some impression as to how changes in technology save one factor input at the expense of another, e.g. technological advance might favour capital at the expense of labour. The actual measures of bias are numerous, the one we have in mind here is the definition due to Hicks.

Bias is related to rates of factor augmentation which in turn are defined as the rates at which technological advance is increasing the productivity of the different inputs. Technological advance may augment capital and labour at different rates and thus raise capital productivity and labour productivity at different rates. From these rates of factor augmentation one can move to a consideration of the bias implicit in technological advance. Also, a weighted sum (with weights usually being the shares of factors in total cost) of the rates of factor augmentation, called the rate of total factor productivity growth, is usually used to measure the overall rate of technological advance.

These rates of augmentation, biases and the rate of technological advance are all factors that are considered technologically determined. We should note, however, that by its concentration upon production function analysis, this view of the technological change process takes inadequate account of the effect of technological advance on product quality, e.g. it emphasises process innovation at the expense of product innovation.

As technological advance occurs and total factor productivity is increased through factor augmentation, the required amount of each input per unit of output will change. If both capital and labour are being augmented, less labour and capital will be needed to produce a unit of output.

If labour and capital are being augmented at different rates, then at given factor prices, the effective relative cost of the two inputs will change. Profit maximising firms will, if technologically possible, wish to substitute the now relatively cheaper input for the more expensive input. The possibilities for such substitution are measured by the elasticity of substitution of the production function.

The reduced input requirements per unit of output will, for given output, reduce the demand for both inputs. The substitution reaction will act on top of this to change the demand for inputs. Assuming there are only two inputs, the substitution reaction, when rates of augmentation differ, will have the effect of counteracting the initial effect for one input while reinforcing the effect on the other.

The reduced input requirements per unit of output, plus the reorganisation of inputs in line with their effective costs, will both, given fixed factor prices, generate lower total and marginal costs of production. Again assuming profit maximisation, the lower costs will generate a desire to increase output and the price in the market will be lower. This increase in output will counteract the reduced labour demands generated by the reduced input requirements per unit of output. The extent of the increased factor demand generated by this increased output is determined by the degree of scale economies in production.

The extent of the increase in output generated by the lower costs will depend upon the extent to which these costs are reflected in lower prices and the increase in demand generated by the lower prices. In the absence of monopoly power on the part of producers, the full reduction in costs should be reflected in prices. The increased demand brought forward by these lower prices is measured by the (own price) elasticity of demand.

Table 1

EFFECTS OF TECHNOLOGICAL CHANGE ON FACTOR DEMAND: FIRM OR INDUSTRY LEVEL, CONSTANT RETURNS TO SCALE, FIXED FACTOR PRICES

		\multicolumn{4}{c}{Labour saving/Labour augmentation}	\multicolumn{2}{c}{Neutrality/ Product augmentation}	\multicolumn{4}{c}{Capital saving/Capital augmentation}
		\multicolumn{2}{c}{Pure}	\multicolumn{2}{c}{Relative}			\multicolumn{2}{c}{Pure}	\multicolumn{2}{c}{Relative}
		\multicolumn{2}{c}{$\frac{da}{a}=0\ \frac{db}{b}>0$}	\multicolumn{2}{c}{$\frac{db}{b}>\frac{da}{a}>0$}	\multicolumn{2}{c}{$\frac{da}{a}=\frac{db}{b}>0$}	\multicolumn{2}{c}{$\frac{da}{a}>0\ \frac{db}{b}=0$}	\multicolumn{2}{c}{$\frac{da}{a}>\frac{db}{b}>0$}
		L	K	L	K	L	K	L	K	L	K
$\sigma>1$	$\sigma<\eta$	+/−	+	+/−	+	+	+	+	+/−	+	+/−
	$\sigma=\eta$	+	0	+	+	+	+	+	+	0	+
	$\sigma>\eta$	+/−	−	+/−	+/−	+/−	+/−	+/−	+/−	−	+/−
$\sigma<1$	$\sigma<\eta$	+/−	+	+/−	+/−	+/−	+/−	+/−	+/−	+	+/−
	$\sigma=\eta$	−	0	−	−	−	−	−	−	0	−
	$\sigma>\eta$	+/−	−	+/−	−	−	−	−	+/−	−	+/−
$\eta>1$	$\sigma<\eta$	+/−	+	+/−	+	+	+	+	+/−	+	+/−
	$\sigma=\eta$	+	0	+	+	+	+	+	+	0	+
	$\sigma>\eta$	+	−	+	+/−	+	+	+/−	+	−	+
$\eta<1$	$\sigma<\eta$	−	+	−	+/−	−	−	+/−	−	+	−
	$\sigma=\eta$	−	0	−	−	−	−	−	−	0	−
	$\sigma>\eta$	+/−	−	+/−	−	−	−	−	+/−	−	+/−
$\sigma=1$	$\sigma<1$	−	−	−	−	−	−	−	−	−	−
	$\sigma=1$	0	0	0	0	0	0	0	0	0	0
	$\sigma>1$	+	+	+	+	+	+	+	+	+	+

Note: + Positive effect.
 − Negative effect.
 0 No effect.
 +/− Effect cannot be signed.

Signs calculated from equations (2) and (3) in the text assuming $\frac{dw}{w}=\frac{dr}{r}=0$.

To derive the overall impact of a technological change on the demand for different factors, we thus have to consider rates of factor augmentation, elasticities of substitution, economies of scale, and elasticities of demand. In the Annex to this paper, we derive mathematically an expression for the rate of growth of factor demands for both an industry and a single firm in that industry under the following assumptions:

a) there is a fixed number of firms in the industry, each firm is the same, and all introduce any new technology at the same time;

b) there are constant returns to scale;

c) the elasticity of demand is a constant;

d) there are only two factor inputs, capital and labour;

e) technological change is factor augmenting.

We may write, that at the level of the industry,

$$\frac{dL}{L} = \alpha K(\sigma - \eta) \frac{(dr}{r} - \frac{da}{a} - \frac{dw}{w} + \frac{db)}{b} + \frac{db}{b}(\eta - 1) - \frac{\eta dw}{w} \qquad (2)$$

$$\frac{dK}{K} = \alpha L(\sigma - \eta) \frac{(dw}{w} - \frac{db}{b} - \frac{dr}{r} + \frac{da)}{a} + \frac{da}{a}(\eta - 1) - \frac{\eta dr}{r} \qquad (3)$$

where $\alpha K, \alpha L$ = share of capital and labour in output

σ = elasticity of substitution of the production function

η = industry elasticity of demand (multiplied by -1)

$\frac{dr}{r}$ = rate of increase of the price of capital services

$\frac{dw}{w}$ = rate of increase of labour costs

$\frac{db}{b}$ = rate of labour augmentation

$\frac{da}{a}$ = rate of capital augmentation

$\frac{dL}{L}, \frac{dK}{K}$ = rate of change of demand for labour and capital services respectively.

In Table 1, we show under an assumption of fixed factor prices the signs of $\frac{dL}{L}$ and $\frac{dK}{K}$ for different values of σ, η and σ/η. As is clear, labour-saving technological advance (1) does not necessarily lead to a reduction in labour demand nor capital saving a reduction in capital demand. The effects depend on a number of factors. In general, it is not simple to draw conclusions from the results in Table 1. However, perhaps the following are on reasonably safe ground.

a) If the industry elasticity of demand is greater than unity, then technological change of any type is in the majority of cases going to increase the demand for both inputs.

b) If the industry elasticity of demand is less than unity then technological change of any type is in the majority of cases going to decrease the demand for both inputs.

c) Neutral technological change (or biased technological advance with $\sigma = 1$) will increase the demand for both inputs if the elasticity of demand is greater than unity, decrease it if the elasticity of demand is less than unity.

d) The effects of technological change depend not only on the absolute sizes of the elasticity of substitution and the elasticity of demand, but also on their sizes relative to each other.

e) A technological advance that is defined as purely saving one factor affects not only the demand for that factor but also the demand for other factors. This point will be pursued below.

From this and the above analysis, it is clear that to predict for any particular industry how technological change will affect factor demands, we need a considerable amount of information on substitution and demand elasticities, rates of factor augmentation and movements in factor prices. To a large extent, it is to these ends that much of the rest of this project is directed.

We are not, however, only interested in movements in factor demands. We are also concerned with output growth, and the framework above enables us to consider this simultaneously with factor demand growth. The point we wish to make is best illustrated by the following. Given any technological change that leads to lower marginal costs, the impact on output of this change is going to depend on the slope of the demand curve (i.e. the elasticity of demand). The shift in the original cost curve brought about by a change in technology will depend on rates of augmentation, biases, etc., but given these, the less steep the demand curve the greater will be the increase in output. The less steep demand curve is associated with a higher (absolute) value for the elasticity of demand, thus the greater is this elasticity the greater will be the increase in industry output.

Moreover, output from an industry may also increase for other reasons. In particular the demand for any good may be considered to be related to income. As income increases so for most products will demand. Thus, if as a reaction to technological change, the economy as a whole expands, this will produce income effects increasing output, and these in turn will stimulate employment. Although such effects are perhaps best treated in the section below, we raise them here, for the impact of income changes may differ across products. The estimates of such income effects are referred to as income demand elasticities. Thus if we are to separate out declining from growing industries, we will require estimates of such elasticities as well as estimates of the parameters discussed above.

Finally, we must say something about market imperfections. In essence the analysis above takes little account of the market power of firms. At this stage we are not able to deal adequately with the case where it is the technological change that is yielding the market power, but we can make some comments on the case where new technology is being introduced in a monopololistic industry. Consider Diagram 1. The industry demand curve is represented by the curve DD^1 with associated marginal revenue curve MR. MC_1 and MC_2 are the marginal cost curves using the old and new technologies respectively. Theory states that a competitive industry would produce output Q_1^c with old and Q_2^c with new technology. A monopolist on the other hand would product outputs Q_1^m and Q_2^m.

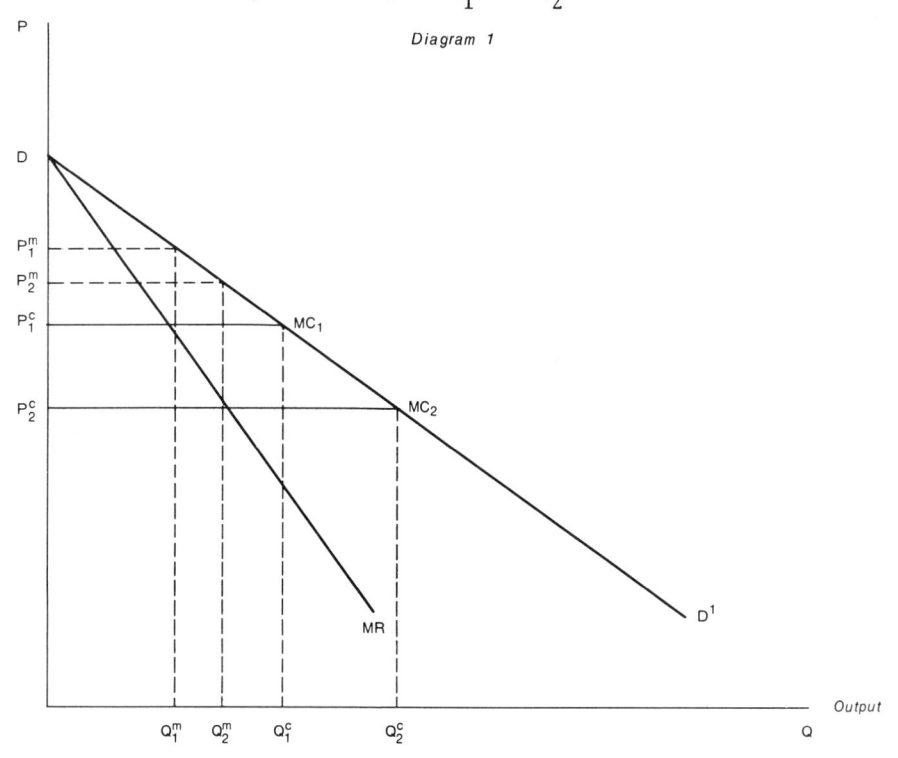

Diagram 1

It is clear that relative to the competitive case the monopolist will produce lower output. However, what is not clear is whether the increase in output under monopoly will be greater or less than under competition. In the simple case detailed here, where demand curves are linear and marginal costs are constant, it is the case that $Q^m = .5Q^c$. Thus $Q_2^m - Q_1^m = .5(Q_2^c - Q_1^c)$ and the increase in monopoly output is only half the increase in competitive output. If this case is not too unrepresentative then monopoly power may well represent a barrier to growth and employment. The work of Encaoua (1983) may lend support to this proposition. Of perhaps even more concern is the case where new technology yields monopoly power. Say that a new technology is introduced by a single firm into a competitive industry that gives the new technology user a competitive advantage. The new technology user may price below p_1^c and drive out other producers. If there are barriers to re-entry he may then price at p_2^m reducing output to Q_2^m, and the net result is a fall in industry output. Although this is an extreme case, it illustrates well the potential importance of the monopoly creating power of new technology. The upshot of this discussion is that when looking at the impacts of technological change we must say something on monopoly power.

In sympathy with our rather eclectic view of the neo-classical framework, we must raise a number of points on which the paradigm is weak or perhaps uninformative.

The first point to raise is that in our discussion the disembodiment of technological change has meant that each firm in an industry adopted the new technology simultaneously and we thus undertook comparative static analysis at the industry level. If new technology is embodied then firms must make positive decisions to install new machines/methods and in general the resulting diffusion processes are often very lengthy [see Stoneman (1983)]. At any moment in time some firms could have new technology and some old technology.

Given that this transition phase could last for a considerable period of time, it is important to analyse what is happening to the output and employment of individual firms and the industry in this phase. In some recently publicised theoretical work, Waterson and Stoneman (1985), it is shown that as diffusion proceeds, those firms adopting new technology increase their output at the expense of non adopters. Non adopters reduce their output and employment continuously as diffusion proceeds. It is also argued that as diffusion proceeds industry price continually falls and industry output continually increases. However, it is suggested that industry employment may not follow such a monotonic path. A first stage sees a fall in employment, the next stage an increase in employment, in a wide variety of market situations. If this argument is valid, then it suggests that our results produced so far do not tell the whole story. However, this work is very recent and based on a number of particular assumptions about functional forms and the whole question of transition effects needs much more work before great emphasis can be placed on such results.

We can perhaps be more precise in the case where early users are importers and late users are domestic firms. As importers innovate, they are enabled to drive down the price of the product. There is thus an expansion in sales. However, the lower price leads to a lower output level by domestic producers and thus lower employment. If domestic producers never innovate, there will be a net loss of jobs. However, if they also innovate then they will increase output above its reduced level. [A good example of this sort of effect at the regional level is given in Goddard and Thwaites (1984).] Given the correct demand and substitution elasticities and the correct biases, this could enable previous reductions in employment to be partially or completely reversed. Alternatively, early innovation by domestic exporters could have a similar but reverse effect. The open nature of the economy requires that the appropriate demand elasticities to use in detailing the effect on factor demands must be those appropriate not to the national but the world market. It is worth noting that elasticities may be much greater if innovation is not occurring overseas (but is occurring at home) than if innovations were also occurring overseas.

The analysis so far presented has considered technological change as mainly factor augmenting. Such representations deal inadequately with product innovation. The effect of pure product innovation will be to shift the demand curve rightwards (to increase demand) and if production methods stay the same this should increase factor demand in the innovating industry [see Katsoulacos (1986)]. Again in a battle between innovators and non-innovators, the latter would most probably lose employment and the former gain. The possibility of product innovation raises the issue of how responsive is demand to new product technology, what we might term, innovation demand elasticities. As it is clear that a large part of innovation is of the product improvement type, if one is to detail future perspectives some feel for the size of such elasticities is important.

The next point we wish to raise is a more general version of the monopolisation point discussed above. The monopolisation point suggested that with the existence of market power, cost reductions may not be fully reflected in price reductions and thus output and factor demands may not increase in reaction to technological change. At the general level, there are two required steps for the demand increases to be realised:

i) that cost reductions actually generate price reductions; and

ii) that demand is sufficiently responsive to these price reductions.

The latter is measured by demand elasticities and the former is where monopoly power has a role to play [e.g. Encaoua, Geroski and Miller (1983) suggest that the link between price change and cost change is significantly affected by concentration]. However a further issue is also relevant, and that is whether total demand is responsive to price change or whether gains in demand by one sector are purely at the expense of another. If total aggregate demand is fixed, one industry's employment gain may be another industry's loss.

This issue, however, is really a macro-economic issue, and there are a number of such issues that merit further consideration. It is to these that we turn next. However, before doing this, I think we should summarise the outcome of this partial equilibrium, micro-economic approach. Firstly on output perspectives; if we are to identify industries with growth prospects, we require knowledge on:

a) potential changes in their technology and some insights into how quickly the potential is likely to be realised;

b) some knowledge of demand elasticities with respect to price and quality;

c) some information on income elasticities; and

d) some insight into the degree of monopoly power in the industry.

On the factor demands, as well as the above, we require some information on the bias of technological change and the elasticities of substitution in the industry.

4. MICRO/MACRO ISSUES

Although these issues are to be discussed more fully later, there are a number of points that immediately arise from the analysis above that can usefully be detailed here. Some of these points relate to the impact on other industries of technological change in a given industry, others to less specific impacts.

We have shown above that augmentation of any one factor will in general affect the demand for all factors, the sign of the knock-on effect depending on whether other factors are complements or substitutes. Thus, labour augmentation could lead to increased material or capital demands. To the extent that this occurs, there will be an impact on factor demands in industries supplying material or capital. This effect will have to be taken into account in looking at the overall effect of technological change.

In the analysis above we have treated technological change as disembodied. This will be a rather unrealistic assumption for most advances which really require new machines to be installed for those technologies to be introduced. Thus, in addition to changes in the demand for net investment resulting from the technological change, boosts in gross investment with their resulting effect on factor demands in the capital goods industry must also be considered.

The consideration of factors such as those above indicates that the interrelated nature of different industries in the economy may be an important element in determining the impact of technological change. It is largely for this reason that our analysis has been limited to an industry level of aggregation. Although one could apply similar analysis to that above at an economy wide level, the use of aggregate production functions would hide/ignore many such inter-industry effects and thus be much less useful to us.

We can show that introducing new technology would affect profit levels (2). In essence, if the elasticity of demand were greater (less) than unity, the profit level would rise (fall) as costs fell. Given that these profits may be distributed and spent on consumption goods or may stimulate investment, a demand creating (reducing) possibility arises.

Further knock-on effects of technological change may arise through non-zero cross price elasticities of demand. Given the reduction in prices that technological change is assumed to generate in the innovating industry, this will stimulate the demand for complements and reduce the demand for substitutes with consequent effects on factor demands and outputs in their supplying industries.

The detailed analysis above largely proceeded on the assumption of given factor prices. As the expressions above indicate, however, any factor demand effect of technological change can be counteracted by changes in the relative price of that factor. In neo-classical analysis, factor prices would be determined at the aggregate level to equalise demand and supplies in aggregate. If such a mechanism does exist, this could guarantee full employment in the economy as a whole but it would not necessarily generate constant factor demands in any one industry. There may be considerable switching of factors from one industry to another.

At the macro level one must also consider the question of how the openness of an economy might affect the impact of technological change. We discussed above how a non-innovating firm may reduce factor demands in the face of innovation by other (perhaps overseas) firms. However, this is not the whole story. Given two countries innovating at different rates, one would expect to see different patterns of foreign payments balances developing. In a world of flexible exchange rates, the consequent changes will have some impact on employment in each economy that must be taken into account in the overall analysis.

The outcome of this discussion is that there are a number of factors affecting economic prospects that cannot be adequately dealt with at the micro-economic level. It is therefore necessary to supplement our micro analysis by some macro-economic work.

5. THE SPEED OF DIFFUSION

We have suggested above that if one firm (country) innovates earlier than others, then that firm/country (in the absence of exchange rate changes) may increase its factor demands and outputs relative to those of the other. The factors that influence the speed of take up thus become important in determining the effect of technological change. As a summary, the literature suggests that inter-alia, the following elements are important:

1. Entrepreneurial attitudes.
2. Information and knowledge.
3. Profitability.
4. Adequate factor supplies.
5. Sufficient skills.
6. Institutional factors.

One could extend this list, but the main point is that if governments are to intervene to gain competitive advantage it is by working on such factors that the use of new technology is to be speeded up.

6. A GUIDE TO OTHER CONTRIBUTIONS

We have shown above that a number of key parameters are involved in determining the impact of technological change. These parameters include biases, elasticities of demand and substitution, speed of diffusion, degree of embodiment and a number of macro-economic reactions. The other papers of this study represent an attempt to provide some "guesstimates" of the values of such parameters on the basis of largely case study work, while at the same time providing important detail on the real world phenomena of technological change that would be excluded by too closely restricting the analysis to consideration of the neo-classical paradigm. The paper by Patel and Soete (Information Technologies and the Rate and Direction of Technical Change) is an attempt to investigate intertemporal industrial capital labour ratios in a quest for information on biases in technical change. This is complemented by a more speculative paper by Eliasson on similar issues. Then, the papers by Wilson (Evidence from Econometric Studies of Production Functions) and Bosworth (Prices, Costs and the Elasticity of Demand) investigate the demand and production sides essentially surveying econometric estimates of demand and substitution elasticities, etc. Next, there are a series of industry and sectoral case studies where, as well as detailing their views on the technological change process, the authors present information on "guesstimates" of substitution elasticities, diffusion speeds, biases, etc., of technologies likely to be diffused in those industries in the next 10-15 years. Finally, there are the two micro-macro analyses of Eliasson (Dynamic Micro-Macro Market Co-ordination and Technical Change) and Whitley and Wilson (Quantifying the Impact of Information Technology using a Macro-econometric Model).

The contributions together should enable one to draw some conclusions partly by inserting the parameter "guesstimates" in the framework above and partly by consideration of the wider overview. The Analytical Summary (Part II) performs this task and on its basis a number of the relevant policy issues are discussed.

7. CONCLUSION

We have considered a neo-classical approach to analysing the impact of new technology on factor demands and output. When a firm installs new technology it will generate either cost reductions (process innovations) or demand shifts (product innovation) that allow it to expand (at least partially at the expense of its rivals). Whether this increases the firms factor demands depends upon substitution and own price or quality demand elasticities. However, in the face of such innovation a non-innovator will lose market share, and thus employment. The impact on factor demand at the level of the whole industry depends on one firm's gain relative to other firms' losses. To see the balance of these, we have concentrated on the case where the whole industry is taking up the new technology simultaneously. At this level we have isolated those parameters that determine whether industry factor demands will increase or decrease. The factors include the extent and bias of technological advance, elasticities of substitution and elasticities of demand. However, these industry level effects are only realised once the whole industry has adopted the new technology. During the diffusion period while this is occurring one firm/country may gain at the expense of another. These industry effects do not, however, complete the story, for macro-implications may arise from the advances in any one industry or simultaneous advances in a number of industries. In the studies, key parameters and the nature of technological change processes are studied in more detail, so that one may add some flesh to the bare bones of this analytical framework.

NOTES AND REFERENCES

1. In Table 1, we have taken some liberties in classifying different combinations of rates of factor augmentation as labour saving or using, or neutral, etc. A more "correct" classification would require consideration of the size of the elasticity of substitution.

2. Seade (1983) shows that in an oligopoly world with identical firms and a constant elasticity of demand, that if costs fall industry profits fall when $\eta < 1$, and profits rise when costs fall if $\eta > 1$.

BIBLIOGRAPHY

R.G.D. Allen, Mathematical Analysis for Economists, Macmillan, London, 1956.

D. de Meza, "Generalised Oligopoly Derived Demand with an Application to Tax Induced Entry", Bulletin of Economic Research, 34, 1982, pp. 1-16.

I. Dobbs, M. Hill and M. Waterson, "Industrial Structure and the Employment Consequences of Technical Change", Oxford Economic Papers, 1986.

D. Encaoua, P. Geroski, R. Miller, Price Dynamics and Industrial Structure, OECD Economics and Statistics Department, Paris, July 1983.

P.R.G. Layard and A.A. Walters, Microeconomic Theory, McGraw-Hill, London, 1978.

A. Friedlander, C. Winston and K. Wang, "Costs, Technology and Productivity in the US Automobile Industry", Bell Journal of Economics, 14, 1, 1983, pp. 1-20.

J. Goddard and A. Thwaites, "Unemployment in the North; Jobs in the South", in P. Marstrand (ed.), New Technology and the Future of Work and Skills, Frances Pinter (Publishers), London, 1984.

Y. Katsoulacos, The Employment Effect of Product and Process Innovation, Harvester Press, Brighton, 1986.

E. Mansfield, Industrial Research and Technological Innovation, W.W. Norton, New York, 1968.

R. Nelson, "Research on Productivity Growth and Productivity Differences", Journal of Economic Literature, XIX, No 3, 1981, pp. 1029-64.

R. Nelson and S. Winter, "Neoclassical vs Evolutionary Theories of Economic Growth: Critique and Prospectives", Economic Journal, 84, 1974, pp. 886-905.

J. Schumpeter, The Theory of Economic Development, Harvard University Press, Cambridge, Mass., 1934.

J. Seade, "On the Effects of Entry", Econometrica, 40, 1980, pp. 479-89.

J. Seade, "Prices, Profits and Taxes in Oligopoly", University of Warwick, May 1983 (mimeographed).

P. Stoneman, The Economic Analysis of Technological Change, Oxford
    University Press, Oxford, 1983.

M. Waterson and P. Stoneman, "Employment, Technological Diffusion and
    Oligopoly", International Journal of Industrial Organisation, 3.3.,
    1985, pp. 327-344.

Annex

THE RESPONSIVENESS OF LABOUR DEMAND TO TECHNOLOGICAL CHANGE

The material in this Annex is mainly a development of the work of Dobbs, Hill and Waterson (1986) (referred to below as DHW) and Seade (1985) which in turn depend on de Meza (1982) and Seade (1980). The principle behind this approach is that the impact on factor demand of a factor augmenting technological change can be related to the impact of a change in factor prices on factor demands. As the latter impact is a standard text book study, we can proceed by the use of standard text book results.

We use lower case letters for the firm and upper case for the industry. Let the production relationship for a firm be summarised by the production function A.1.

$$y = f(\bar{\ell}, \bar{k}) \qquad (A.1)$$

where y = output of the firm and $\bar{\ell}$ and $\bar{k}$ are related to the inputs of labour and capital, ℓ and k respectively, by the relationships A.2 and A.3.

$$\bar{\ell} = b(t)\ell \qquad (A.2)$$
$$\bar{k} = a(t)k \qquad (A.3)$$

We may define* $\dfrac{db}{b}$ and $\dfrac{da}{a}$ as the rates of factor augmentation.

If $\dfrac{db}{b} = \dfrac{da}{a} = \dfrac{dc}{c}$, then technical progress will be Hicks neutral (if the production function is homogenous of degree one), and $\dfrac{dc}{c}$ is termed the rate of product augmentation.

Assume that the firm maximises profits and determines its desired input levels by the equality of marginal products and factor prices. One can then write from A.1 the implicit factor demand functions A.4 and A.5

$$\ell = \dfrac{\bar{\ell}}{b} \; (\dfrac{r}{a}, \dfrac{w}{b}) \qquad (A.4)$$

---

* All these rates are implicitly considered as derivatives with respect to time and time subscripts are omitted where no confusion arises.

$$k = \frac{\bar{k}}{a}(\frac{r}{w}, \frac{w}{b}) \qquad (A.5)$$

where r and w are the prices of capital and labour inputs. Taking the total differential of A.4, we obtain

$$d\ell = \frac{1}{b}(\bar{\ell}1\left[\frac{1}{a}dr - \frac{r}{a^2}da\right] + \bar{\ell}2\left[\frac{1}{b}dw - \frac{w}{b^2}db\right]) - \frac{1}{b^2}\bar{\ell}db \qquad (A.6)$$

where $\bar{\ell}1$ and $\bar{\ell}2$ are the partial derivatives of ℓ with respect to $\frac{r}{a}$ and $\frac{w}{b}$, respectively. Given

$$\frac{\partial \ell}{\partial r} = \frac{1}{ab}\bar{\ell}1 \text{ and } \frac{\partial \ell}{\partial w} = \frac{1}{b^2}\bar{\ell}2$$

we may substitute into A.6, and generate

$$\frac{d\ell}{\ell} = \frac{\eta\ell r}{r}dr - \frac{\eta\ell r}{a}da + \frac{\eta\ell w}{w}dw - \eta\ell w\frac{db}{b} - \frac{db}{b} \qquad (A.7)$$

In a similar way we can derive

$$\frac{dk}{k} = \frac{\eta kr}{r}dr - \frac{\eta kr}{a}da + \frac{\eta kw}{w}dw - \frac{\eta kw}{b}db - \frac{da}{a} \qquad (A.8)$$

Equations A.7 and A.8 indicate that for the firm the impact of technological change on factor demands depends upon own price and cross price elasticities of factor demands and the direction of technological change. However, the factor demand elasticities are derived elasticities and are determined by more basic parameters. To derive these elasticities we really have to consider the industry as a whole rather than an individual firm.

The most general approach is to assume an oligopolistic industry containing n firms. Let us assume that n is fixed and all the firms are the same. Then using the following assumptions:

(a) that each firm's costs are given as $C^i = c(w,r)h(y_i) + F$, where F is fixed costs;

(b) all firms profit maximise;

(c) all firms form conjectural variations on rivals' behaviour such that

$$\frac{dY}{dy_i} = \lambda_i, \quad Y = \sum_{i=1}^{n} y_i$$

(d) that the industry inverse demand function can be written as $P = P(Y)$;

(e) n, the number of firms, is fixed;

then DHW shows that at the industry level

$$\eta \, Lr = \alpha_K(\sigma + Z)$$
$$\eta \, Kw = \alpha_L(\sigma + Z)$$
$$\eta \, Kr = \alpha_L \sigma + \alpha_K Z$$
$$\eta \, Lw = \alpha_K \sigma + \alpha_L Z$$

where α_L, α_K are the shares of labour and capital in total output

σ = elasticity of substitution of the production function

and $\quad Z = \dfrac{\gamma(1+m)}{E+q+m}$

where $\gamma = \dfrac{yh'(y)}{h}$ the elasticity of scale

η = industry elasticity of demand

$m = \dfrac{n}{\lambda}$, the number of effective firms

E = elasticity of the slope of industry demand

$$\left(d\dfrac{(P'(Y))}{dY} \cdot \dfrac{Y}{P'}\right)$$

$q = \dfrac{1-c(w,r)h''(y)}{\lambda \, P'(y)}$ and $h'' = 0$ if there are constant returns to scale.

One could proceed with these expressions but they are more complicated than we can really deal with. We thus consider a more special case. Allen (1956) derives a case where (a) $\gamma = 1$; (b) the elasticity of demand is constant so $E = \dfrac{1}{\eta} - 1$; (c) there are constant returns to scale so $q = 1, \alpha_K + \alpha_L = 1$; and (d) the number of firms is large so all firms are price takers. Under these conditions we obtain A.9 - A.12.

$$\eta \, Lw = -\alpha_K \sigma - \alpha_L \eta \tag{A.9}$$
$$\eta \, Lr = \alpha_K(\underline{\sigma} - \eta) \tag{A.10}$$
$$\eta \, Kw = \alpha_L(\sigma - \underline{\eta}) \tag{A.11}$$
$$\eta \, Kr = -\alpha_K \eta - \alpha_L \sigma \tag{A.12}$$

If the number of firms in the industry is fixed, then the industry demand for a factor is just n times each firm's demand. If all firms are the same and all change technology at the same time, we may then write that:

$$L = n\ell$$

$$K = nk$$

$$\frac{dL}{L} = \frac{dn}{n} + \frac{d\ell}{\ell}$$

$$\frac{dK}{K} = \frac{dn}{n} + \frac{dk}{k}$$

and given $\frac{dn}{n} = 0$, $\frac{dL}{L} = \frac{d\ell}{\ell}$ and $\frac{dK}{K} = \frac{dk}{k}$. Thus, to obtain expressions for changes in factor demands for either the industry or one firm in that industry we may substitute from A.9 - A.12 into A.7 and A.8 to yield

$$\frac{dL}{L} = \frac{d\ell}{\ell} = \alpha K (\sigma - \eta) \left(\frac{dr}{r} - \frac{da}{a} - \frac{dw}{w} + \frac{db}{b}\right) + \frac{db}{b}(\eta - 1) - \eta \frac{dw}{w}$$

$$\frac{dK}{K} = \frac{dk}{k} = \alpha L (\sigma - \eta) \left(\frac{dw}{w} - \frac{db}{b} - \frac{dr}{r} + \frac{da}{a}\right) + \frac{da}{a}(\eta - 1) - \eta \frac{dw}{w}$$

which are the expressions used in the text above.

In generating these results, we have made two perhaps objectionable assumptions about the number of firms in the industry. The first is that it is fixed, the second that all firms are the same. The work of DHW illustrates that if n is variable, then the final outcome is much more opaque and the implications more difficult to derive but perhaps not very different in a qualitative sense. The work of Seade (1983) suggests that the symmetry assumption is not really very important to the results derived. We do not feel, therefore, that our assumptions are too constraining. The assumption that the number of firms is large is dealt with in the text in an ad hoc manner.

Although it is standard in neo-classical theory to model with only two factors, when discussing technological change the possibility of material saving technological change arises. If we allow for materials in the production function and write it as

$$Y = G(a(t)K, b(t)L, g(t)M)$$

where M is the input of raw materials and $\frac{dg}{g}$ is the rate of material augmentation we may observe in a manner similar to that used above, that

$$\frac{dL}{L} = \eta_{Lr}\frac{dr}{r} - \eta_{Lr}\frac{da}{a} + \eta_{Lw}\frac{dw}{w} - \eta_{Lw}\frac{db}{b} + \eta_{Ls}\frac{ds}{s} - \eta_{Ls}\frac{dg}{g} - \frac{db}{b}$$

$$\frac{dK}{K} = \eta_{Kr}\frac{dr}{r} - \eta_{Kr}\frac{da}{a} + \eta_{Kw}\frac{dw}{w} - \eta_{Kw}\frac{db}{b} + \eta_{Ks}\frac{ds}{s} - \eta_{Ks}\frac{dg}{g} - \frac{da}{a}$$

$$\frac{dM}{M} = \eta_{Mr}\frac{dr}{r} - \eta_{Mr}\frac{da}{a} + \eta_{Mw}\frac{dw}{w} - \eta_{Mw}\frac{db}{b} + \eta_{Ms}\frac{ds}{s} - \eta_{Ms}\frac{dg}{g} - \frac{dg}{g}$$

where s is the price of raw materials.

Given that η_{ij} is the price elasticity of demand of factor i to the price of factor j, we may take from Layard and Walters (1978, p. 270):

$$\eta_{ij} = \alpha_j(\eta + \sigma_{ij})$$

where α_j is the share of j in total cost

η is the industry elasticity of demand

and σ_{ij} is the Allen elasticity of substitution. Assuming constant factor prices

$$\frac{dL}{L} = -\frac{da}{a}(\alpha_K(\eta + \sigma_{LK})) - \frac{db}{b}(1 + \alpha_L(\eta + \sigma_{LL})) - \frac{dg}{g}(\alpha_M(\eta + \sigma_{LM}))$$

$$\frac{dK}{K} = -\frac{da}{a}(1 + \alpha_K(\eta + \sigma_{KK})) - \frac{db}{b}(\alpha_L(\eta + \sigma_{KL})) - \frac{dg}{g}(\alpha_M(\eta + \sigma_{KM}))$$

$$\frac{dM}{M} = -\frac{da}{a}(\alpha_K(\eta + \sigma_{MK})) - \frac{db}{b}(\alpha_L(\eta + \sigma_{ML})) - \frac{dg}{g}(1 + \alpha_M(\eta + \sigma_{MM}))$$

This is obviously a much more complicated set of expressions from which to generate any easily interpretable results. The elasticities of substitution indicate whether any two inputs are substitutes or complements in the production process (note that $\sigma_{ij} = \sigma_{ji}$). If we take, for example, material augmenting technical changes then the impact on material demand includes a direct effect, given output can be produced by less material input; an effect generated by changes in output resulting from lower prices (the elasticity of demand); plus an effect through substitution induced by the relatively lower price of materials. For capital and labour input demands the output expansion effect still operates and a substitution effect exists but whether this is positive or negative depends on whether the input is complementary ($\sigma_{ij}>0$) or a substitute ($\sigma_{ij}<0$).

One can note that $\sigma_{ii} \leq 0$, i.e. the own price elasticity of substitution is always negative. Thus, the effect of augmentation of a factor on its own demand will be positive if

$$1 + \alpha_i(\eta + \sigma_{ii}) < 0$$

i.e., if $\frac{-1}{\alpha_i} - \sigma_{ii} > \eta$

and thus the relative size of demand elasticities and substitution elasticities is always important. For the effect on the demand for j of augmentation of factor i, the demand for j will increase if

$$\alpha_j(\eta + \sigma_{ij}) < 0$$

i.e., if $\eta < -\sigma_{ij}$

If i and j are complements, then $\sigma_{ij}>0$ and given $\eta > 0$, we always have $\eta > -\sigma_{ij}$ and the demand for the factor must rise. If i and j are substitutes and $\sigma_{ij}<0$, then the relative sizes of η and σ_{ij} matter. We can, however, say that augmentation of factor j will increase the demand for factor i if i and j are complements ($i \neq j$). For experimental purposes only, we will take estimates of σ_{ij} (i,j = K,L,M) as calculated by Friedlander, Winston and Wang (1983) for the US automobile industry. They calculate that $\sigma_{LL} = -1.49$, $\sigma_{KK} = -9.04$, $\sigma_{MM} = 0.80$, $\sigma_{KL} = 2.19$, $\sigma_{LM} = 0.71$, $\sigma_{KM} = -0.54$. Let the shares of capital, labour and materials in total cost be 15%, 30% and 55%, respectively. Then

$$\frac{dL}{L} = -\frac{da(.15(\eta + 2.19)}{a} - \frac{db(1 + 0.3(\eta - 1.491)}{b} - \frac{dg(.55(\eta + 0.71))}{g}$$

$$\frac{dK}{K} = -\frac{da(1 + .15(\eta - 9.04)}{a} - \frac{db(0.3(\eta + 2.19)}{b} - \frac{dg(.55(\eta - 0.54))}{g}$$

$$\frac{dM}{M} = -\frac{da(.15(\eta - 0.54)}{a} - \frac{db(0.3(\eta + 0.71)}{b} - \frac{dg(1 + .55(\eta - 0.80))}{g}$$

Then for purely material augmenting technological change $\frac{da}{a} = \frac{db}{b} = 0$, $\frac{dg}{g} > 0$, we have that $\frac{dL}{L} < 0$; $\frac{dK}{K} > 0$ if $\eta < 0.54$, $\frac{dK}{K} < 0$ if $\eta > 0.54$; and $\frac{dM}{M} > 0$ if $\eta < -1$, but $\eta > 0$ ∴ $\frac{dM}{M} < 0$. Of course these results are purely illustrative.

II. GENERAL STUDIES

1

INFORMATION TECHNOLOGIES AND THE RATE AND DIRECTION OF TECHNICAL CHANGE

by

Pari Patel and Luc Soete
Science Policy Research Unit
University of Sussex
(United Kingdom)

SUMMARY

Objective of the paper

This paper discusses briefly the role and effect of innovation on investment behaviour and economic growth, and provides a historical analysis of the post-war trends in capital/labour ratios and both labour and capital productivity in manufacturing in some of the major OECD countries. In order to assess more directly the impact of past technical changes on these post-war capital/labour trends, use is made of a vintage-capital simulation model, which allows one to identify trends in both best-practice labour and capital-productivity, as well as estimates of capital stock, based on a more directly related capacity-utilisation scrapping criterion.

Because of data constraints the analysis is at present limited to the aggregate manufacturing level, except for the United Kingdom, where sectoral trends in "best-practice" labour and capital productivity have also been identified. Also in the last section of the paper, some of the implications for future capital/labour requirements are analysed and their possible effect upon future growth and implicit investment requirements touched upon.

Position within the overall project

The focus being on "capital accumulation" and technical change, the approach chosen in this paper falls within the broad "Schumpeterian" tradition, focussing in the first instance on the long-term relationship between technical innovation, investment and employment and the possible link with the existence of structural unemployment. Such an approach while starting from a set of different assumptions in relation to the speed of the various "adjustment" and compensation mechanisms assumed to exist in the economy, is nevertheless by and large complementary to the more traditional approaches presented elsewhere, in that it focusses in particular on the way technical innovation as embodied in new investment, might have limited ex-post capital-labour substitution, allowing for the possibility of a "temporary" lack of physical and/or human capital needed to achieve full employment.

Main findings and conclusions

Structural and labour mismatch unemployment represent now a significant proportion of total unemployment in the majority of the major OECD countries. The exception was to some extent the United States, where demand-deficient unemployment remained a significant component in the increase of unemployment over the late 70s, early 80s. The dramatic decline in unemployment over the last three-quarters of 1983, first quarter of 1984 corresponds however mainly to a decline in the cyclical, so-called "demand-deficient" component. Over time, the increase in "capital shortage" unemployment appears to be related to the labour-saving bias in the rate of technical change. The exception is Japan, where a pattern of near "Harrod-neutral" technical change seems to have characterised its trend in "best-practice" capital productivity growth. This Japanese productivity pattern fits well with the low overall levels of, and increase in, unemployment.

Using evidence limited to the United Kingdom, the trend in labour-saving technical change appears to occur across most sectors of the economy.

Electronics emerged however as the most important major sector displaying a unique pattern of both rapid best-practice labour and capital productivity growth. This appeared to be primarily the result of the dramatic gains in best-practice labour and capital productivity in the United Kingdom computer industry. The growth implications of such a pattern of technical change for future recovery were, it was argued, quite significant. That growth impact would be most significant in those sectors of application of electronics where productivity growth has been the hampering factor behind output growth: such as many service sectors. Furthermore, there could be significant growth potential for those areas of application of electronics where the significantly increased productivity growth might improve the international competitiveness of the sector.

There are also however, straightforward growth implications in the replacement of electro-mechanical, or first (and possibly second) generation electronic capital equipment by new, third-generation electronic capital equipment which should lead to significant savings in terms of capital expenditure and thus in principle to higher profits. The result might well be the restoration of the profit rate in a number of capital-intensive sectors which have been suffering from low profits. Characteristically the new technology also permits, when fully and efficiently deployed, major capital savings in inventories and in work-in-progress. More straightforwardly, if these gains from technical change, and from capital-saving technical change in particular, are translated into lower prices, this should again lead to increasing demand for that sector's output.

What the implications of such a capital-saving diffusion pattern are for employment remains, however, an open question. On the one hand, one can expect further significant employment displacement effects in those areas of application of electronics where straightforward "substitution" of capital for labour will occur and might not be fully "compensated" for by output growth. On the other hand, there is at least potential for employment growth in those areas where the diffusion of electronics will lead to significant output growth and especially in labour-intensive "software" areas.

Shortcomings and future work

In conclusion, though, the speculative nature of these arguments for long-term employment growth must be stressed. The evidence of the electronics industry is limited to the United Kingdom and might itself be subject to severe measurement problems. Furthermore in carrying out the present analysis, no attempt has been made to separate out the contribution of possible capital/labour substitution effects, "induced-innovation" effects or autonomous technical change effects.

An econometric analysis of the major determinants of the trends in best-practice labour and capital productivity could in principle though be carried out, and would provide a complementary approach to the simulation method followed. Such an exercise would probably be even more worthwhile once the analysis could be carried out at the sectoral level for all the major OECD countries.

2

INFORMATION TECHNOLOGY, CAPITAL STRUCTURE AND THE NATURE OF TECHNICAL CHANGE IN THE FIRM

by

Gunnar Eliasson
The Industrial Institute for
Economic and Social Research
Stockholm (Sweden)

ABSTRACT

This paper presents statistical evidence on:

1) the importance of "soft" capital spending items like marketing and R&D investments, and

2) the dominant service content of production in the modern manufacturing firm.

It pictures the firm as a dominantly information processing entity that has been gradually shifting its competitive base from process cost efficiency toward a product technology. The paper argues:

3) that during the post-war period technical change has been gradually pivoting in a relatively more (hardware) capital saving direction.

The growing service content of manufacturing production consists of various forms of information gathering and using activities, product development, marketing and management being the most important items, using up more than half of the resources in the largest Swedish manufacturing firms. Rather than competing with simple products and lower prices the advanced manufacturing firms are based in sophisticated customer markets and compete with improved product qualities, to a large extent through extensive marketing networks located in foreign countries. Sometimes the information gathering and using activities take place within the administrative framework of the firm and are statistically measured as a manufacturing activity, sometimes the activities are run through separate agents, and are statistically observed as private services. The institutional delimitations are becoming increasingly unstable. (This development suggests that the current concern with the employment consequences of information technology in automation of factory production is a misdirection of attention. Far more significant developments are occurring in other dimensions. It also makes the notion of price elastic export functions, commonly used in international trade models and macroeconomic models, somewhat suspect.)

I. FROM A PROCESS TOWARD A PRODUCT-BASED INDUSTRIAL TECHNOLOGY

A large body of literature conventionally assumes that technical change has been, and still is, predominantly labour saving. These results come out of standard production function analysis, the bulk of which is from econometric analysis of macro time series data. (This quality of technical change is sometimes thought to have permanent consequences for employment; see Eliasson, 1985c.)

The econometric studies practically always see capital as consisting of machinery and constructions to be used in factories. Occasionally, goods in process inventories are included. The notion of a firm from this (macro-economic) perspective is that of a factory.

The argument in this paper is that this kind of analysis fails to capture the evolution of the modern manufacturing firm. Statistical data as a rule do not exhibit the large "soft" part of investment spending, devoted to product development (almost all R&D), marketing and knowledge accumulation in general. Lacking, or disregarding, this information, we do not understand the change in the nature of technical progress that has taken place gradually, from a process efficiency ("cost cutting") based industry toward a product-based ("value added increasing") industrial technology oriented toward specialised customer markets.

Internal data on production activities in a modern firm used for analysis in several IUI studies suggest that technical change has been gradually shifting in the direction of relatively more capital saving technical change. With "capital" we then mean machinery, constructions and possibly inventories, or the data that usually enter macro production function analysis. New co-ordination and information management techniques work in that direction and the higher share of interest costs in total costs during the 70s has provided an economic incentive to adjust faster to what has been technically feasible.

This change in the nature of capital invested in industry also mirrors a parallel shift in technology in which economies of scale in processing is diminishing in importance, while significant economies of scale in marketing and finance are emerging, forcing the organisation and institutional delimination of the modern firm to change (Eliasson, 1985a, b).

This paper broadens the concept of capital to include all inventories, accounts receivable and all other assets appearing on the active side of a balance sheet, as well as a spectrum of debt categories directly linked to the ongoing production process. This is exactly where capital saving technology is predominantly applied in the non-hardware production process which appears to be a major part of value added creation within a modern business entity.

If the analysis is extended to cover all external, institutionalised information and distribution activities that are directly related to manufacturing goods production and the carrying of the goods to the final users, this conclusion as to technical change would no doubt be further reinforced and the notion of a shrinking "manufacturing sector" in a modern industrial society would most likely be falsified as a statistical artifact, based on badly designed statistical taxonomies.

The point of my argument is that if we continue to stick with the old notion of capital in industry as being machinery and construction capital directly linked to the process side of production, and think that this is all that matters, we are being deceptive to ourselves and our readers.

This paper will present some recent statistical and qualitative evidence on the nature of capital accumulation in Swedish manufacturing to support this view.

II. THE MODERN MANUFACTURING FIRM -- A KNOWLEDGE-USING AND INFORMATION PROCESSING ENTITY

Most of capital invested in a modern manufacturing firm applies to the non-hardware side of production. Take human capital away and the same conclusion probably still holds. Practically all non-hardware capital and much hardware capital (computers being a case in point) are related to the gathering, analysing and use of information in various forms, or information handling in general. The following set of Tables 2 (A to C), derived from Swedish firms, illustrate this. Sweden seems to be one of the few places where such data are systematically gathered (1). The data are neither representative for all Swedish manufacturing firms, nor for average industry in the advanced industrialised countries. However, the data should be indicative of the direction in which manufacturing in advanced industrial nations will eventually be heading.

The basic information technology in the sophisticated fringe of large Swedish firms is devoted to developing the right products and moving the products to the right customers around the world. In the early 80s these firms employed some 50 per cent of the industrial labour force in Sweden. Their product development and marketing competence have been the vehicle for making them competitive during the 70s, thus displacing basic industries to second rank in the hierarchy of size, performance and as competitive exporters. (Table 3 lists all large Swedish companies by size as exporters in 1965, 1978 and 1981) (2). Those firms are of special interest as indicators of the future structure of industry. The tables show that at least half of "measurable" capital spending has been invested in marketing and R&D. The bulk of marketing capital is invested abroad, and even if it is largely of a goodwill nature associated with the development of new markets, it is still "physically" or geographically tied to these markets. R&D capital has largely been invested domestically in Sweden as is also the case with the bulk of process installations.

Marketing and R&D capital are decisive for the competitive situation of the entire corporation. Capital for marketing and R&D defines the unique knowledge base of the firm, and explains whatever profitability that can be derived from process activities. A supplementary indication of this is that practically all statistically measured R&D spending in Swedish industry goes into new product development (see Table 4) and that new product changes usually initiate and carry major productivity advances in ongoing process activities (see section III).

With at least half of capital spending devoted to development and improvement of products for specialised customer-markets and to moving them to these customers across borders, within the internal distribution system of the firm, the bulk of the latter investment being located outside the country, the whole notion of estimating traditional macro export functions and export price elasticities for industrial sectors in advanced OECD countries is becoming increasingly irrelevant.

Since the competitive edge of these firms is only secondarily based on process knowledge one can safely conclude that further investment will shift capital structures in the direction of relatively more non-process, product and market investments, and away from plant and equipment installations. If any part of the entire operation perishes for economic and technical reasons it will be the manufacturing process part. This is already evident from a firm by firm and sector comparison. Hardware intensive firms, producing simple goods and selling them through external traders, like basic industries, iron and metal manufacturing and parts of intermediate goods and heavy engineering industries constitute a relatively declining industrial base. These firms live on process cost performance and cost efficient technology is relatively easy to imitate in, for instance, the newly developed industrial countries. Technical innovative activities are oriented toward process improvements, where the payoffs from R&D spending appear not to be as large as in R&D investments closer to the product. While R&D intensive production seems to be competitive through exports from Sweden, simpler process dependent production, like textiles, seems to be more prone to be allocated abroad, away from a high wage economy like Sweden.

The change in aggregate capital structures thus observed has mainly come about through a generally faster growth of those firms, whose competitive edge was based on new product creation to begin with, rather than on cost efficient production. Technological and market development, however, has made marketing and product development (R&D investment) relatively more profitable than new process installations (Eliasson, Bergholm, Horwitz and Jagrén, 1985). Hence, also within firms, one can observe a shifting in emphasis toward upgrading product qualities through R&D spending and marketing investments. This is typical of the industries in the upper left hand corner of Figure 1.

Swedish manufacturing industry was heavily based on process performance through skilled workers by the late 60s. For instance, internal budgeting and control procedures in Swedish firms appeared to be relatively more biased toward cost and process control than the pronounced product and market orientation of similar management procedures observed in the United States firms (Eliasson, 1976, p. 227). The process-based industries in Western industrialised countries suffered heavily in the post oil crisis years of the 70s. Perhaps as much as 20 per cent of manufacturing capacity in Sweden, almost all of it in the unsophisticated basic industry firms (3) in practice went bankrupt with little advanced notice, and the bulk of remaining industries went into a reshape period. Only some of the already R&D, product and marketing oriented firms weathered the 70s more or less unscathed. Some firms went for process rationalisation of existing lines, with not very successful outcomes. Others pulled ahead, restructuring their organisations, emphasizing product and knowledge-based activities, and closing unsophisticated product lines, emerging, if successful, at the top of Table 3. These reorganisations would probably not have been possible without a prior build up of the necessary knowledge and competence base. To understand the nature of, and the prerequisites for a successful reorganisation of a firm a much more profound and comprehensive knowledge is needed of the interior activities of an industrial firm than economics currently has. This in particular holds for the accumulation and transmission of knowledge within a firm (Item 10 in Table 1).

To serve as a systematic background for understanding the content of ongoing activities within a modern firm, Table 1 lists the important functions. The equation below is a breakdown of costs allocated on the functions in Table 1. They have been used to calculate Table 2B and 2C. The argument above is that the performance of the materials processing function is no longer the critically important one, and will be even less so in the future in the more advanced industrial economies. Non-processing [all other items than (6) in Table 1] activities are mainly oriented toward innovating and co-ordinating the entire business entity. Such stocks of knowledge we do not measure well, but the rough estimates presented in the table suggest that they are sizeable and at least comparable to machinery, equipment and buildings on a reproduction value basis. The co-ordination activities require sizable capital stocks to keep the flow performance of the firm efficient. Ingoing, intermediate and outgoing inventories of the process stage is one well-known example.

Table 1

MAIN OPERATIONAL TASKS OF A LARGE MANUFACTURING FIRM

1. Innovative
2. Internal reorganisation
3. Product development
4. Investment (bank) allocation
5. Commercial bank (cash management)
6. Insurance, risk reduction
7. Materials processing (the hardware function)
8. Purchasing
9. Marketing and distribution
10. Education and knowledge accumulation
11. Welfare and income redistribution.

To measure the input content of total value added let us decompose total costs (TC) of a division or a firm into:

$$TC = \sum_{n} w.L + \sum_{n} p^I.I + \sum_{n} (r+p-\frac{\Delta p}{p})p^K.\bar{K} \tag{1}$$

n lists the number of tasks or functions (i.e. n = 10 in Table 1).

The first item to the right is labour costs (w = wage, L = labour input). The second item adds up purchases [p^I(= price), times I (= volume)].

Figure 1. **FROM A PROCESS COST EFFICIENT TOWARD A PRODUCT-BASED INDUSTRIAL TECHNOLOGY**

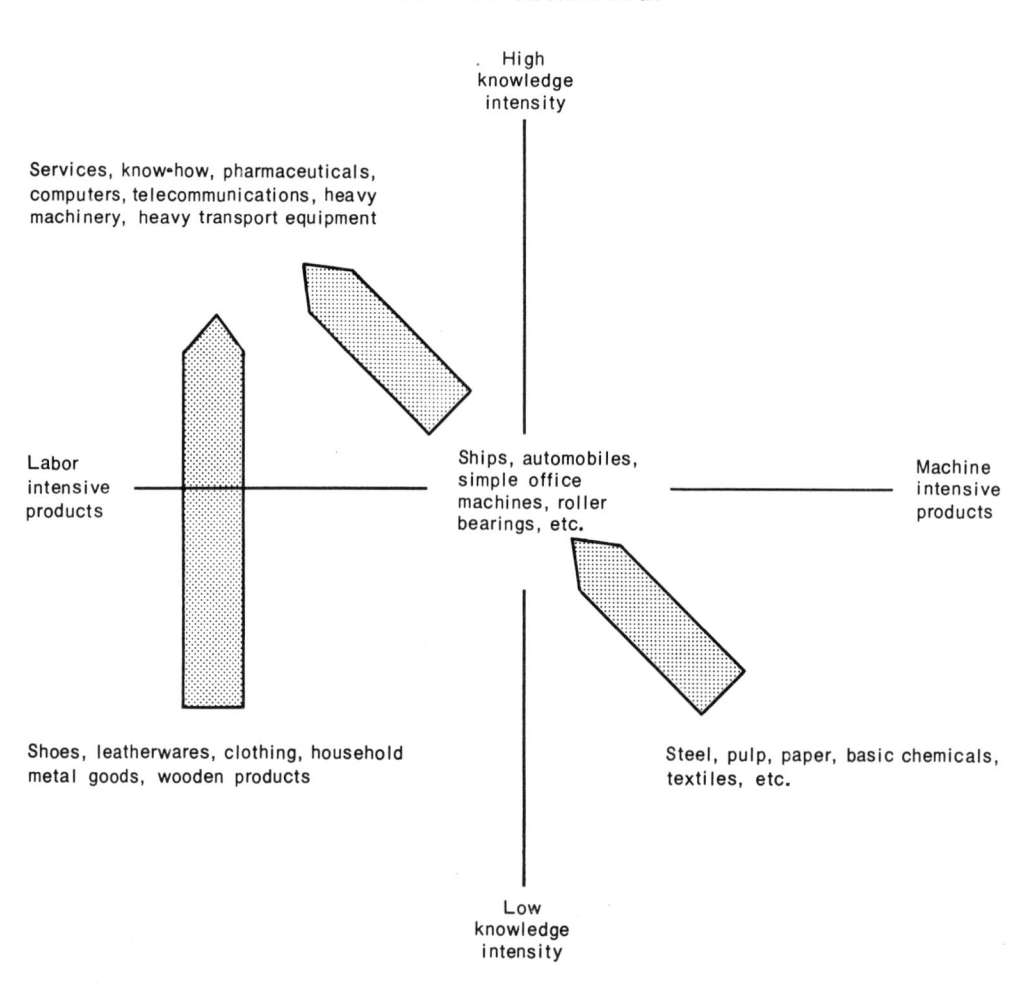

High knowledge intensity

Services, know-how, pharmaceuticals, computers, telecommunications, heavy machinery, heavy transport equipment

Labor intensive products

Ships, automobiles, simple office machines, roller bearings, etc.

Machine intensive products

Shoes, leatherwares, clothing, household metal goods, wooden products

Steel, pulp, paper, basic chemicals, textiles, etc.

Low knowledge intensity

The third item is the standard definition of capital costs associated with each function. The price of the service of a unit of capital is p^K (the price of a unit of capital) multiplied by the sum (within brackets) of the interest rate, the depreciation rate and the change (with negative sign) of the capital goods price index. The latter measures the capital gain on K, which has to be subtracted from the capital service charge.

Define

$$\epsilon = R - r$$

where R is the nominal rate of return on capital (K) and r is the nominal loan rate. Then the sales value (= S) of the firm can be expressed as

$$S = TC + \epsilon \cdot K$$

If the return to capacity is equal to the loan rate then $\epsilon = 0$ and total sales equal total costs, if properly measured. From an analytical point of view it is interesting to know how the various functions n (that draw labour, materials and capital costs) contribute to the overall return to capital, measured by ϵ. We argue in this paper that the major contributions to a positive ϵ in the 70s have been R&D spending on product development (item 3) and marketing (item 9) in Table 1. We would also argue that items 1, 2 and 10 have been critical in developing the product and marketing skills although it is close to impossible to pinpoint these activities in statistical terms. In Tables 2B and 2C we have disregarded the ϵ item in dividing total costs, and in Table 2B we have disregarded all costs but labour costs when distributing costs on functions 3, 9 and everything else.

The internal structure of the modern firm is such that each function listed in Table 1 has its own departmental domain well defined within the firm and in its cost account classification. To some extent, most of these "internal" activities can be made both cost and profit responsive. Notably, in small firms the services of many of the non-processing activities are bought in the market. This highlights two important factors in productivity change, namely institutional or organisational change as a result of the changing importance of different activities within the firm. This can also take the form of acquisitions and through exits. We also observe that each of the ten operational tasks and departments has its own capital endowment, that can sometimes be measured and isolated on an investment accrual basis. We can now rephrase our previous argument by saying that much of total factor productivity growth or improved profit performance of a firm can be traced to a changed allocation of resources on the various items in Table 1, (Eliasson, 1985c).

III. FINANCE AND ORGANISATION

Finance in its various manifestations has a much more significant impact on the real side of the behaviour of firms than is generally recognised in the economic theory of the firm, a circumstance that makes it natural to view a firm as a financially defined entity. It is dominated and co-ordinated from the top down by the capital market and the owners, who set rate of return requirements, that also define the outer limits of the firm as an organisation, namely when, on the margin, it begins to attract and/or leak external funds (Eliasson, 1976, p. 256; 1984d).

Table 2A

INVESTMENTS (a) IN THE FIVE AND THE 37 LARGEST SWEDISH
MANUFACTURING GROUPS, 1978

Firms have been ranked by foreign employment (percentages)

	The five largest groups		The 37 largest groups	
	All group	Foreign subsidiaries only	All group	Foreign subsidiaries only
R&D	25	10	21	6
Machinery and Buildings	45	41	52	42
Marketing	30	49	27	52
Total	100	100	100	100

(a) Investments in marketing and R&D have been estimated from cost data.

Table 2B

WAGE AND SALARY COSTS IN DIFFERENT SPENDING CATEGORIES
IN THE FIVE AND 37 LARGEST SWEDISH GROUPS, 1978 (Percentages)

	The five largest groups		The 37 largest groups	
	All group	Foreign subsidiaries only	All group	Foreign subsidiaries only
R&D	7	3	7	2
Processing and other	63	52	70	58
Marketing and distribution	30	45	23	40
Total	100	100	100	100

Note: We have been unable to separate administrative costs, etc., from production process cost data, and wages and salaries in marketing and distribution are probably underestimated. The "other" item should be in the neighbourhood of 15 per cent of total costs according to preliminary data from an ongoing IUI study.

Source: Eliasson G., De intlandsetablerade företagen och den Svenska ekonomin, Research Report No 26, IUI, Stockholm, 1984.

Table 2C

TOTAL COSTS DISTRIBUTED OVER DIFFERENT ACTIVITIES IN A LARGE
SWEDISH ENGINEERING FIRM, 1981 (SWEDISH OPERATIONS ONLY) (Percentages)

1. R&D, design and technical documentation	17
2. Work scheduling	15
3. Production	44
4. Marketing and distribution	9
5. Finance and administration	5
6. Other	10
Total	100

Source: Fries, H., "The Firm, Productivity and the Emerging Technology", in Microeconometrics, IUI Yearbook 1982/83, Stockholm, 1983.

Risk finance and ownership control is usually associated with decisions that fundamentally restructure the organisation of the firm and that appear to be the main vehicle for large and fast advances in productivity. Venture capital is a special form of risk finance. The term is usually associated with new innovative entry activities, often thought of as "high tech" innovative entry (see Granstrand, 1985). The long-run importance of such innovative entry activities for the macro economy appears to be very large. Much more theoretical and empirical research is, however, needed for this working hypothesis to be gainfully used in policy making (Eliasson, 1984a,e). In addition, the bulk of innovative activity seems to take place within the large firms, financed through internal cash flow, which is the quantitatively most important form of risk capital.

In addition to supplying risk finance aiming for long-run economic performance, owners also exercise a short-term cost and rate of return control function. This is operated indirectly through top level management. Either owners sell out (vote with their feet) or apply pressure on, or change top management. Efficient profit control is partly a matter of being informed, partly a matter of taking action on the basis of information. Modern information technology is rapidly increasing the transparency of large corporations for owners and top management in terms of cost and profit performance allowing, as a consequence, more "flat" hierarchical organisations. However, access to information, control and the ability to take effective action fast have much to do with how the firm is organised. Divisionalisation or the organisation of the firm as a group of separate corporate entitities owned and controlled by a financial holding company (the investment company function, item 4 in Table 1) began long ago, but is still in progress.

Table 3

THE LARGEST SWEDISH (MANUFACTURING) EXPORTERS, 1965, 1978 AND 1981

Name of firm	Rank by size of exports 1981 1978 1965	1965 Exports from Sweden in percent of total Swedish goods exports	1965 Percentage of total employment in foreign subsidiaries	1978 Exports from Sweden in percent of total Swedish goods exports	1978 Percentage of total employment in foreign subsidiaries	1981 Exports from Sweden in percent of total Swedish goods exports	Year of establishment	Type of activity
Volvo	1 1 1	5.0	Percentage share for group 1-5: 13.0	9.2	Percentage share for group 1-5: 29.3	10.6	1926	Automobiles, trucks, etc
ASEA	2 4 5	2.6		3.4		5.2	1883	Heavy electrical, robots
Saab-Scania	3 3 13	1.6		3.8		4.2	1937/1891	Trucks, automobiles, aircraft
Electrolux (a)	4 6 25	0.8		2.3		3.6	1910	Whitewares, etc.
Sandvik	5 5 9	2.2		2.6		2.6	1862	Hardcore metal, tools
Ericsson	6 2 8	2.3	Percentage share for group 6-10: 48.8	4.0	Percentage Share for group 6-10: 31.3	2.5	1876	Telecommunications
SCA	7 8 3	3.0		2.1		2.3	1929	Paper & pulp
Boliden (b)	8 19 18	1.4		1.2		1.8	1925	Metal & mining
SKF (a)	9 15 6	2.5		1.5		1.6	1907	Ball bearings, etc.
Alfa Laval	10 11 20	1.1		1.6		1.5	1878	Dairy systems, centrifugal equipment
LKAB	11 10 2	4.6		1.8		1.5	1890	Iron ore
Stora Kopparberg	12 14 12	1.7		1.5		1.5	13th cent	Copper mining, steel
Svenska Vary	13 7 -	-		2.1		1.5	(1977)	Shipbuilding
Södra Skogsagarna	14 16 -	0.6		1.5		1.5	1943	Pulp & paper
SSAB	15 13 -	-	Percentage share for group 11-20: 0.9	1.5	Percentage share for group 11-20: 2.2	1.5	(1978)	Pulp & paper
MoDo	16 18 7	2.4		1.3		1.3	1873	Pulp & Paper
Bofors	17 17 21	1.0		1.3		1.2	1873	Weapons, steel, electronics
Holmen	18 21 23	1.0		1.2		1.2	1609	Paper
Billerud	19 - 19	1.2		(1.0)		1.2	1883	Paper
Papyrus	20 - -	0.3		0.9		1.1	1895	Paper

a. Including large parts of Facit (1978) and, for 1981, also Gränges.
b. The reason for the large advance of Boliden in the export ranking is partly the rapid increase in relative raw materials prices 1978 to 1981, and partly an increase in trade activities.

Source: Eliasson, G., De utlandsetablerade företagen och den svenska ekonomin, op. cit.

Table 4

ORIENTATION OF R&D INVESTMENTS IN SWEDISH MANUFACTURING, 1981
(Percentages)

1.	On general increases in knowledge	4
2.	On new product	19
3.	On products already in market but new to firm	26
4.	On improvements of existing products	36
5.	On improvements of existing _processes_	8
6.	On development of new processes	7
	TOTAL	100

Source: Swedish Central Bureau of Statistics, 1984:20.

Finance buffers, furthermore, operate as a risk reducer that makes it possible to plan ahead and to smooth other activities over time, something that has been demonstrated over and over again to be productivity enhancing.

Of course, any firm that cannot efficiently finance its own trade is placed at a disadvantage, when it comes to the planning of production, distribution and marketing. The advantage of a large investment capital becomes even more important when allocating investment and in the carrying out of long-term, risky investment programmes.

In addition to this -- of growing significance because of the high interest rates during the 70s -- large, idle financial balances, that are not profitably invested, are costly. That is one of the reasons why both the investment allocation, the commercial bank and the insurance function have been increasingly internalised and centralised in large firms in an effort to economise on the costs of finance, while preserving financial independence. Arguments resembling these have been used to include a "real balance" variable in macro production function analysis, [for instance Fisher (1974), You (1981)]. In principle, there is a good point here, even though I doubt these are the effects that show up in macroeconometric production function analysis. [Jagrén (1984) demonstrates how productivity on the construction side of the OIII nuclear reactor in Sweden was deliberately lowered to complete the project ahead of schedule in order to reduce total costs and start an income stream earlier. Toward the completion of the project accumulated interest costs were much larger than total construction costs.]

Financial strength on the margin of course also defines the outer limits of the firm seen as a financial entity. If rates of return on some marginal activity within a firm are consistently below the market loan rate or the rate of return on some alternative interior activities, strong pressures build up to sell off or close down that activity, or at least to deprive it of new resources. There are few factors that hold back efficient long-term planning as much as insufficient financial size and strength. It reduces the ability to take on risks. If management knows what it wants, inefficiency breeds if they cannot launch ahead on full scale, but have to take one cautious step at a time. This is particularly emphasized by the shifting of economies of scale during the post-war period, between the items in Table 1, away from factory production toward marketing in particular. The ten largest firms in Table 3 have been devoting a rapidly growing share of their capital spending on international marketing efforts, investments that are extremely risky.

Pratten (1976) reports another intriguing and related result. In his comparison of matched Swedish and British firms he notices that Swedish firms were much smaller in financial size but larger if compared by process/factory scale of operations. Productivity in the latter sense in Swedish firms was much above the same measures in British firms, that also invested less and grew much more slowly, even though they exhibited a somewhat higher return to capital according to the three definitions used. These are data from the late 60s. They do, however, suggest that there may be financial factors at work both on the formation of firms as institutions and on the real, GNP contributing performance of manufacturing activities. Financial durability is critical for longer-term innovative ventures, where a positive cash flow may take years to show. A large and somewhat "over-sized" financial base is therefore instrumental in running a large modern firm efficiently. The larger and more heterogeneous the firm, however, the more complex it is to operate and the more easily internal inefficiencies develop. The firms may simply be too large to be efficiently run, or the technology and competence to run them may be lacking. Rigidities and inefficiencies associated with big corporate bureaucracies have been increasingly discussed in the last decade (Dearden, 1972; Eliasson, 1976; Hayes-Abernathy, 1982). As an introduction to the next section I venture to say that this competence (vested in items 1 through 6 and 10 in Table 1) may be a most fundamental industrial technology that defines the comparative advantages of firms in the advanced OECD nations. The efficient use of information is the critical matter.

IV. TECHNICAL CHANGE IN A MODERN FIRM

From the macro-econometrics of production technology, the residual "after labour and capital", for a long time "explained" most of output growth among the industrialised countries as a measured time trend, or in a "mystic way". Technical change so measured faded away in the 70s (Aberg, 1984). Denison (1967) removed part of the shift by redefining input volumes through ad hoc adjustments for quality. Griliches-Jorgensen removed much of the United States residual in the 50s and the 60s through appropriate adjustments of prices on factor inputs. Why the residual came in the 50s and the 60s and why it went in the 70s, however, still remains a mystery to paraphrase Denison (1979).

When seen from a macro-economic point of view, technical change can occur at roughly three levels of aggregation in the production process, and at a fourth level in terms of the market environment.

Items 3 and 4 separate the firm from its environment, or the market. It is significant in my view that much of the measured productivity improvement at the macro production function level appears to lie in the intersection between 3 and 4, notably between the firm on the one hand, and the capital and equity markets on the other.

Table 5

STAGES OF TECHNICAL CHANGE

---

1. Process
2. Product (normally establishment level)
3. Management (firm level)
4. Economic policy (macro level).

The most widely "acknowledged level" of technical change on the other hand, again, is at the process stage, where process techniques are improved so that the same products can be manufactured by the application of smaller inputs of one, several or all factors, or rather more interesting from the economic point of view, at lower total unit costs. In some industries, notably capital intensive, basic process industries, technical change oriented toward a more cost efficient production of simple products undoubtedly is very important. However, such improvements as a rule occur as a consequence of a redesign of production process flows associated with the installation of new capital goods (new products). In engineering industries, however, technical improvements of existing production lines appear to be the least important of the four types of technological improvement, even though it can be large and rapid at small, well-defined segments of the production process (Figure 2A illustrates this).

Major shifts in productivity at a production line in engineering industries normally occur simultaneously with a redefinition, or a redesign of a product, like a new automobile model, or the high speed printer in Figure 2B. This redesign of the product and a simultaneous redesign of the production line, after the initial shift, often leaves ample scope for further piecemeal improvements. The major initial shift seems to be dependent upon a reorganisation of process activities that have been planned and thought of when designing the product, not necessarily with the installation of new, faster and more sophisticated machinery. The research carried out by the Swedish Computers and Electronics Committee includes many examples of how a reorganisation of existing machines, to obtain a new flow pattern, significantly improved aggregate productivity performance. It is not by accident that recent engineering literature is so occupied with the optimal factory design and that the availability of engineers trained in "systems thinking" has been found to be insufficient in advanced industrial nations.

In fact, improved overview and better co-ordination of the entire factory process appear to be the major simple notion that is extremely conducive to productivity increase in a general sense. I will begin at the production line level and move upwards through the product design and process levels, including also distribution. Finally it will reach stage 3 in Table 5. With regard to the art of holding the firm together financially and optimising productivity performance at that level, non-process equipment begins to dominate and to become a large cost item in total costs. The technological possibility to overview of the entire system can significantly cut stock requirements and significantly increase flow efficiency.

Figure 2. **CHANGE IN PRODUCTIVITY, 1969-81**
Percent

A. LABOUR PRODUCTIVITY IN THE PRODUCTION OF A PARTICULAR PART WHICH REMAINS IDENTICAL OVER TIME

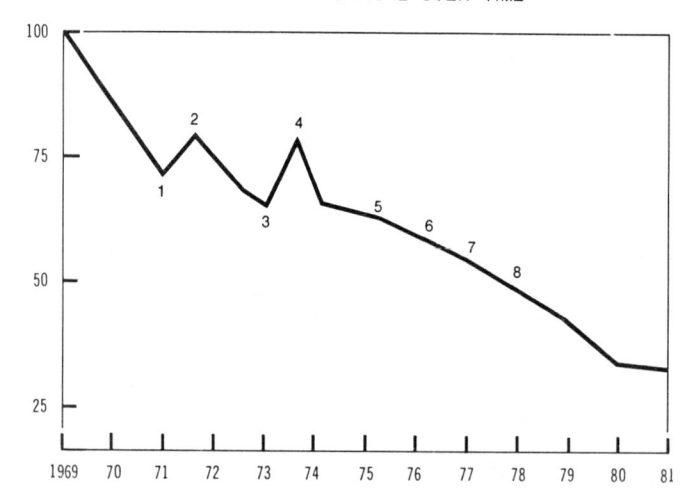

1. Learning phase, hours for supervision and quality control gradually reduced.
2. Subcontractor takes over, new learning phase.
3. Production moved back to own factory.
4. New subcontractor.
5. Pick and place robot installed.
6. Automatic engraving + multiple machine servicing begins.
7. Electrochemical + extra robot, etc.
8. Automatic grading begins.

B. TOTAL FACTOR PRODUCTIVITY FOR A FAMILY OF SOPHISTICATED ENGINEERING PRODUCTS

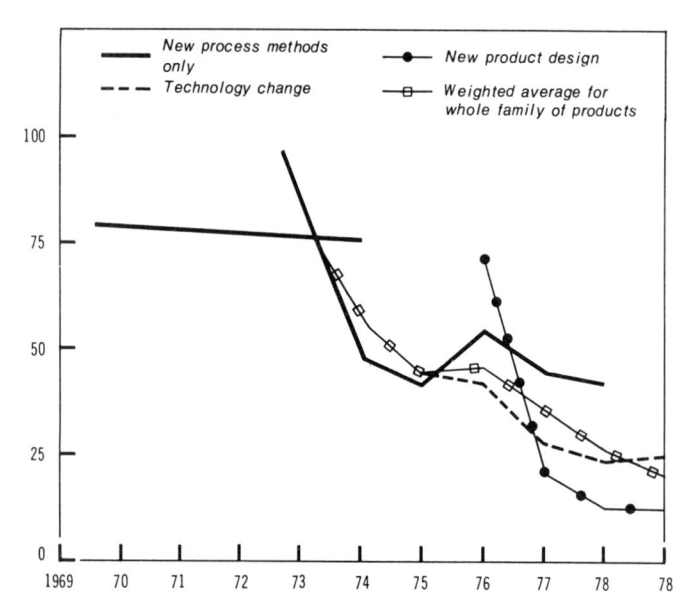

— New process methods only
--- Technology change
—●— New product design
—□— Weighted average for whole family of products

Note : The figures show the use of factor inputs (labour hours in A and a weighted index of all factors in B) per unit of output. Index = 100 initial year.
Source : Gunnar Eliasson, "Electronics, Economic Growth and Employment – Revolution or Evolution", in Giersch (ed.) *Emerging Technologies, Consequences for Economic Growth, Structural Change and Employment,* Tübingen, 1982.

It is clear from much of the analysis carried out at IUI that the productivity potential of the so-called new information technology lies in making the business organisation more transparent and in the more efficient co-ordination that becomes possible. Improved, central profit control makes it technically possible to decentralise operational decisions and responsibilities (Eliasson, 1984c, Fries, 1984). Improvements begin to show already at the parts production stage where better overview and a faster flow allow savings in inventories at all stages. Positive systems effects, however, expand rapidly from there to financial control at the firm level. Labour saving improvements may dominate at the lower process stages of production (numerically controlled machines, robots), but capital (costs) saving improvements escalate from there on.

Let us begin by seeing a product as a particular constellation of parts. Some parts may be standard parts while others are uniquely fashioned for the particular product. Competitiveness of a product of a particular producer lies in:

i) the manufacture of parts (or purchasing of parts);

ii) the design of the combination of parts (product design);

iii) the design of new parts and new combinations of parts (and new product design);

iv) the assembling of parts to a product.

Competitiveness under i) and iv) is normally based on process cost efficiency, under ii) and iii) on unique human skill endowments. Parts production employs most of the heavy machinery in a firm. (In the extreme case, where a bulk commodity like pulp or steel is the output and little assembling or combinating activity is needed, the entire process can be seen as "parts production".) Numerically guided machine tools, robots and automation (in process industries) have become increasingly important at this stage. The smaller the part the more labour saving such installations appear to be. The longer the parts production process, with several sequences of machine installations like in Figure 2A, or complete automation of a line (see Nilsson, 1981), the more of machine capital saving is achieved through faster flows but also, and more importantly, the more savings on stocks of goods in process are achieved.

It should be remembered, however, that a part in a product, is a product in itself, that may be the main (final) product of a subcontractor (for instance ball bearings in an automobile). The earlier in the production stage the simpler the product as a rule, and the more process-oriented production (steel, parts, automobile) the more of automated processes we find. However, also at this stage major innovative product design activity has been taking place recently. New materials are entering engineering industries making it possible to integrate, or rather cut across several production stages, using different technologies, i.e., to "shape" materials (casting and gluing rather than turning and grinding). It was noted already by Hicks (1977, p. 147 ff) that the basic functions of machine tools used in engineering production are the same as those about 150 years ago. Plastics and composite materials are becoming increasingly superior to steel in standard products and -- above all -- as basic materials, in the new, advancing industries (aircraft, etc). Entirely new tools to cut (for instance lasers) and to form and fasten are used, and costs are coming down rapidly. It is no wonder that the traditional machine tool makers are finding themselves in a competitive squeeze from two ends, new materials and distressed customers. (The frequent worries about robots and distressed machine tool manufacturers by industrial policy authorities may simply be beside the point. It is the combination of new materials and new types of tools that will reshape factory processing of goods in the advanced industrial countries and rapidly shift performance upwards.)

Capital costs increase in relative importance as we approach the later assembly stages of a given combination of parts (a given automobile). Automated equipment is still relatively rare at this stage, but technology is improving fast. The more comprehensive the production process, the more stocks are needed to handle flow interruptions in order to keep up flow speeds. Information techniques, and designs to monitor the production flows to achieve overview of the production line become instrumental in the capital savings process. Hence, what we are observing is the substitution of one form of capital for the other used in the co-ordination of production and all activities of the firm. In the old type of decentralised operations, inventories are needed to prevent flow interruption. Particular designs of flows and feedback adjustments cut stock, and also machine capacity requirements even further. The more in this direction we move, the more of information technology and accumulated human capital is, however, needed to achieve the observable capital savings.

The design and change of the product itself is the third competitive factor, and the decisive one in advanced industries. It is quite resource using in itself (see Tables 2 and 4). Electronics enter into the product, replacing mechanical techniques. Major advances are currently on the way in design (service) production in the form of CAD and (even) CAD/CAM techniques linking parts inventory and parts production directly to product design. This is inventory saving, while labour inputs in the design stage may even increase. The important technical improvements, however, come with the interaction of product design with process organisation and techniques. (In saying so I am thinking more of designing the product with the requirements of the process technique in mind than of actually integrating design work with work preparation and processing. The latter is the idea of CAD/CAM which is still (1985) in its embryonic stages, with few applications outside specific industries like chip manufacturing. The former is probably the major instrument behind currently observed productivity advances.)

Standard parts in the manufacturing of increasingly complex and variable product designs are becoming common. The automobile is a case in point, and the relative competitive superiority of small producers of design-based manufacturing is a double case in point.

CAD technologies coupled with flexible process designs make it possible to achieve more frequent product changes using standard parts all the time and without fundamentally new investments in factory equipment. All this is dominantly capital saving technical change. In addition to this the major advances in total factor productivity performance (see Figure 2B) are normally associated with major product design changes. Robotisation, for instance, to be profitable normally requires a minimum product life. Hence, existing production lines for old products are not automated if the remaining lifelength of the product is short. When a new product is introduced and a new production line designed, new techniques, like robotisation, can normally be planned in advance.

A division or a profit centre of a firm can be seen as a bundle of products of the above type. At this stage the combination of products is truly what matters for competitiveness, and in some firms a division may be buying semi-manufactured products or the whole product, simply applying its own brand label, or maybe adding some design features to the product.

This is the situation in important areas for many of the world's leading firms, notably several in Table 3. The design, marketing, distributing and financing activities increase in importance. Overview, often global overview, becomes important and technical change at this level operates significantly on the capital (stock) requirement side. Global inventory control systems are easily recognisable illustrations of this, where large technological steps forward have already been taken, but these are not necessarily the potentially most important areas.

A firm, finally (we are now reaching stage 3 in Table 5), can be seen as a bundle of divisions. Technology now is almost entirely management or its various forms of co-ordination. We can distinguish between four different categories:

i) Cost control.

ii) Profit control (short term).

iii) Investment allocation (medium term).

iv) Organisational change (long term).

Cost control dominates the interior activities of the firm. Profit control enters at a level of aggregation when the firm opens up to both product and input markets, for instance, the division level. It is normally associated with the budgeting process (see Eliasson, 1976a). In practice, this process is concerned with improving cost performance over a given divisional product structure, eliminating cyclical slack. Hence, budget profit control is closely related to the economists notion of static efficiency. The comprehensive budget process in a large firm means co-ordination through total cost control through the application of advanced, predominantly capital-saving information technology.

The problem of comprehensive profit control of course becomes even more important and difficult at higher decisions levels in the firm. Investment allocation was closely related to the long-term planning process which was very popular during the late 60s. As a formal management procedure, however, it has not been successful (see Eliasson, 1976a). Investment allocation is a typical corporate headquarter task. It means changing the composition of output through remixing a given bundle of products, through the varying of investment. Efficiency, here in the sense of equating the marginal product of capital to some chosen interest rate, is closely associated with the neoclassical notion of dynamic efficiency. Reweighting of output composition has been demonstrated to be a significant factor behind shifts in the macro production function (see Eliasson, 1985c). Again, short-term profit control in the budget appears to be the important information technique currently used in achieving such results.

What I prefer to call Schumpeterian dynamics (see Dahmén, 1984) is dominated by the entrepreneurial, or the capitalist, ownership function. It enters under category 4. This time we are concerned with institutional change or reorganisation within a firm defined as a financial entity (a group, a conglomerate) through entry, exit and internal changes at all levels. (Entry corresponds to the use of new, unique parts in a new product design.) Large step improvements in competitiveness and productivity, as we measure them at the firm level, are normally associated with such internal reorganisations.

This is not the place to present quantitative evidence on such structural changes. Very little, in fact, exists and research in that area has recently been started in IUI. However, a few observations can illustrate this. Over the past seven-year period, for instance, Swedish Match has bought 40 subsidiary companies and sold off 45 companies. Electrolux has acquired ca 325 producing units and sold off ca 30 firms since 1967. This is the kind of structural change that can be observed rather easily. But if one looks deeper into the aggregates a much more lively recombinatorial activity appears. Parts of subsidiaries or divisions are purchased or sold. So far, we have only impressionistic evidence of this, even though IUI is currently doing a detailed study on a group of firms.

These changes are geared to concentrate and reduce the number of activities to a few rather than many knowledge bases and to achieve economies of scale both in product development, marketing and production. Interestingly enough the patterns we have observed point in one direction. Economies of scale in increasingly costly R&D spending require larger and larger volume shipments. To achieve larger volume shipments either new markets have to be developed or -- which is more typical of mature product firms -- market shares have to be increased, notably through increased marketing efforts in customer markets. Investments in marketing are both long term and expensive and increased competitiveness does harm to competitors. Marketing skills draw on a rather homogeneous, product-related knowledge base and a specific, market-dependent knowledge base that relates to many products in that same market. Furthermore, it is often less expensive -- and much faster -- to buy an existing market network than build it from scratch. Hence, one observes firms, in particular in the mature product markets, that expand their administrative control system to internalise also the significant value added created through marketing services, that was earlier often run through independent agents or sales agencies.

At least for Swedish firms, the bulk of foreign direct investments is related directly or indirectly to such extensions of directly (controlled) marketing networks in foreign markets.

Larger volumes bring larger production and economies of scale. Most firms want to concentrate processing of hardware production in a few places. It is typical and most economical for most Swedish multinational companies, as in all activities of any degree of sophistication, requiring skilled or educated workers, to concentrate goods processing to Sweden. Local markets, national trade policies and existing production facilities in purchased companies, however, do not always make this homeward production possible, practical or economical.

However, at the other end, service production at earlier stages of production and R&D development demand a much larger variety of very specialised service activities.

As a rule it is not economical even for large firms to keep all these activities inhouse, at least as long as they are not vital for commercial product innovations or for reasons of commercial secrecy.

Hence, while manufacturing firms are integrating vertically downstream, closer and closer to the final consumer, the need for more and more specialised services at earlier stages of production has been spinning off a varied, institutional fragmentation and specialisation. In countries where taxes are high and labour markets are regulated, the economic incentives for this are also strong, since skilled, specialised and valuable talent normally does not fetch its right remuneration within a large organisation. The employee does not want to take on responsibility for a very expressive and specialised service that is needed now and then. The specialist wants to be compensated at a level comparable to his value for the user of his service. Hence, there is a mutual interest for institutional separation. These tendencies are difficult to measure statistically, but they can be observed to occur abundantly around high-tech industries like electronics. This development will clearly put pressure on the unintentional welfare and income redistribution arrangements that have always been typical within large "teams", like large factory installations. With high productivity "workers" separated off in self-employment or small consulting firms the remaining factory operation will lose some of its potential internal generosity.

It is clear that the organisational and internal institutional changes that we are discussing are decided at the very top of companies, at the highest executive level, at the board of directors and by the dominant owners.

Very little systematic research on the importance of the capitalist ownership function has been published. IUI has recently began a large scale project with this intention.

As it emerges from our analysis the major advances of productivity at the firm level seem to be associated with structural changes of the kind mentioned at the product and higher levels that are closely linked to the ownership function of a firm where risk finance and industrial competence enter a form of symbiosis. The next important step in the shifting of the macro production function appears to be the capital market allocation function between firms.

Technical change currently appears to be working against traditional economies of scale in factory production while, at the same time, an often neglected scale function has been on the advance for decades, and increasingly so during the disorderly 70s (see Eliasson, Sharefkin, Ysander, 1983), i.e., financial scale, financial risk reduction being the key factor at work. Figure 3 summarises these tendencies.

In the first place, the international market environment has become increasingly less predictable.

Secondly, product technologies and continuous innovative product change have become key competitive edges for the advanced manufacturing firm.

Figure 3

TENDENCIES

<u>From cost efficient production of simple goods toward
a product-based industrial technology</u>

---

1. Uncertainty up and predictability down in the international business environment.

2. Product technology is becoming relatively more important for competitiveness than cost efficiency.

3. Products are characterised by:

    -- more complex technology and design;
    -- longer development periods;
    -- larger development costs;
    -- larger demand for risk capital;
    -- shorter life lengths; and hence,
    -- higher risks.

4. Competing technological development and higher business uncertainty together places a premium (ceteris paribus) on financial size.

New products, however, are characterised by longer gestation periods, larger development costs, larger requirements of internal risk finance. But once in the market product life cycles have shortened.

Together, this means a higher level of risk taking on the part of the firm. Disorderly market behaviour and reduced environmental predictability mean that the larger financial commitments receive a premium. Risks can be spread over a larger number of activities, and most importantly by concentrating cash flows from many operations to one point at a time. The financing of high risk product developments can be internalised.

However, the larger and the more heterogeneous the financial organisations under which all these activities are gathered, the more complex and the more information demanding the task of managing the system. This becomes obvious when we look again at for instance, Electrolux Corporation, headquartered in Stockholm, with approximately 89 000 employees, approximately 270 subsidiaries and operating in approximately 50 countries. The typical characteristics of such a company is that top level management has far from complete knowledge of what goes on below them. This is particularly true for how things are done. On the other hand, the top managerial staff of a well managed large company has a clear view of its objectives and a quite clear view of what, in terms of performance, can be demanded of the various subsidiary operations of the company.

The top level is to set the right targets and to devise a reliable reporting and control system against these targets. Targets have to be close to what is feasible; only slightly above, to be taken seriously and to stimulate increased efforts. But if targets are set too low, performance invariably adjusts downwards. The art of remote control and guidance of a large business organisation affects productivity performance of the entire organisation and clearly is a matter of how to design an efficient information system (4).

There is a trend toward the delegation of operations (how to do things) and increased centralised control (what to do). This is exactly the opposite to automation which involves centralising process knowledge (how) in enough detail to run a production process centrally. This orientation of modern business information and management systems also runs contrary to the "old" idea of scientific management, which was based on the naive idea of centralised management. The reason for the the changed orientation was the clash with reality. Complexity of top management decisions and built-in inconsistencies (see Table 1) between various functions make centralised management techniques impracticable.

Table 6 illustrates that important parts of key elements of operations knowledge simply are not available at the top. The resolution of top level routine access to information rarely goes below the product group level [item (3) in Table 6] and the reasons are entirely practical, namely costs of designing and updating the database.

V. WHY IS TECHNICAL CHANGE SHIFTING IN A CAPITAL SAVING DIRECTION?

A typical development of the modern firm that accompanied the post-war advancement of industrial technology in the Western world, has been the increased emphasis on product technology and a relative decrease in the importance of process techniques and cost efficiency as a basis for competitiveness. This development is witnessed by the emerging importance of engineering industries, while basic industries have been in relative decline. The relative growth of a white-collar, educated labour force in manufacturing tells a similar story.

Perhaps even more important in a future perspective is the so far neglected emergence of service production and information handling as the dominant production activity of a manufacturing firm. It is often more important to know how to design the product and the production process and to know where the right customers are, than to manufacture the product. A consequence of this has been a rapid institutional change -- also in typically non-manufacturing sectors -- and a growing dependence of the manufacturing firm on human knowledge and skills.

A side effect of this development has been a rapid deterioration in the quality and relevance of official statistics, that so far has not been adequately taken into account in economic analysis. Above all, the delimitations of statistically defined sectors have become shifty and dependent upon the organisation of firms. With a signficiant part of total resources in manufacturing devoted to service production that can be administered within the firm as a manufacturing activity or in a separate

Table 6

ORGANISATIONAL AND INFORMATION HIERARCHIES IN A LARGE FIRM

Level of Aggregation (1)	Organisational Unit (2)	Activity (3)	Objective (Criterion) (4)	Database (Measurement System) (5)	Market Contract (a) (6)
1.	Group	Financial guidance and control	Return to equity	Profit and loss statement and balance sheet	I, L, P, K
2A.	Division	Financial & profit control	Return to total capital	Profit and loss statement and partial balance sheet	I, L, P
2B.	Subsidiary	Profit control	Return to total	Ditto	I, L, P
3.	Product Group	Factory Production	Profit margin	Profit and loss statement	I, L, P
4.	Product	Process	Sum of cost elements	Cost accounts	I, L
5.	Component (part)	Process-stage	Cost element	Cost accounts	I, L

a) I = Market for components, etc. (purchasing).
L = Labour market (hiring).
P = Product market (selling).
K = Credit market (borrowing).

Source: Eliasson, 1984c.

business unit (a consulting firm, a distribution or a sales agent, a firm devoted to technological innovative development work, etc.) statistically classified as private service, the information content of official national accounts statistics is on the decline. A traditional economic analysis of standard aggregates may make us believe in "de-industrialisation", while a careful analysis may suggest that this is all nonsense.

Industrial technology will probably push further in the direction of using relatively less hardware than software capital. And at least to judge from Swedish experience, the locus of manufacturing competence has already shifted toward product technology, where most of R&D spending goes, and marketing and distribution, which also -- in fact -- means a broadening of the product concept. The enhanced product orientation has already demonstrated itself in:

   i) more diversity and complexity in product offerings;

  ii) longer product gestation periods;

 iii) shorter product life cycles;

  iv) that successful manufacturing firms have their base in competitive customer markets in advanced industrial economies.

A direct consequence of the growing product orientation of manufacturing industry and the longer gestation period between product initiation and final delivery is:

   i) The growing importance in total value added of service production of various kinds and the increasing share of both;

  ii) Information and transaction costs;

 iii) Capital costs in total costs.

The accumulation and application of information is a common denominator of those activities. The development of a new product, preparing for its production, perhaps in a different country, making it known to customers, marketing it, distributing it and servicing it, etc., are all reflections of the increased role of information use in manufacturing production.

These activities are not hardware capital intensive. They are based on people and human skills (5). This development, however, at the same time increases the total risk exposure of the entire business entity. It takes longer before investments begin to generate a positive cash flow, and if mistakes are made, product lives in the market will be short and the whole firm may be in jeopardy. Such technical, commercial and market risks are normally carried within the company as a financial unit and by the owners, risk carrying being an important production activity of the modern firm. The increased exposure has already induced, and will continue to induce, the formation of larger multiproduct, multinational firms seen as financial units, that can absorb greater mistakes internally.

We have already observed from a number of studies that better co-ordination of factory processes and distribution networks has been a typical capital-saving technology based on new information techniques. This above mentioned development, hence, means that these monitoring and control techniques are now becoming even more important in co-ordinating the entire set of activities in even larger business units.

Better co-ordination of the entire organisation means a faster flow of products (cf. global inventory control) and is a typical capital-saving technological change.

VI. SUMMING UP

This paper does not present a strict econometric test of some well-defined hypotheses. We have rather brought together a wealth of scattered facts. This fragmented evidence has been merged with some reasonable guesswork into a rather complex working hypothesis about the nature of, and change in technological progress in modern manufacturing industries. The following five statements make up our main conclusions.

First, total factor productivity as observed at sector or macro levels is mainly economic in nature, rather than technical; the dynamics of allocation of resources within firms ("management") and through markets, between firms being the vehicle for advance.

Second, the focus of technical change, and the application of R&D spending are shifting from achievement of cost efficient processing towards product quality upgrading. This shifting of emphasis reflects the orientation towards customer markets and large and elaborate resource applications in marketing.

Third, points 1 and 2 highlight the modern manufacturing firm as a predominant "information processor". Exploiting new, emerging technologies for sophisticated product designs and intense marketing to find the right "paying" customers globally is a more profitable focussing of resource use than efficient production of simple hardware. The not very successful idea of a world car compared with the successful performance of specialised, customer-oriented automobile designs is a good example. This development will probably knit the advanced industrial OECD nations together economically even more, further alienating the group from the not so developed economies.

Fourth, this shifting of activities from hardware processing towards various forms of information processing appears to be pivoting the nature of technical change in a relatively more capital saving direction than was earlier the case.

Fifth, finally, even though the service content of manufacturing production may dominate, the services are still linked to a product that can be traded (Lindberg-Pousette, 1985). The changing nature of manufacturing production and institutional reorganisation brought about by both technological advance and other economic factors are blurring our statistical observation instruments. We may wrongly believe that we are observing a process of "de-industrialisation".

A proper scientific foundation of these results requires much more empirical research. The evidence so far accumulated suggests that industrial policy-makers should take careful note of this movement of the industrial locus away from blue-collar factory production.

NOTES AND REFERENCES

1. At the Industrial Institute for Economic and Social research (IUI) as part of the database project associated with the micro-to-macro model project (see Eliasson, 1978, 1984; Lindberg-Pousette, 1985) codenamed MOSES Database.

2. A supplementary conclusion of this paper is that the existence of this technology washes away the importance for medium-term employment of the crisis industries (accounting for more than 10 per cent of manufacturing employment in the mid-70s) and the enormous industrial subsidies during the crisis years of the 70s, spent to save employment. In the longer term, the effects of these subsidies appear insignificant or perhaps even worthless. I would even argue for a sizeable negative value, since industrial subsidies probably stimulated substantial domestic factor cost overshooting and retarded output growth in the frontier firms: see Eliasson-Lindberg, 1981; Eliasson, 1984; and Carlsson-Bergholm-Lindberg, 1982.

3. This figure comes on top of a normal share of distressed industries. See Chapter 10, Section 6.6 in Eliasson-Carlsson-Ysander et al, 1979.

4. See again Eliasson, 1976, on MIP targeting (op.cit., pp. 236 ff., 258 ff.). MIP targeting characterises the firm in the micro-to-macro model used for simulation experiments in Eliasson, 1985c.

5. Information processing has also become more hardware intensive (see Barras' paper), for the simple reason that computers are replacing clerks with pens at desks.

BIBLIOGRAPHY

Aberg Y., Produktivitetsutvecklingen i olika OECD-länder 1953-1980, IUI Research Report No. 25, Stockholm, 1984.

Carlsson B.; Bergholm F; Lindberg T., Industristödspolitiken och dess inverkan pa samhällsekonomin (Industry Subsidy Policy and its Macroeconomic Impact), IUI, Stockholm, 1981.

Dahmén E., "Schumpeterian Dynamics: Some Methodological Notes", JEBO, Vol. 5, No. 1, March, 1984, also IUI Booklet No. 162, Stockholm, 1984.

Day R., Eliasson G., The Dynamics of Market Economies, IUI and North Holland, 1986.

Dearden J., "MIS is a Mirage", Harvard Business Review, January-February 1972.

Denison E.F., Why Growth Rates Differ, The Brookings Institution, Washington, D.C., 1967.

Denison E.F., Accounting for Slower Economic Growth -- The United States in the 70s, The Brookings Institution, Washington, D.C., 1979.

Eliasson G., Business Economic Planning -- Theory, Practice and Comparison, John Wiley & Sons, Stockholm, London, New York, etc., 1976.

Eliasson G., A Micro-to-Macro Model of the Swedish Economy, IUI Conference Reports, No. 1, Stockholm, 1978.

Eliasson G., Electronic, Technical Change and Total Economic Performance, IUI Research Report, No. 9, Stockholm, 1980.

Eliasson G., "The Micro (Firm) Foundations of Industrial Policy", in European Industry: Public Policy and Corporate Strategy, Oxford University Press, also IUI Booklet No. 173, Stockholm, 1984a.

Eliasson G., De utlandsetablerade företagen och den svenska ekonomin (foreign Established Companies and the Swedish Economy), IUI Research Report, No. 26, Stockholm, 1984b.

Eliasson G., "Informations- och styrsystem i stora företag" (Information and Guidance Systems in Large Companies), in Eliasson-Fries-Jagrén-Oxelheim, Hur styrs störforetag?, IUI/Liber, Kristianstad, 1984c.

Eliasson G., The Firm and Financial Markets in the Swedish Micro-to-Macro Model (MOSES) -- Theory, Model and Verification, IUI Working Paper No. 122, Stockholm, 1984d.

Eliasson G., "Micro Heterogeneity of Firms and the Stability of Industrial Growth", JEBO, Vol. 5, Nos. 3-4 (September-December), also IUI Booklet No. 183, Stockholm, 1984e.

Eliasson G., Theory Construction and Economic Measurement at Different Levels of Aggregation -- Parallel Theories and Data on Families and Firms, IUI Working Paper, 1985a.

Eliasson G., "The Knowledge Base of an Industrial Economy -- The OECD Human Resources Project", IUI Working Paper, 1985b.

Eliasson G., "Dynamic Micro-Macro Market Co-ordination and Technical Change", forthcoming IUI Working Paper, 1985c.

Eliasson G., Nya institutioner, förändrad marknadsorganisation och modifierade samhälls-värderingar -- horisont 2000. (New institutions, a changing market organisation and modified social values -- Horizon 2000), in Eliasson-Björklund-Pousette tec., 1985d.

Eliasson G., The Stability of Economic Organisational Forms and the Importance of Human Capital, IUI Working Paper No. 143, Stockholm, 1985e.

Eliasson G.; Bergholm F.; Horwitz E.C.; Jagrén L., De svenska storföretagen -- en studie av internationaliseringens konsekvenser för den svenska ekonomin (The Large Swedish Companies -- A Study of Corporate Internationalisation and the Swedish Economy), IUI, Stockholm, 1985.

Eliasson G.; Björklund A.; Pousette T., Att rätt värdera 90-talet (Evaluating the 90s), IUI, Stockholm, 1985.

Eliasson G.; Carlsson B.; Ysander B.C. et al, Att välja 80-tal (Choosing the 80s), IUI, Stockholm, 1979.

Eliasson G.; Fries H.; Jagrén L.; Oxelheim L., Hur styrs storföretag? (How are Large Companies Operated?), IUI/Liber, Kristianstad, 1984.

Eliasson G.; Granstrand O.; The Financing of New Technological Investments, IUI Booklet No. 121, Stockholm, 1981.

Eliasson G.; Sharefkin M.; Ysander B.C., Policy Making in a Disorderly World Economy, IUI, Stockholm, 1983.

Fischer S., "Money and the Production Function", Economic Inquiry, 12, 1974, pp. 517-33.

Fries H., "Datateknik och koncernstyrning", in Hur styrs storföretag?, IUI/Liber, Kristiansand, 1984.

Granstrand O., "Measuring and Modelling Innovative New Entry in Swedish Industry", forthcoming in Day-Eliasson 1986, also IUI Working Paper, No 140, 1985.

Griliches Z.; Jorgenson D.W., "The Explanation of Productivity Change", Review of Economic Studies, Vol. 34, 1967.

Hayes R.H.; Abernathy W.J., "Managing our Way to Economic Decline", Harvard Business Review, July-August, 1982.

Hicks J., A Theory of Economic History, London, 1977.

Jagrén L., O III -- organisation, kostnader och säkerhet, IUI Research Report No. 23, Stockholm, 1983.

Lindberg T.; Pousette T., Services in Production and Production of Services in Swedish Manufacturing, IUI Working Paper, forthcoming.

Nilsson S., Förändrad tillverkningsorganisation och dess aterverkningar pa kapitalbildningen -- en studie vid ASEA, IUI Booklet No. 115, Stockholm, 1981.

Pousette T., Datakommunikation i företag, IUI Research Report No. 24, Stockholm, 1983.

Pratten C., A Comparison of the Performance of Swedish and United Kingdom Companies, Cambridge University Press, 1976.

Sinai A.; Stokes H.H., "Real Money Balances: An Omitted Variable from the Production Function", AER 58, 1972, pp. 713-54.

You J.S., "Money, Technology, and the Production Function; An Empirical Study", The Canadian Journal of Economics, August, 1981.

III. PRODUCTION AND DEMAND: ESTIMATION OF ELASTICITIES

1

EVIDENCE FROM ECONOMETRIC STUDIES OF PRODUCTION FUNCTIONS

by

R.A. Wilson
University of Warwick
(United Kingdom)

SUMMARY

In this study an alternative approach to the analysis of technological change is considered -- the use of econometric techniques to examine the nature of the underlying technology of production and to assess how it has altered over time. The paper reviews the various econometric studies that have been conducted in recent years and assesses the extent to which the parameter estimates can throw light on the questions addressed in the workshop.

It is very difficult to assess the extent to which the econometric estimates of the economic parameters are biased by the nature of models and data sets used. In all cases the results refer to particular sectors in particular countries over a certain period of time. The specific problems associated with the data base used and methodological approach adopted will therefore limit the generality of the results obtained. In many studies some of the key parameters are fixed by assumption rather than being freely estimated which makes interpretation difficult. Clearly, therefore, great care is necessary in summarising the evidence and interpreting its implications.

Virtually all studies find that input demand does respond to price changes and that the parameters estimated are generally consistent with the axioms of production theory (although there are some notable exceptions).

However, the precise estimates of the degree of substitutability between any pair of inputs is subject to very wide margins of uncertainty. Very different results are obtained using time series or cross-sectional data and depending upon whether one starts from the production function itself or its dual-cost function. Overall, an elasticity of substitution between capital and labour of around unity is probably about the average but nearly all explicit attempts to test whether the technology is Cobb-Douglas or some more general form rejects the Cobb-Douglas function. Most studies suggest that there is a very different cross price response with respect to capital for blue collar (non-information) and white collar (information) labour. The former have usually been found to be substitutes for capital, the latter complements. Finally, with regard to bias in the direction of technical change, nearly all of the studies looking for it have found it. However, it is not always in accordance with prior expectations and often contradictory between different studies.

In conclusion, while in general the econometric approach appears to offer the possibilities of obtaining estimates of the key parameters with which the overall project was concerned, for all sorts of reasons (e.g. theoretical problems, measurement problems, relevance of the past to the future) there are considerable doubts about the value of the results obtained to date. This is particularly true when attempting to find some guidance as to the likely effects of IT. The results of empirical work based on data from the 1950s and 1960s may be of very limited value in attempting to assess how things will develop in the 1980s and 1990s. A key issue is the question of whether in the future white collar/information labour will continue to be a complement to capital or whether, as the case study evidence suggests, IT will result in increased capitalisation of office functions and substantial substitution of capital for labour.

2

PRICES, COSTS AND THE ELASTICITY OF DEMAND

by

Derek Bosworth
Polytechnic of Central London
(United Kingdom)

SUMMARY

1. Objectives

The introductory contribution by Stoneman, "An Analytical Framework for Analysing the Impact of Information Technologies on Economic Perspectives", outlined a neo-classical framework for the analysis of the impact of technological change on employment. This work highlighted the potentially important role of demand elasticities in determining the output expansion effects which to some degree, off-set the factor saving aspects of process changes. The higher the elasticity of demand, other things being equal, the greater the output expansion effect. Thus, this paper reports estimates of the own price and income elasticities of demand by country and product area, in an attempt to isolate industries and countries in which output expansion effects are (or are not) likely to be favourable to employment.

The theory recognises that the elasticity of demand alone is not sufficient to determine the output expansion effect. For any given value of the elasticity, the precise effect of any given cost reducing innovation will depend on the degree of monopoly power of firms in that market. Comparison of the theoretical results for the polar cases of perfect competition and monopoly suggest that, the higher the degree of monopoly power, the lower will be the expansionary effect. This paper provides estimates of industrial concentration as an indication of the degree of monopoly power.

When estimating price elasticities, it is important to recognise the international nature of most markets. The magnitude of import and export elasticities indicate countries with combinations which favour early process innovation (e.g. high import and export elasticities) and those with less favourable combinations (e.g. low import and export elasticities). Two things should be noted. First, high trade elasticities are a double edged weapon: early innovation should ensure a relatively favourable employment effect; a failure to innovate may mean particularly adverse employment effects. Second, success in ensuring favourable employment effects by one country will tend to mean an even more acute employment decline in another country.

The neo-classical framework also suggests that output expansion and positive employment effects may accrue from increases in product quality. The hedonic, or technical characteristics theory of prices, asserts that consumers are willing to pay a higher price for every unit of the good they purchase because of its improved quality (an outward shift in the demand curve for the product). Quality indices constructed by this method can be used to show that product improvements lead to increases in demand for a particular manufacturer's output (or for the product group as a whole).

Again, the theory of international trade is moving towards recognising the importance of quality improvements in determining the magnitude of trade flows. The theory now links product quality with either a "factor abundance" or a "technology gap" explanation of trade. In the former, it is the relative abundance of highly qualified manpower, R&D or innovative activities that determine relative prices and, therefore, the sorts of products that will be imported or exported (even though the production function is assumed identical across countries). In the second approach, the differences in efficiency of production, rather than relative factor endowments, determine the sorts of products traded.

2. Summary of Results

Elasticities of Demand

A survey was undertaken of studies that estimate elasticities of demand. Ideally, the results could be tabulated in matrix form, by product area and country, separately for price and income elasticities. In practice, a number of major problems were encountered: the results related almost entirely to final goods; different models tended to yield different estimates of the elasticities; a comprehensive coverage of countries proved impossible. Nevertheless, it has proved possible to tabulate some of the results in this form, although differences in the elasticities across product areas appear to be better determined than differences across countries.

For most product groups, the own price and income elasticities tend to move together. This simplifies matters somewhat when tabulating the results, which, corresponding with a priori expectations, broadly divide into two groups: basic necessities (e.g. food, drink, housing and perhaps clothing) and habit forming goods (e.g. tobacco and certain types of drink) associated with relatively low own price and income elasticities; luxury items (e.g. durables, services and expenditure abroad), associated with relatively high values of both the own price and income elasticities.

It seems likely that consumer tastes are probably sufficiently alike across many countries (at least for those countries for which the results were readily available) to make it more difficult to isolate differences in elasticities across countries. Differences may well be obscured by imperfections in the adopted models, by variations in national classifications, etc. Nevertheless, if the results can be taken at face value, Italy appears to have relatively high income and own price elasticities. The United States appears to have high own price, but somewhat lower income elasticities. The United Kingdom, Belgium and France are more difficult to disentangle, but, if anything, the values of the United Kingdom appear somewhat higher than for the other two. The income elasticity for France is higher than for Belgium, both have relatively low own price elasticities.

Import and Export Elasticities

Again, ideally, it would be most useful to be able to produce a matrix of results by product group and by country. In this instance this is not possible, although something can be said about both dimensions. Unlike the domestic demand elasticities, the import and export elasticities are probably better determined by country than by product group. However, the country results are open to criticism insofar as they are derived from aggregate import or export functions.

The results suggest that import elasticities by product area can be divided into two groups: food, drink and tobacco, raw materials and fuels tend to have relatively low import elasticities; manufactured goods tend to have higher elasticities. There is a considerable degree of variation within the group of manufactured goods, but there are a number of similarities in the results for different countries: transport equipment appears to have a high own price import elasticity in both the United Kingdom and the United States; the equivalent elasticity for textiles and clothing is also relatively high in both countries. While this division into high and low categories does not quite so clearly apply, there are nevertheless some points of similarity between UK import and export elasticities, for example, the low own price elasticities for food and drink and the relatively high elasticity for textiles.

The majority of countries have relatively price elastic trade on either the import or the export side. Only a minority appear to have trade elasticities which are both high or both low. According to this criterion, the United States, France, Denmark and Switzerland appear to be favourably placed to take advantage of process innovation; the United Kingdom, Netherlands, Finland and Australia appear to be relatively unfavourably placed. However, any final conclusions on this front require knowledge not only of the elasticities, but also of the relative importance of international trade within the overall economic activity of the economy.

Quality and Performance

While the work on elasticities is far from comprehensive, it is relatively well established in the economics literature compared with the more recent research on the importance of quality change in the determination of demand. Nevertheless, an increasing volume of results are becoming available about quality. At this stage, however, they are far from sufficient to produce systematized results by product group or country. On the other hand enough evidence exists to suggest that this will be an extremely important area of research in the future.

Results indicate that, at least for most types of durable goods, quality change is a key variable in explaining demand. The work on tractors indicated extremely high technical improvements. Combining the results of two separate studies, the index of quality for tractors increases by a factor of more than six over a thirty year period post-war. Similar sorts of increases seem to be going on in other areas, such as mainframe computers, but, intuition suggests that the quality improvement here would perhaps be even greater. There is immense scope for further research into quality indices and quality adjusted prices for goods with IT components.

Quality and Trade

The early indications are that the empirical evidence supports the hypothesis of the central role played by technical change in determining the types of products imported and exported, as well as the magnitude and direction of world trade. This modelling is at the very earliest stages of development. Patent data, which are available internationally on a broadly comparable basis, could be more fully exploited in empirical tests of such models. The work on hedonic prices (technical characteristics) can also be applied to the question of the role of quality in trade. In particular, it has been shown that, in the case of tractors, a small foothold is often obtained in the higher quality end of the market by new entrants, prior to an attack on the larger, often somewhat lower quality end of the market.

Monopoly Power

Statistics relating to the degree of market power are becoming increasingly available on a broadly comparable basis, particularly for member States of the EEC. A matrix of concentration measures, giving product area by country detail is established, but a number of important caveats should be mentioned. First, there are differences between countries in their product classifications. Second, there appear to be problems in interpreting concentration measures (e.g. adjustment for country size appears to change the ranking of countries in terms of their levels of concentration). Third, the evidence on concentration tends to emphasize the heterogeneity within industries, making it difficult to draw hard and fast conclusions about the output expansion effect of a process change in any particular industry.

Taking Europe as a whole, both the traditional four and twelve firm concentration ratios appear to indicate that, ranking from lowest to highest, textiles, paper, mechanical engineering and food are amongst the least concentrated groups; metal industries and chemicals are fairly highly concentrated; and transport equipment and electrical engineering are highly concentrated. If we take the percentage of each industry's turnover accounted for by firms that fall into the largest of all 1 000 firms in the EEC, the ranking again remains unchanged. The individual country returns (rather than for the EEC as a whole) also give a similar pattern.

As for the different degree of concentration across countries for each product area, the picture is far more difficult to interpret. If the different absolute sizes of the economy are ignored, the European countries covered can be ranked (from lowest to highest concentration): Italy, France, Netherland, Belgium and the United Kingdom. Allowing for the absolute sizes of the economies appears likely to alter the rankings somewhat, but not in the extreme cases of Italy and the United Kingdom. All the normal sorts of provisos about the use of concentration measures seem to apply. In particular, in making aggregate comparisons of this type, the importance of competition from foreign competitors through international trade should be borne in mind.

3. Conclusions

Globally, there are two "games" going on. The first is the (probable) overall reduction in world employment opportunities resulting from process innovation. The second is the transfer of employment opportunities between countries by the adoption of appropriate innovation strategies. In this discussion, we look at the problem from the point of view of a particular country. The main conclusions can be summarised under two main headings: product and country results.

Product Results

As might be anticipated, basic necessities and habit forming goods tended to have low own price elasticities. It is the group of more luxurious goods and service activities that tend to have higher own price and income elasticities. A further result was that own price and income elasticities tended to move in the same direction: products with low own price elasticities also possess low income elasticities. In addition, the import and export elasticities tend to split along very similar lines. It is more difficult to supplement these results with information about monopoly power.

There do appear to be some product groups with both relatively low domestic and international price elasticities (as well as low degrees of concentration), such as food, drink and tobacco. On the other hand, there are other components of manufactured (final) goods which have, at least, somewhat higher own price elasticities (e.g. clothing, parts of transport and communication goods, durables, etc.), which also comprise the group with a high import elasticity. This seems to be an area where further research is required and, at this stage, no further comparisons are undertaken.

Other things being equal, those groups with low domestic elasticities are likely to have unfavourable employment consequences where process innovation occurs. However, a failure of domestic industry to innovate in areas with low elasticities will not necessarily protect jobs in these industries because of innovation amongst foreign competitors. Nevertheless, the rate at which markets are lost to foreign innovators will still tend to be relatively slow in such areas because the associated import and export elasticities are also likely to be relatively low. High domestic price elasticity products are likely to have less unfavourable employment consequences associated with a domestic process innovation. In this case, however, insofar as such products tend to be associated with higher import and export elasticities, they will be particularly susceptible to process innovations amongst their foreign competitors.

The evidence on the role of quality improvement tends to reinforce these views. While at this stage the lack of results make conclusions rather speculative, it seems likely that technical characteristics and their improvement are likely to be more important in the luxury manufactured goods categories. Again, therefore, insofar as product improvements tend to raise demand, other things being equal, employment opportunities depend heavily on quality improvements. Again, these should be considered internationally. What counts from a national point of view are the quality improvements vis-à-vis foreign competitors. It is also clear from the rather limited evidence already available that technical characteristics can be pitched at different relative levels to establish a foothold in a new market or to aid market penetration.

Country Results

It appears unlikely that, at the present stage, we can simply provide a ranking of countries in terms of the degree of benefit or cost associated with early innovation. On the other hand, there are some pointers as to which countries are likely to be at the extremes. It is fairly easy to pick out countries with potentially favourable portents in one or other respect, for example:

   i) Domestic price elasticities: appear to indicate that Italy and, possibly, the United States have relatively high values, while the other countries covered are lower; the United Kingdom is towards the lower end, although not the very lowest;

   ii) Trade elasticities: the United States, France, Denmark and Switzerland appear to have trade elasticities that favour early innovation; the United Kingdom, Netherlands, Finland and Australia appear to be relatively unfavourably placed;

   iii) Quality improvements: are more speculative, but there is clear evidence of Germany and COMECON countries using a high technology strategy in certain markets; it seems likely that the United States and Japan, amongst others, also fall into this category;

   iv) The degree of industrial concentration appears to indicate significant differences between countries, with Italy amongst the least and the United Kingdom amongst the most concentrated.

Given the lack of comprehensive coverage, it is extremely difficult to combine these results to obtain an overall picture. Nevertheless, there are grounds for believing certain countries to be relatively well placed for early innovation: take for example the case of Italy (with its relatively high domestic elasticities, coupled with trade elasticities of around unity, plus relatively unconcentrated manufacturing industry) and the United States (with its particularly favourable import and export elasticities, coupled with reasonably high domestic own price elasticities and, probably, reasonably low concentration levels. These countries at least form a contrst with others less favourably placed for early innovation, such as the United Kingdom (with its relatively low domestic elasticities, its unusually low combination of low import and export elasticities, its failure to exploit technical product improvements, and its relatively concentrated industries).

4. Shortcomings and Future Research

The shortcomings of this paper fall into three main categories: first, those imposed by the design of the project; second, areas of improvement within the existing framework discovered during the project; and third, those arising from the limitations of the current state of economic research.

Design of the Project

There are obvious problems encountered in constraining the project to a neo-classical framework. It is doubtful, however, that any alternative (or mix of alternatives) would have proved superior and, it must be admitted that the neo-classical framework does give some extremely important insights about the implications of new technology. We leave further discussion of this question to one side. There is a more practical problem of the sheer enormity of the task of reviewing and pulling at least four extremely large and diverse sets of empirical results together, e.g. domestic demand elasticities, trade elasticities, technological characteristics/hedonic prices results, and market structure. It seems highly likely that the first, second and fourth of these are referred to so frequently in all kinds of international studies, that the OECD might consider a detailed position paper in each of the areas. The third area is so central to a broader understanding of technological change that it deserves attention in its own right, and we return to it below.

Extending the Results within the Existing Framework

It is fairly clear from the results reported that the inherent logic of the framework adopted in this paper could be tightened considerably. There is, for example, a fairly obvious connection between the component micro elements studied in this paper (e.g. product elasticities, monopoly power, trade elasticities, etc.) and the implications of new technology for employment in each country. The connection is made via the product mix and the magnitude and mix of imports and exports of each country. In addition, it is fairly certain that there are a number of connections, which are assumed to be independent in the analysis, that are, in fact, causally linked. For example, the elasticity of demand in any one country is not independent of the level of technical characteristics embodied in the product and, therefore, the innovation process.

Areas of Further Economic Research

The work has served to highlight areas where economic research might be supported. The whole area of the employment implications of product innovation deserves attention, both from a theoretical and empirical point of view. There is a specially important gap in the empirical literature with respect to hedonic prices and quality indices for micro computers (and, more generally, other goods relating to IT). There is immense scope for work on the role of technical quality in international trade.

I. INTRODUCTION (1)

This section addresses the question of what impact a cost reducing technological change, resulting from the application of new information technology (IT), will have on the level of prices and, thereby, on product demands, output and the demand for labour inputs. Neo-classical theory suggests that the answer to this question depends crucially on the elasticity of demand for the product in question and the degree of monopoly power. The associated theoretical framework and, therefore, the grounds for focussing on these influences have already been discussed at length in the contribution by Stoneman, "An Analytical Framework for Analysing the Impact of Information Technologies on Economic Perspectives".

The theory suggests that, other things being equal: the greater the own price elasticity of demand (E_p), the larger the employment creating effects of any given price reduction resulting from the introduction of an IT process innovation; the greater the income elasticity of demand, the greater the employment creating effects of any growth in income in the economy. Thus, the empirical evidence about elasticities of demand for various types of products lies at the heart of the analysis reported below. In practice, however, the provision of a consistent set of product categories (particularly in the context of the industry or product groupings adopted in other contributions in this study) proves to be an almost impossible task.

The simple neo-classical framework tends to stress the role of the characteristics of the demand curve within the domestic economy. In practice, the extent of employment creation effects depend crucially on the degree to which domestic production goes to export and domestic demand is met by foreign production. In other words, the elasticity estimates and the measures of market structure need to be interpreted in the light of import and export behaviour.

There are, in addition, a number of other issues that require an extension to the simple neo-classical framework. In particular, there is the question of the extent to which IT innovations improve the quality of products and services. The effect of such improvements will be an outward shift in the demand curve for the product at each price, raising the quantity of output purchased and ameliorating the employment consequences of any associated IT process innovation. A related question concerns the extent to which the new technologies give rise to completely new products and services, with their own employment implications. Thus, we examine in some detail the literature on hedonic prices and technical characteristics.

Again, there may be grounds for believing that improvements in the quality of products and the introduction of entirely new products may have an important influence on an innovating country's import/export performance. If it could be shown, for example, that imports and exports are more sensitive to quality than to price changes, then the emphasis of the discussion might well shift to the hedonic price literature and to the role of relative factor endowments and technology in world trade.

In isolation, however, data about elasticities of this type are not sufficient to enable any hard and fast conclusions to be drawn about the off-setting employment creating effects of the associated price reduction. A further consideration is the extent to which the reduced costs resulting from the innovation are passed on to buyers in the form of lower prices. This phenomenon will be related to the degree of monopoly power of firms producing that type of output. Thus, adopting a simple structure-conduct-performance (SCP) approach, evidence can be sought about the level of industrial concentration (CR) in the various industry groups.

Using both the elasticity and market power information in concert, it may be possible to isolate those low Ep/high CR industries in which the employment creating effects of the product innovation are likely to be least, and high Ep/low CR industries, where the effects are likely to be greatest. In practice, it proves much more difficult to isolate such industries than this simple framework would suggest. In particular, there is an important mismatch between the product groups for which elasticities are generally estimated and the industry groups for which measures of market structure are available.

There are a number of other areas which it would be useful to explore, but where, at this stage, the state of knowledge is such that the returns from doing so promise to be slight. First, there are some important question marks about the existence of a monotonic relationship between industrial concentration and market power. Second, conclusions about employment based on market power are complicated by what firms do with the extra economic profits gained in lieu of lower prices (e.g. they may be spent in creating employment in research and development, R&D, marketing, or investment, functions). Of these, the discussion touches on the role of R&D in producing a technological advantage in certain industries and countries which results in a dominant demand position. Considerations such as R&D, advertising, etc., lead to the third problem, that the model as it stands only considers the first order relationships:

   i) in a dynamic setting, some proportion of economic profits are paid in dividends and taxes, which form income for shareholders and government, and stimulate spending (generally) outside of the sector;

  ii) the spending on investment in new plant and machinery, etc., creates employment in capital goods industries;

 iii) the output of an innovating firm may pass through other processing before being sold, and firms at these later stages influence the extent to which there is an associated expansion in demand.

In the following, Section II examines the empirical evidence on the own price and income elasticities of demand; Section III looks at data on the price elasticities of imports and exports; Section IV focusses on the role of improvements in technical characteristics in determining product demands; Section V examines the role of quality improvements in determining performance in international trade; Section VI looks at measures of industrial concentration; Section VII attempts to bring the estimated elasticities and measures of industrial structure together to try and isolate those industries with potentially important or insignificant employment creating effects; Section VIII examines some of the more important caveats outlined above and draws the main conclusions, providing a number of suggestions for future research.

II. ELASTICITIES OF DEMAND

The theory outlined in Stoneman's contribution indicates the role played by the own price elasticity of demand (Ep) for the expansion of demand, counteracting the contraction of employment arising from the cost reducing innovation. This section, therefore, focusses on the available empirical estimates of elasticities, to give some clues about where the employment maintenance effects will be least and where they will be greatest, other things being equal. In practice, this task turns out to be far from easy. While the elasticity concept is one which is taught to students of economics at a very early stage, the number of comprehensive studies of demand is very limited and, those that are available tend to focus attention almost exclusively on consumer demands for final goods. As we will see, this imbalance forms an important limitation in terms of the aims of this study, although a great deal can still be learnt from this more limited class of goods.

There are several comprehensive studies of consumer demand curves. In particular, there is the work by Houthakker and Taylor (1966), Goldberger and Gamaletsos (1970), Phlips (1974), Deaton (1974, 1975) and Barker (1976). The work of Houthakker and Taylor (1966) is the least useful in the context of this paper. Their central goal is forecasting and different models are adopted in different product areas, making comparison of elasticities (where they are available at all) extremely difficult. On the other hand, other authors, for example, Phlips (1974) and Deaton (1974), investigate the Stone-Geary utility function and the associated linear expenditure system. The results of these exercises give direct measures of own-price (Ep), cross-price (Ec) and income (Ey) elasticities. From this information, certain authors also construct compensated price elasticities of demand (CEp). The work of Deaton (1975) goes on to look at the hierarchical demand system; the work of Phlips considers a dynamic demand system. Both still provide information about the associated elasticities.

1. UK Elasticities

Table 1 summarises the estimated Eps from the work of Deaton (1974, 1975). These results are obtained from the basic linear expenditure system.

In practice the price estimates of Ep are suspect for a number of reasons which the author himself outlines (Deaton, 1975, p.63). Certainly the Ep values, if taken at fact value, indicate that all goods are price inelastic, which seems to be unreasonable. Nevertheless, the ranking of the goods into low, medium and high Ep categories, outlined in Table 1, appears more acceptable. The allocation of basic foodstuffs, certain habit forming goods, housing, etc., to the low Ep category, at least corresponds with a priori expectations. Similarly, a number of the high Ep goods such as wines, spirits, recreational goods, expenditures on foreign holidays, etc., could also have been anticipated. However, the positive values of Ep for so large a number of quite unexceptional goods is more difficult to explain. These positive values of Ep correspond with negative values of Ey, associated with inferior goods.

The problem is, to some degree, overcome by recognising that the

Table 1

OWN PRICE ELASTICITIES FROM THE LINEAR EXPENDITURE
SYSTEM FOR THE UNITED KINGDOM

Low Ep(a)	Medium Ep	High Ep	Positive Ep
Meat/bacon	Fruit	Electricity	Bread/cereal
Fish	Other food	Wines/spirits	Sugar/sweets
Oil/fats	Footwear	Car operating costs	Coal
Dairy produce	Clothing	Expenditure abroad	Gas
Potatoes and veg.	House repairs	Recreation goods	Rail
Beverages	Other fuels	Chemist goods	Other travel
Rents/rates	Post/telephone	Other goods	Books/magazines
Beer	Texts/hardware		Newspapers
Cigarettes/tobacco	Catering		Domestic service
Match/soap/etc.	Entertainment		
	Other services		

a) Low Ep 0.0 to -0.2; Medium Ep -0.2 to -0.4; High Ep less than -0.4.

Source: From Deaton, 1975, pp.60-61.

Table 2

THE BROAD GROUPS

Product Group	Ep -ve	Ey +ve	Range of Eps +ve	Range of Eps -ve 0.0-0.4	0.4-0.7	0.7-1	1+
Food	.251	.493	1	4	4	0	1
Drink/tobacco	.350	.953	0	2	1	0	0
Clothing	.493	1.501	0	0	2	0	0
Housing	.236	.651	0	2	0	0	0
Fuel	.365	1.208	0	1	0	2	1
Transport/communications	.505	1.551	0	1	1	1	2
Other goods	.504	1.542	0	0	3	3	1
Other services	.374	.990	1	3	0	0	0

Source: From Deaton, op.cit., pp.173, 175-181.

demand relationships change over time. In this way, gas can be seen to change from an inferior good to a normal good (indeed, a luxury good) and its own price elasticity becomes negative in the second half of the period. However, the problems seems to arise more form the underlying specification of the model. The adoption of a hierarchical approach to modelling consumer demands in place of the overall simultaneous system for all commodities, appears to ameliorate many of the earlier problems.

Table 2 reports the aggregate elasticities arising from the hierarchical model of demands.

Based on the disaggregated results for the hierarchical model, it is possible to construct Table 3, which is directly comparable to Table 2.

Table 3

OWN PRICE ELASTICITIES FOR THE HIERARCHICAL EXPENDITURE SYSTEM

Low Ep(a)	Med/low Ep	Med/high Ep	High Ep	Positive Ep
Bread/cereal	Meat/bacon	Coal	Other foods	Fish
Oil/fats	Sugar/sweets	Other fuels	Gas	Entertainment
Pots & vegs	Dairy products	Oper. car	Other travel	
Beverages	Fruit	Texts/hard.	Exp. abroad	
Rent/rate/etc.	Footwear	Recre.goods	Chemist goods	
House repairs	Clothing	Other goods		
Electricity	Wines/spirits			
Beer	Rail			
Cigs/tobacco	Match/soap/etc.			
Post/telephone	Books/mags.			
Dom. service	Newspapers			
Catering				
Other services				

a) Low Ep 0.0 to -0.4; medium/low Ep -0.4 to -0.7; medium/high Ep -0.7 to -1.0; high Ep less than -1.0.

Source: From Deaton, op.cit., pp.175-181.

Finally, in this discussion of results for the United Kingdom, we reproduce the results of empirical analysis of consumption based on the Cambridge model (Barker, 1976, p.102).

The results are again both interesting and largely consistent with those reported above. All goods appear to be characterised by low own price elasticities. Of these, drink and tobacco, food and housing are the least price elastic of all. These three categories also exhibit expenditure elasticities of less than unity (food and housing are particularly low), while

Table 4

EXPENDITURE AND PRICE ELASTICITIES, NON-DURABLES, 1980

Expenditure Category	Expenditure Elasticity	Price Elasticity
Food	0.428	-0.233
Housing	0.164	-0.317
Fuel	1.254	-0.547
Clothing	1.235	-0.576
Drink & tobacco	0.873	-0.220
Transport & communication	1.820	-0.937
Other goods	1.459	-0.678
Other services	1.716	-0.999

Source: Barker, op.cit., p.102.

Table 5

ELASTICITIES BASED ON STATIC LINEAR EXPENDITURE SYSTEM: BELGIUM

Commodity	Ey	CEp	Ep
Food & drink	0.55	-0.21	-0.40
Tobacco	0.93	-0.44	-0.46
Clothing	0.86	-0.38	-0.46
Housing	0.69	-0.28	-0.43
Durables	1.83	-0.69	-0.90
Services	1.88	-0.73	-0.92
Recreation	1.06	-0.46	-0.55
Expenditure abroad	3.51	-1.57	-1.63

Sources: Sanz-Ferrer, 1972; Phlips, 1974, pp. 128-130.

other services and transport and communication have expenditure elasticities closer to two.

2. Belgian Elasticities

Values of own price (Ep) and expenditure (Ey) elasticities, along with the income compensated own price elasticities (CEp), are reported for Belgium by Phlips (1974, pp.127-131). The main results, summarised in Table 5, are based on the linear expenditure system, although the product groupings are somewhat different. The tables again correspond with a priori expectations, insofar as basic foodstuffs, tobacco, clothing and housing have both low Ey and Ep. On the other hand durables, services (excluding recreation) and expenditures abroad, have significantly higher Ey and also greater Ep, although only the last category has an Ep which exceeds unity.

Table 6

ELASTICITIES BASED ON DYNAMIC EXPENDITURE SYSTEMS: USA

Commodity		Linear Expenditure System			Quadratic Model		
		Ey	CEp	Ep	Ey	CEp	Ep
Food and	S	0.5	-0.2	-0.3	0.6	-0.2	-0.3
beverages	L	0.6	-0.4	-0.5	0.3	-1.1	-1.0
Clothing and	S	1.1	-0.4	-0.5	1.1	-0.4	-0.5
shoes	L	1.0	-0.9	-1.0	0.4	-1.5	-1.5
Housing	S	0.2	-0.1	-0.1	0.2	-0.1	-0.1
	L	3.5	-1.0	-1.4	-1.4	7.5	7.3
Household	S	0.6	-0.2	-0.2	0.6	-0.2	-0.3
operation	L	2.2	-1.3	-1.4	2.0	-8.2	-8.1
Furniture and	S	2.4	-0.8	-0.9	-2.0	-0.7	-0.8
household	L	0.9	-0.8	-0.9	0.6	-2.4	-2.4
Automobiles	S	7.6	-1.6	-2.1	7.6	-1.9	-2.3
and parts	L	1.7	-1.3	-1.4	0.7	-3.2	-3.1
Transport	S	0.8	-0.3	-0.3	1.0	-0.4	-0.4
	L	1.0	-0.8	-0.9	0.0	-1.6	-1.6
Other durable	S	1.3	-0.5	-0.5	1.1	-0.5	-0.5
goods	L	1.9	-1.5	-1.5	-1.4	6.4	6.4
Gasoline and	S	0.4	-0.1	-0.2	0.2	-0.1	-0.1
oil	L	1.8	-1.1	-1.2	3.6	-14.5	-14.4
Other non-	S	0.8	-0.3	-0.3	0.8	-0.3	-0.4
durables	L	1.2	-0.8	-0.9	9.5	-6.2	-5.3
Other	S	0.6	-0.2	-0.3	0.6	-0.2	-0.3
services	L	-1.0	0.7	0.9	-0.3	1.4	1.3

Source: Phlips, op.cit., pp.195 and 201; and Weiserbs, 1972, 1973.

3. US Elasticities

Phlips (1974, pp.258-263) reports estimates of Ey, Ep and CEp for the United States. In this instance, however, the results are based on a dynamic system (in which habits are allowed to modify gradually over time, at a constant rate). Thus, two elasticities are reported, for the short-run and the long-run. The main results are reported in Table 6.

4. International Comparisons of Demand Elasticities

It would be extremely hazardous to attempt to draw any hard and fast conclusions about the relative rankings of the elasticities for Belgium, the United Kingdom and United States from the results presented so far, because of different definitions of product groups and different models used in estimation. General conclusions about own price elasticities by product group appear somewhat less problematic. Although a complete ranking of products is probably none too meaningful, it seems reasonable to assume that they can be broadly divided into the relatively low elasticity group (including food, drink, tobacco, housing, etc.) and the relatively high elasticity group (including consumer durables and services). More detailed conclusions than this really depend on uncovering studies which have, as far as is practically possible, produced results according to consistent product headings in different countries.

The work of Goldberger and Gamaletsos (1970), reported in Mayes (1981), provides estimates of demand elasticities for five different countries and five categories of expenditure. The main results are reported in Tables 7, 8 and 9. The two estimates reported for each country/product category are calculated from different forms of the demand function. The first row for each country reports the results of the linear expenditure system and the second row gives analogous results for the log-linear model. It should be added that the results discussed must be treated with a great deal of caution. In particular, there is a considerable degree of inconsistency between the results (and rankings) for the two models.

Based solely on the results for the linear expenditure system, it is possible to rank the resulting estimates of income elasticities shown in Table 7 by product and by country. The product rankings are considerably more consistent than the country rankings. Based on the average of these rankings, durables has the highest income elasticity, followed by (in rank order), other goods, clothing, housing and (the least income elastic) food.

Table 7

INCOME ELASTICITIES OF DEMAND IN FIVE COUNTRIES

Country	Food	Clothing	Rent	Durables	Other
Belgium	0.63	0.99	0.21	2.45	1.17
	0.87	0.87	0.11	1.91	1.00
France	0.68	1.09	0.69	2.55	1.02
	0.53	1.53	1.19	2.55	1.03
Italy	0.85	0.67	0.96	2.27	1.19
	0.78	0.59	0.27	2.78	1.22
United Kingdom	0.57	1.28	0.60	3.33	0.88
	0.57	1.17	0.70	1.16	0.87
United States	0.35	0.56	1.54	0.85	1.34
	0.12	0.57	1.63	1.37	1.75

Source: Table 8.

Bearing in mind that the country ranks are considerably less consistent, Italy and France had equal highest ranks, the United Kingdom was next, and Belgium and the United States had the lowest ranked income elasticities.

Based on the own price elasticities calculated from the linear expenditure model reported in Table 8, average rankings can again be calculated both by country and product group. These results suggest that own price elasticity is highest for other goods (consistently ranked highest in

Table 8

OWN PRICE ELASTICITIES OF DEMAND IN FIVE COUNTRIES

Country	Category of Expenditure				
	Food	Clothing	Rent	Durables	Other
Belgium	-0.16	-0.06	0.02	-0.17	-0.43
	-0.67	-1.36	0.21	-1.07	-0.34
France	-0.22	-0.11	-0.00	-0.09	-0.39
	-0.52	-0.33	-0.29	-0.29	-0.41
Italy	-0.49	-0.19	-0.21	-0.46	-0.53
	-0.71	-0.25	0.08	0.21	-0.33
United Kingdom	-0.16	-0.10	-0.03	-0.20	-0.36
	-0.08	-0.19	-0.13	-2.93	-0.25
United States	-0.13	-0.13	-0.37	-0.20	-0.66
	-0.48	-0.11	-0.41	-0.56	1.45

Source: Goldberger and Gamaletsos, 1970, taken from Mayes, 1981.

all countries), and then (in rank order) follow durable goods and food (with an equal average ranking), clothing and (with the lowest ranking) housing. These results are not too far from those we might have expected in terms of the earlier individual country findings. The country rankings revealed that Italy appeared to have the highest rank (formed from being consistently ranked with the first or second highest elasticities in each product group), followed by the United States, the United Kingdom and then Belgium and France (with equal lowest average ranks). The country results appear to indicate a quite clear distinction between Italy and the United States, and between the United States and the other three countries. However, it is very much more difficult to disentangle the relative positions of the lowest ranked three countries.

III. PRICE ELASTICITIES OF DEMAND IN INTERNATIONAL TRADE

A considerable amount of empirical research has been undertaken on the movement of products between countries. Many of these models include relative product prices, from which it is possible to estimate the price elasticities of imports and exports. Fortunately, much of this information has been summarised and can be found in Stern, Francis and Schumacher (1976). In this section, we reproduce some recent data on the UK export and import elasticities and, in addition, reconstruct parts of two principal tables about other countries, from Stern et al.

1. UK Export and Import Elasticities

Table 9 provides estimates of UK export elasticities by country; Table 10 gives analogous results by product group. Based on the results contained in Table 9, Barker (op.cit., p. 148) reports that:

> "The weighted average of 0.647 clearly reflects the United Kingdom's declining share of world trade even after allowing for other factors, since the elasticity of world production is slightly above unity."

Table 9

UK EXPORT ELASTICITIES

Area	Average Share of UK Exports 1954-1971	Elasticity with respect to Index of Industrial Production	Elasticity with respect to Own Price (long run)
North America	14.7	0.983	0.000
Latin America	3.9	1.557	0.652
Eastern Europe	2.8	1.145	-0.406
Australia and New Zealand	8.8	0.550	-0.356
EEC (pre-1970 basis)	18.2	0.734	-0.601
EFTA (pre-1970 basis)	14.0	0.649	-0.343
Ireland	3.8	0.581	-0.127
South Africa	4.7	0.322	-0.438
Rest Sterling Area	18.6	0.407	-0.086
Rest of World	10.5	0.230	-0.362
All areas	100.0	0.647	-0.253

Source: Barker, op.cit., p. 147.

In addition the author claims that:

> "Our results broadly confirm that exports to developed countries are more responsive than exports to less-developed countries to changes in area industrial production, and that manufactures are generally more income elastic than non-manufactures."

The long-run own price elasticities show considerable variation, both by area and by product group. North and Latin America exhibit relatively low values, while exports to Europe have a relatively high own price elasticity. Finally, manufactured goods appear more price sensitive than non-manufactured goods.

Table 11 presents analogous estimates of the import elasticities. In this instance, the figures indicate the response to a 10 per cent increase in total demand, personal disposable income and relative price respectively.

Table 10

UK EXPORT ELASTICITIES

Commodities	Average Share of UK Exports 1954-1971	Elasticity with respect to Index of Industrial Production	Elasticity with respect to Own Price (long run)
Food	3.8	-0.102	-0.071
Drink	2.8	0.804	-0.052
Textile fibres	2.3	-0.843	-0.069
Petrol products	2.8	0.151	-0.617
Rest non-manufacture	3.8	-2.367	0.226
Chemicals	9.6	-0.247	-0.601
Textiles	7.0	0.731	-1.864
Iron and steel	5.3	0.312	-0.001
Non-ferrous metals	3.4	0.037	-0.482
Metal manufactures	3.3	0.371	-1.187
Mechanical engineering	19.9	0.194	-0.291
Electrical engineering	7.2	0.140	-0.666
Transport equipment	16.2	-0.161	-1.479
Instruments, etc.	2.2	-0.384	-0.869
Travel, clothing, etc.	1.7	0.666	-2.557
Rest of manufactures	8.7	0.000	-1.285
All commodities	100.0	-0.003	-0.778

Source: Barker, op.cit., p. 147.

Thus, the first column shows the first round effects of an increase in the demand for each commodity; the second column shows the final result when all repercussions on prices and other demands are taken into account; the final column is again based on the first round effects. The author reports (Barker, op.cit., p. 169) that:

> "The elasticities with respect to total demand show a clear break into two groups: manufactures and fuels on the one hand with elasticities over 1.9 and the rest of imports on the other hand with elasticities just over 1.1."

The overall figure for manufacturing, however, conceals a wide variation from 1.0 to nearly 3.5. The total figure for the second column shows:

> "In aggregate, a 10 per cent increase in real disposable income increases imports by 8 per cent; the effects on individual imports depend very much on the elasticity of the consumers' expenditure to income and the importance of that expenditure in the demand for the commodity. Thus motor vehicles and leather, clothing and footware both show much larger responses to incomes than other imports shown in the table."

The relative price elasticities are: very low for food, drink and tobacco and for raw materials; somewhat higher (although still well below unity) for fuels and services; high (well over unity) for manufactured goods. Again, the manufactured goods agreggate conceals a wide variety of values: from approximately 0.9 in chemicals to nearly 3.7 in leather, clothing, etc.

Table 11

EXPENDITURE AND PRICE ELASTICITIES FOR UK IMPORTS

	Elasticities of Imports with Respect to:		
Import Group	Total Demand for Each Commodity	Real Personal Disposable Income	Each Relative Price
Food, drink, tobacco	1.118	0.743	-0.130
Raw materials	1.160	0.426	-0.108
Fuel	1.906	0.931	-0.444
Manufactures	1.995	0.751	-1.371
Chemicals	1.490	0.674	-0.915
Engineering products	2.400	0.778	-1.430
Motor vehicles	2.681	1.224	-1.441
Metal goods	1.222	0.440	-1.307
Textiles	1.000	0.615	-2.014
Leather cloth, etc.	3.437	1.561	-3.651
Paper and board	1.421	0.413	-1.365
Services/adjustments	1.115	0.721	-0.567
Total	1.638	0.776	-0.869

Source: Barker, op.cit., p.168.

2. An Overview of Trade Elasticities

The discussion in Barker reveals the existence of "... substantial disagreement about the influence of prices on imports ...". The author concludes that, "the aggregation bias is demonstrably sufficient to discredit any results from an aggregate import function". Thus, there are strong grounds for looking at more disaggregated studies. Even here, however, there are important theoretical and practical problems in obtaining an appropriate index of relative prices. Problems such as these should be borne in mind in considering the results reported below.

Table 12 indicates the best estimates of the long-run, point elasticities of demand, by country (Stern, et al, op.cit., p. 20). Separate estimates are given for imports (Em) and for exports (Ex), although only the results for imports are sufficiently detailed to enable disaggregation by broad industry group. The industry groups adopted are: SITC 0+1(Food, beverages and tobacco); SITC 2+4(Crude materials, oils and fats); SITC 3(Mineral fuels); SITC 5-9(Manufactured goods); SITC 0-9(Total, all goods).

Table 12

BEST POINT ESTIMATES OF LONG-RUN ELASTICITIES FOR
IMPORTS AND EXPORTS BY SITC COMMODITY GROUP AND COUNTRY

	\multicolumn{5}{c|}{Imports}	Exports
	SITC 0+1	SITC 2+4	SITC 3	SITC 5-9	Total	Total
United States	-0.80	-0.47	-0.96	-1.84	-1.66	-1.41
Canada	-0.80	-0.58	-0.52	-2.06	-1.30	-0.79
Japan	-0.66	-0.91	-0.57	-1.42	-0.78	-1.25
France	-0.58	-0.80	-1.11	-2.36	-1.08	-1.31
Germany	-0.78	-0.25	-1.17	-2.53	-0.88	-1.11
United Kingdom	-0.87	-0.25	-0.44	-1.22	-0.65	-0.48
Belgium/Luxembourg	-1.06	-0.22	-1.35	-1.34	-0.83	-1.02
Denmark	-1.52	-0.47	-1.00	-2.61	-1.05	-1.28
Ireland	-1.59	-0.93	-0.44	-2.64	-1.37	-0.86
Italy	-0.96	-0.50	-1.16	-1.02	-1.03	-0.93
Netherlands	-0.26	-0.94	-0.01	-0.88	-0.68	-0.95
Austria	n.a.	-0.27	n.a.	-0.74	-1.32	-0.93
Finland	-0.09	-0.50	-0.33	-0.99	-0.50	-0.78
Norway	-0.58	-1.15	-1.36	-1.65	-1.19	-0.81
Sweden	-0.47	-0.52	-0.24	-1.05	-0.79	-1.96
Switzerland	-0.15	-0.17	-2.78	-1.21	-1.22	-1.01
Australia	-0.73	n.a.	n.a.	n.a.	-0.42	-0.74
New Zealand	-1.12	-0.75	-0.34	-1.23	-1.12	-0.70
Average	-0.77	-0.57	-0.86	-1.58	-0.99	-1.02
Median	-0.78	-0.50	-0.96	-1.34	-1.06	-0.93
Low	-0.09	-0.17	-0.01	-0.74	-0.42	-0.48
High	-1.59	-1.15	-2.78	-2.64	-1.66	-1.41

Source: Constructed from Stern et al, op.cit., p. 20.

The mean elasticity (calculated as a simple arithmetic average), the median value and the range of values (e.g. lowest and highest) are given at the foot of each column of Table 12. Taken at face value, the estimates indicate that, for imports, the industries can be ordered from least to most elastic, in the following way: crude materials, oils and fats; food, beverages and tobacco; mineral fuels; and manufactured goods.

Scanning the all industry totals across countries reveals that: Australia, Finland, Sweden, Netherlands, Benelux, the United Kingdom, Germany and Japan have relatively low import elasticities (values under 1.0); while the United States, Canada and Ireland appear to have relatively high import elasticities (e.g. greater than 1.25). The estimated values of the export elasticities indicate that: the United Kingdom has the lowest value of all; Australia, New Zealand, Finland and Canada are also relatively low (values of 0.7-0.8); while the United States, France, Denmark and Sweden are relatively high (values over 1.25).

The range of values (reported at the foot of each column) stems partly from the imperfections in the models adopted in the various studies drawn upon by Stern et al, op.cit. However, they are also a reflection of the product mix for each country and within each industry. Nevertheless, the table may give us some clues to those countries that, potentially, will benefit most from a cost reducing-price decreasing technological change. These are countries with higher import and export elasticities: the concomitant price reduction relative to their main competitor nations will lead to greater reductions in imports (replaced by domestic output) and greater increases in exports. However, this appears to be a two edged weapon, because the failure of such high Em and Ex countries to innovate in the face of competitors who do so may leave them in a precarious position.

Although a full interpretation probably requires knowledge about the relative shares of imports and exports in each country's total of economic activity, a certain pattern can be discerned from casual observation. A scattergram, Figure 1, reveals the more important features. Four countries appear to be in the most favourable position to take advantage of a cost reducing IT innovation: the United States, France, Denmark and Switzerland (with Em and Ex both other unity), particularly the United States. Two further groups appear in an intermediate position. First, Canada, Ireland, Italy, Austria, Norway and New Zealand (with Em over unity, but Ex less than unity). Second, Japan, Germany, Benelux and Sweden (with Ex greater than unity, but Em less than unity). Of these, Sweden seems particularly favourably placed. Finally, a group of four countries which appear to have an unfavourable combination of ratios, comprised of the United Kingdom, the Netherlands, Finland and Australia. Of these, the United Kingdom and Australia seem particularly unfavourably placed.

Finally, in this section, we examine the results for the detailed product breakdown, again reported in Stern et al, op.cit., pp. 21-26. Unfortunately, at this more detailed level, estimates are generally only available for the United States. In Table 13 these are reported in descending order of the absolute value of Em. The variation in the value of Em is very large, ranging from 5.6 for rubber products, to around 1.5 for leather and leather products and for iron and steel, to as little as 0.5 for paper and paper products. The resulting estimates have been rearranged in terms of the broader industrial groups used in later sections. The results are shown in Table 14, which serves to emphasize the range of elasticities found within each of the broader industrial categories. The mean Em are constructed as simple arithmetic averages, however, and should therefore be interpreted with some caution.

IV. TECHNICAL CHARACTERISTICS, PRICES, OUTPUT AND EMPLOYMENT

The traditional neo-classical functions relate the quantity of the product demanded to product prices and consumer incomes. Each product is seen as a homogeneous entity and no attention is paid to the technical characteristics that make this product distinct from any other offered on the market. The work of Lancaster (1966), however, caused a considerable stir in

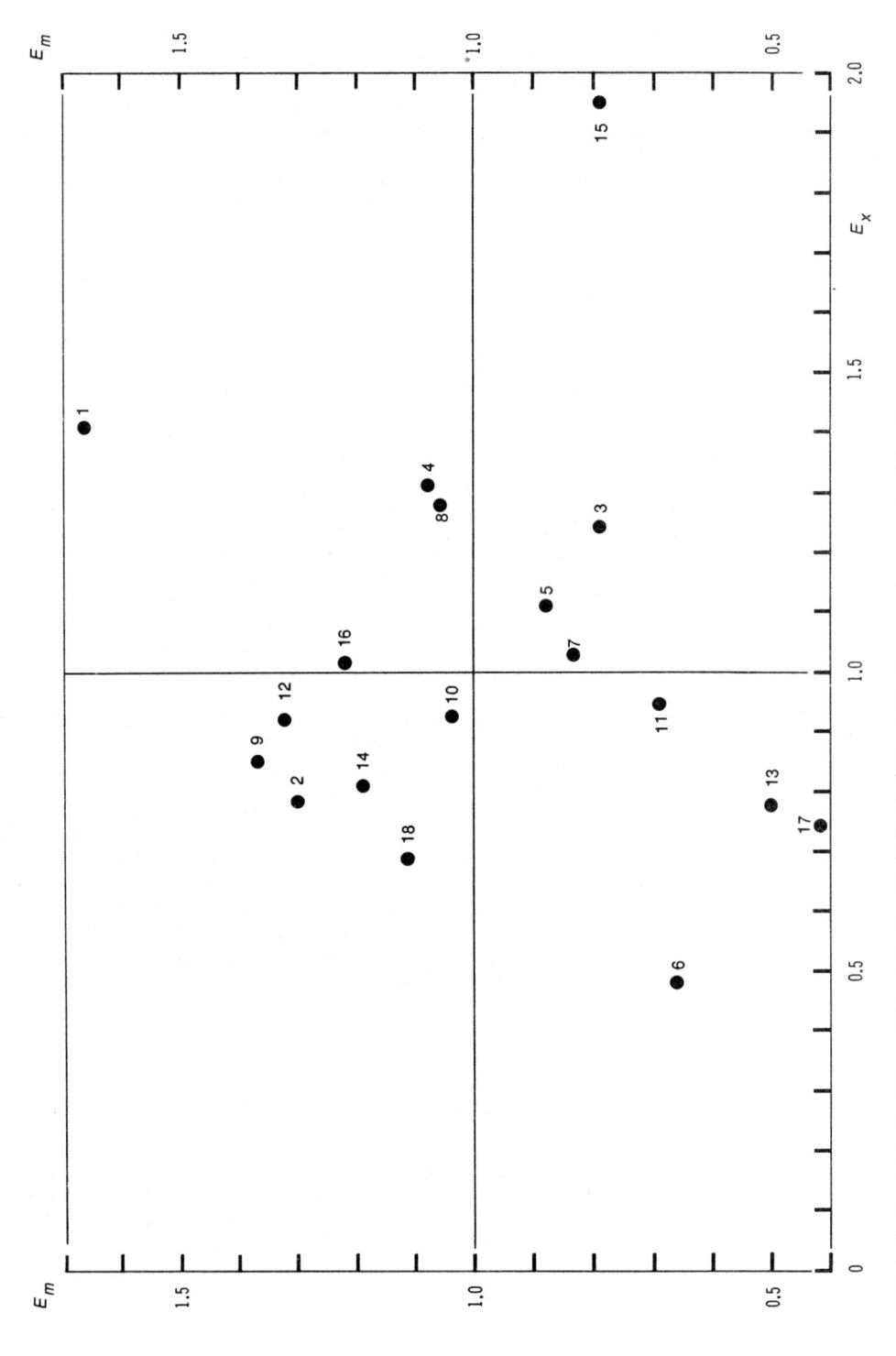

Figure 1. SCATTERGRAM : IMPORT AND EXPORT ELASTICITIES

Note : Numbers refer to the position of the country in Table 12 ; elasticities are given as absolute values.

Table 13
IMPORT ELASTICITIES BY PRODUCT GROUP FOR THE UNITED STATES

Industry	Best Point Estimate
1. Rubber products	-5.26
2. Wearing apparel	-3.92
3. Metal products (excluding machinery)	-3.59
4. Transport equipment	-3.28
5. Furniture and fixtures (excluding metal)	-3.00
6. Printing and publishing	-3.00
7. Pottery, china and earthenware	-2.85
8. Industrial chemicals	
9. Other chemical products	-2.53
10. Plastic products not elsewhere specified	
11. Footware -2.39	
12. Other manufacturing industries	-2.06
13. Other non-metallic mineral products	-2.00
14. Beverages	-1.64
15. Glass and glass products	-1.60
16. Leather and leather products	-1.58
17. Iron and steel basic industries	-1.42
18. Non-ferrous metals basic industries	-1.38
19. Textiles -1.14	
20. Tobacco -1.13	
21. Food products	-1.13
22. Professional photographic goods, etc.	-1.08
23. Machinery (excluding electrical)	-1.00
24. Petroleum refineries	
25. Miscellaneous products of petrol and coal	-0.96
26. Wood products (excluding furniture)	-0.69
27. Paper and paper products	-0.55

Source: Stern et al, op.cit.

Table 14
DISTRIBUTION OF IMPORT ELASTICITIES AND MEAN VALUES

Industry	Mean	0-1	1-1.5	1.5-2	2-3	3-4	4+
Food, drink & tobacco	1.3	0	2	1	0	0	0
Chemicals	2.9	1	0	0	1	0	1
Metal manufacture	1.4	0	2	0	0	0	0
Electrical engineering	1.0	0	1	0	0	0	0
Mechanical engineering	2.3	0	1	0	0	1	0
Transport equipment	3.3	0	0	0	0	1	0
Textiles	2.3	0	1	1	1	1	0
Paper & printing	1.8	1	0	0	0	1	0
Timber & furniture	1.9	1	0	0	0	1	0
Glass, bricks, etc.	2.2	0	0	1	2	0	0
Other manufacturing	1.6	0	1	0	1	0	0
Totals		3	8	3	5	5	1

Source: From Stern et al, op.cit., p. 25.

the literature on consumer theory with the introduction of the idea that, even within a given product group, different brands of the same product might possess different technical characteristics. The work of Rosen (1974) placed the Lancaster approach more clearly into a traditional marginal framework, emphasizing the operation of (implicit) markets, rather than focussing on consumer behaviour. Despite this important contribution, the theory is still under-developed and the vast bulk of the very large literature reports empirical estimates based on largely ad hoc specifications.

Research on the role of (changing) technical characteristics is particularly important to the subject of this paper, because quality improvements can be expected to shift the demand curve outwards. In other words, consumers are willing to pay more for any given number of units purchased, or to buy more at any given overall price level. Other things being equal (e.g. the firms' production, cost curves and supply functions), this should produce an increase in equilibrium output and employment. It would be interesting to analyse directly the impact of IT (as it becomes increasingly introduced and embodied within products) on consumers' willingness to pay. However, little empirical work of this type appears to have been undertaken. Interest has surrounded technical characteristics generally and not just those linked with IT. In certain instances, changes in performance (e.g. fuel consumption in vehicles or accuracy in metal cutting or forming operations), may be linked with the introduction of IT, but this may not be explicitly recognised in the hedonic regression work (e.g. relating the prices paid to the technical characteristics embodied).

The idea that quality improvements result in greater output and employment should be treated with some caution. In particular, improved technical characteristics may be associated with higher costs of production. Any upward shift in the supply function would stultify the output and employment creating effects. In addition, the very nature of product change may be tied up with important process changes, such as the use of different types of equipment or education and skill levels amongst the workforce.

It is impossible to attempt a comprehensive review of the results of the technical characteristics/hedonic price literature here. Nevertheless, an attempt is made to at least list some of the important work in this area, before concentrating in more detail on some of the more interesting results in the context of this study. In order to reduce the task the extremely large literature on housing and accommodation is omittted. This is of limited interest because of its rather more peripheral relationship to IT and because, in relation to Section V below, it is not generally internationally traded. The reader interested in this area can refer to: Baily and Muth (1963), Musgrave (1969), Cubbin (1970), Wabe (1971), Kravis et al (1975, 1978), King (1976/77), Cobb (1976), Harrison and Rubinfeld (1978), Goodman (1978), Freeman (1979), Lang and Jones (1979), Abelson (1979a and 1979b), Witte, Sumka and Erekson (1979), Noland (1979), Li and Brown (1980), Linneman (1980), Palmquist (1980), Goodman and Kawai (1980), Nellis and Fleming (1980), Brueckner and Colwell (1981), Ellickson (1981), Gillingham and Greenlees (1981), Gillingham (1982), Quigley (1982), Dale-Johnson (1982) and Engle, Lilien and Watson (1982) (2).

Consumer durable goods are more interesting for the reasons outlined above (their potential for the embodiment of IT and their role in international trade). The approach has been applied to a wide variety of goods:

i) Cars: Court (1939), Fisher (1962), Griliches (1964), Cagan (1965), Dhrymes (1967), Triplett (1969), Cowling and Cubbin (1971, 1972), Hall (1971), Ohta and Griliches (1973), Boyle and Hogarty (1975), Cubbin (1975), Kravis et al (1975, 1978), Leech and Cubbin (1978), Morris (1978) and Goodman (1982).

ii) Tractors: Fettig (1963), Rayner (1966), Rayner (1967), Rayner and Cowling (1967, 1968), Cowling and Rayner (1970), Cowling, Metcalf and Rayner (1970), Muellbauer (1971), Gibbons, Coombs, Saviotti and Stubbs (1981).

iii) Miscellaneous consumer durables:
refrigerators: Dhrymes (1967) and Triplett and McDonald (1977);
slide projectors: Dawson (1977);
washing machines: Hesselman (1981).

iv) Miscellaneous capital goods:
computers: Chow (1967), Ratchford and Ford (1976, 1979, 1980), Michaels (1979), Brock (1980);
deisel engines: Kravis and Lipsey (1971);
metal working machine tools: Bosworth (1973).

In the remainder of this section our attention focusses on a small number of products where the technical specification appears to be a particularly important factor (not only in determining the strength of demand, but also the degree of import penetration and export achievement) and, to a lesser extent, where IT innovations can be embodied within the product. By far the most commonly investigated products are automobiles, tractors and computers.

The demand for tractors has been the subject of a considerable amount of empirical work. The research in this area is interesting because of the construction of quality (technical change) indices [see: Adelman and Griliches (1961); Griliches (1961); Fettig (1963); Rayner (1966)]. More importantly in the context of this study, however, is the early introduction of technological indices as an explanatory variable in the work on demand functions for tractors [see: Rayner (1966); Rayner and Cowling (1967, 19680; Cowling, Metcalf and Rayner (1970); Gibbons, Coombs, Saviotti and Stubbs (1981)].

The work of Rayner (1966); Rayner and Cowling (1967, 1968); and Cowling, Metcalf and Rayner (1970) all used quality change in various forms in the explanation of the UK demand for tractors. In their main summaries of results [(Rayner and Cowling, 1967, pp. 595-596 and Cowling, Metcalf and Rayner, 1970, pp. 120-122) they report the elasticities shown in Table 15 based on a stock adjustment model of the demand for tractor services.

The short-run elasticity of tractor stock with respect to: constant quality tractor prices alone is -0.90; crop prices alone 0.24; and labour earnings alone 0.66. Despite talking about advertising, market promotional activities do not figure importantly in the estimated models or the reported results. More importantly in the context of this study, while these studies emphasize the importance of technological changes, the methodology adopted (various adjustments to the dependent variable to allow for quality change), does not allow the isolation of the significance of this aspect.

Table 15

SHORT AND LONG-RUN ELASTICITIES OF UK TRACTOR STOCKS

With respect to:	Short run	Long run
Constant quality tractor prices/crop prices:	-0.24	-0.35
Constant quality tractor prices/labour earnings:	-0.66	-0.97
Percentage investment allowances:	0.10	0.01

Source: Rayner and Cowling, 1967; Cowling, Metcalf and Rayner, 1970.

Nevertheless, the slightly greater than threefold increase in quality that their approach indicates (see Table 16) gives an impression of the potential importance of quality change and the problems that will accrue in demand work, at least in certain product areas, where this dimension is omitted.

The study by Gibbons et al (1981) is more interesting for a number of reasons. First, it is more recent. Second, it not only looks at the construction of quality indices, but uses them as an explanatory variable in modelling the demand for tractors. As they appear directly as an explanatory variable (rather than as an adjustment to the dependent variable), their role in explaining demand can be seen directly. Finally, their work examines the use of quality variations as a means of entry and as a strategy for altering market shares.

It is interesting to compare the two quality indices produced by the different studies. Both are characterised by quite slow increases during the early years for which they are available, and by more rapid rises towards the end of each of the periods which they cover. As a result, the CMR index outpaces the GCSS index in the years where they overlap. The GCSS index shows some signs of levelling off during the 1970s, but it is probably too early to tell whether this is a transitory or longer term phenomenon. The CMR index increased by a factor 3.2 over the 18 year period from 1948 to 1965; the GCSS index increased by a factor of 2.5 over the period 1959 to 1977. Any attempt to link the two series should be treated with considerable caution (particularly as they show differences over the short period when they are both available). Nevertheless, both indices are characterised by very rapid growth and the combined index emphasizes this remarkable pattern, rising by a factor of 6.4 over the 30 year period from 1948 to 1977.

V. QUALITY AND INTERNATIONAL TRADE

1. Importance of Quality: Theory

If quality change is important in determining export performance and import penetration, then it may also turn out to be central to determining the employment consequences of IT for any particular innovating country. Process innovations may themselves be associated with improvements in the reliability

Table 16

INDICES OF QUALITY CHANGE

Year	CMR Index	GCSS Index	Combined Index
1948	42.5		42.5
1949	47.7		47.7
1950	49.4		49.4
1951	55.9		55.9
1952	68.1		68.1
1953	77.5		77.5
1954	83.4		83.4
1955	83.9		83.9
1956	80.7		80.7
1957	91.8		91.8
1958	99.8		99.8
1959	103.2	103.2	103.2
1960	105.5	105.8	105.5
1961	111.9	108.4	111.9
1962	114.0	110.9	114.0
1963	120.3	113.5	120.3
1964	126.3	120.7	126.3
1965	136.5	128.0	136.5
1966		135.2	144.2
1967		142.4	151.9
1968		152.0	162.1
1969		161.7	172.4
1970		171.3	182.7
1971		182.0	194.1
1972		192.8	205.6
1973		203.5	217.0
1974		214.3	228.5
1975		225.0	239.9
1976		239.5	255.4
1977		253.9	270.8

Source: Cowling et al, 1970, p. 130 (CMR); Gibbons et al, 1981, p. 47, (GCSS).

and quality of the product; but product improvements alter the bundle of technical attributes more directly, making the product more appealing to potential customers. If improvements take place in the products of one country at a faster rate than the products of another country, then, other things being equal, we can expect the country with the greater relative improvement to raise its exports and reduce its imports from competing nations. The implication appears to be that a successful innovator can ensure that the detrimental employment effects of IT are passed on to its competitors, rather than retained within the domestic economy. We should, however, bear in mind the inter-relatedness of countries through world trade, and the negative pressures of reduced income and expenditure in the less competitive countries feeding back in the form of reduced imports.

Cooper and Clark (1982), in discussing the role of technology on trade and the balance of payments, picture three broad groups of countries. The first group are those countries, "... which have been able to secure comparatively large shares of world trade in product groups where (by virtue of the amounts of R&D they do) they might be expected to have achieved a succession of technological advantages". This group comprises countries such as the United States, Germany and, more recently, Japan. Krugman (1979) develops a model in which the trade advantage of the industrialised countries vis-à-vis the Third World is based on this innovative behaviour. The second group includes those that, while not at the forefront in terms of innovation, imitate rapidly. Such countries need not be at a competitive disadvantage: not only do they follow close on the heels of the primary innovators, but they also learn from their mistakes. They should be able to achieve rapid rates of growth in exports, retard the growth of imports and achieve a healthy balance of payments. It is generally believed that Japan in the 1960s is a good example of this type. Finally, there is the group of countries which are not primary innovators and are slow to imitate. Because of the more rapid responses of their competitors, they seem likely to face important balance of payments problems. It is thought that, amongst the comparatively industrialised countries, the United Kingdom is an example of this type. Cooper and Clark (1982, p.39) note that:

> "... it has been suggested that the so-called 'unfavourable elasticities' in the UK economy -- whereby overall growth in the world economy tends to induce a deterioration in the UK balance of trade, and devaluation is an ineffective response -- are related to it."

2. **Technology in Trade: Evidence**

First, let us examine the hypothesis that quality change is important in determining world trade flows. Some early US work by Gruber et al (1967) indicates that industries that are heavy R&D spenders tend to be more successful exporters. As Stoneman (1983) points out, the underlying philosophy of these studies appears to be that technological change increases the competitiveness of firms and thereby their net exports. He also indicates that there are a number of problems with this sort of approach. There is the fundamental question about the direction of causality. For example, it could be argued that good export performance is reflected in higher profits and thereby higher R&D spending. In practice, causation is unlikely to be unidirectional.

A further problem with the approach is that technological superiority is likely to be less well reflected by R&D expenditures than by measures of inventive output such as patent indices. Pavitt and Soete (1980) and Soete (1981) have adopted patent measures in their study of export performance. In the study by Pavitt and Soete, exports per head are regressed on patents per head, across countries, industry by industry. In the Soete study, the share of each countries exports in total OECD exports is regressed on the analogous share of patents, investment per head, the absolute size of population and a measure of physical distance between trading nations. Again, the regressions were estimated across countries for each industrial sector. Despite the obvious simplicity of the models being estimated, the results appear to support the general conclusion that technological superiority is an important factor determining the pattern of world trade in the majority of (although by no means all) product groups.

The role played by science and technology can be linked with traditional trade theory in two ways. First, if all countries are on the same production function, then relative factor abundances determine the factor services which countries import or export and, thereby, the associated products. Thus, science and technology can be introduced by associating them with highly specific, narrowly defined factor inputs and examining their relative abundance. A second approach effectively assumes different production functions for each country because of differences in the degree to which countries innovate and in the magnitude of lags in the diffusion of knowledge (Krugman, 1979). Based on the first of these two approaches, Sveikauskas (1983, p.551) concludes that it is science and technology (and, in the case of the United States, particularly R&D and major, radical innovations) rather than other more general forms of physical and human capital formation, that are fundamental to the economic advantage of the major industrialised nations in world trade.

3. <u>Technology in Trade: Technical Characteristics Evidence</u>

The discussion in Section IV clearly indicated that, at least in certain areas, there have been significant increases in product quality. The overall increase in quality of tractors was reflected in an increase in the index of about 6.5. Clearly, such indices could, in principle, be constructed for the goods produced by a particular country, rather than an overall index covering all tractors, independent of country of origin. In most product areas, however, little seems to have been done to isolate relative quality changes by country of origin or to establish the importance of such change on import and export performance. Nevertheless, sufficient piecemeal evidence exists to suggest that relative quality changes are likely to play a significant role in world trade.

The primary use of the hedonic approach reported in Section IV above is the quality adjustment of conventional price indices and the analysis of price formation and pricing behaviour. Some authors, however, have attempted to extend their analysis by looking at the use of such indices in the explanation of demand, market share and import penetration [see, for example: Court (1939); Chow (1967); Rayner and Cowling (1967); Cowling and Rayner (1970); Cowling and Cubbin (1971); Leech and Cubbin (1978); Witte et al (1979); Ratchford and Ford (1979); Hesselman (1981) and Gibbons <u>et al</u> (1981)].

The study by Leech and Cubbin (1978) attempted to explain the market shares of domestic and imported makes of cars using advertising expenditure; number of dealers; average delivery time; reliability; guarantee; extras included in the price; quality adjusted prices. The ensuing analysis appeared to reveal that neither delivery performance or extras included in the price significantly affected UK market shares, but reliability did have an important effect.

In the discussion above, other things were assumed constant, but clearly price and quality are not independent: in general, higher quality is brought about at a higher cost and higher price. Thus, the effect of quality improvement on imports and exports cannot generally be judged independently of price. The size of the market is governed by the price-quality combination being offered by companies, not by quality alone. It should be remembered, however, that largest market shares are unlikely to be just a matter of firms offering a high quality at a given price, but doing so in price-quality ranges where the bulk of consumers are located. Cases of extremely high quality products with high prices (but high quality/price ratios) and very low market potential are not too difficult to find. The United Kingdom has often been argued to have more than its share of such examples (e.g. Concord and many technological developments arising from the defence industries where technical quality is extremely high but money is no object).

The study by Hesselman (1981) indicated that UK washing machine manufacturers chose not to produce a model with a spin speed of less than 800 rpm. Thus their models filled the middle quality range, and were good value for money but certainly not cheap. According to Hesselman (1981, p.24):

> "Unfortunately a substantial proportion of domestic consumers chose cheaper imported models with slower maximum spin, models UK manufacturers thought to be more appropriate for sunny Naples than Cloudy Birmingham ... UK manufacturers lost a substantial proportion of the domestic market because they did not supply the cheaper end of it".

The author argues that the UK manufacturers' strategy might be thought more appropriate for higher income, foreign markets and added that, in future research:

> "... it would be interesting to see if they fared better in export markets that in the domestic market".

Some interesting work has looked at the use of hedonic procedures in isolating quality adjusted prices for various US mainframe computer companies in an attempt to look at changes in market structures. Two important caveats should be mentioned at this stage: first, the studies look at US markets and have not, to date, been extended to study international markets; second, theoretical and, more particularly, data problems have led to somewhat different results in the various studies [see, for example: Ratchford and Ford (1979, 1980); Brock (1980); Michaels (1979)]. Despite these limitations, the more comprehensive study by Michaels (1979) does lead to some interesting conclusions. This study attempts to establish the reasons for IBM's dominant position in the US computer industry. Unlike earlier studies the results did not indicate any significant price premium on IBM machines. On the other hand, the absence of any important differences in quality adjusted price make it difficult for the author to explain either, "IBM's 70 per cent of the mainframe market or its persistent profitability" (Michaels, 1979, p. 274). However, the study appears to reveal predatory pricing on one machine which may have helped to establish and protect a specific niche in the market. Clearly, while the data problems may be large, the central links of computers to IT would make the extension of work in this area of immense interest. Two areas might be considered for further research: first, the markets for micros as well as mainframes, given the way in which technological change has tended to bring these two into closer competition; second, the international markets for computers.

The study by Gibbons et al (1981) looks separately at the differing technical quality of tractors sold by various countries in the UK and Dutch markets. The tractor manufacturers were from Britain, Germany, Italy and COMECON countries. The results were almost identical for the British and Dutch markets. The main results, based on a cross sectional analysis for the year 1978, show that: British manufacturers tend to produce moderately priced tractors with low to middle technical specification; German manufacturers produce the technically most sophisticated tractors; the Italian tractors are generally no more sophisticated than the British (with the exception of the early incorporation of four wheel drive); COMECON combine a very low price with some degree of technical sophistication. It appears from the results that new entrants use technical sophistication as an entry strategy (e.g. as a substitute for large, widespread dealer networks, etc., which are built up at a later stage).

VI. MONOPOLY POWER

1. Measures of Monopoly Power and Industrial Concentration

While a number of attempts have been made to construct direct measures of monopoly power, economists still rely heavily on the concept of the structure-conduct-performance hypothesis and use of measures of industrial structure as a proxy for monopoly power. The wealth of literature in the area of Industrial Economics has led to the widespread availability of a number of alternative measures of industrial structure. Of these, the measures of industrial concentration are by far the most common, although they have increasingly been used in combination with other variables in econometric work (such as barriers to entry). The EEC (1982, pp. 163-164) proposes that:

> "... various indicators should be used ... several concentration ratios (CRi), ... at least one composite concentration index (such as the Herfindahl index) and the delimitation of the oligopolistic or quasi-monopolistic nucleus by applying measurements of dominance such as the Linda index or the enlarged Herfindahl index".

While a number of concentration measures are now used, such as the n-firm concentration ratio (CRn), the Herfindahl, the Linda index, etc., the most common is the CRn and this is gradually becoming available in an internationally compatible form. The United Kingdom, for example, reports information on the CR5 for detailed product groups over a long period of time (see, for example, Business Monitor, PQ 1006, 1978). The ratio shows the proportion of the product output that is attributable to the five largest firms in the industry. However, having emphasized the availability of such data, it is much more common for manufacturing than other industries and services. This limitation is even more apparent where international comparisons are attempted.

2. European Findings on Concentration

There is a considerable amount of information available about concentration in European industry thanks in part to a European-wide initiative by EEC member States and partly through the activities of individual researchers. In the EEC-wide tables, in broad terms, the industry groups correspond with those adopted in this study. It should be noted, however, that there may be hidden differences not fully noted here. It is also worth adding that the practical problems of deriving CRs for industries outside the final consumption goods sector are not present in the form faced in the preceeding sections which discussed elasticities.

We turn first to the level of concentration in the EEC by industry, based on data for the 1 000 largest firms in the Community (by turnover). The results of this analysis are shown in Table 17. They indicate that, in 1977, a tiny proportion of the total of firms in the EEC (0.4 per cent by number) account for a large share of total turnover (52 per cent) in the Community market, excluding imports. The table also gives a hint that the largest firms increased their share at the deepest point of the recession, around 1975 (although this is more clearly seen from another EEC table not reported here -- EEC, 1982, p.167). More importantly, Table 17 clearly shows that these 1 000 firms are ensconsed to different degrees in different industries. Firms drawn from this sample account, in 1977, for as little as 13 per cent of turnover in textiles and as much as 74 per cent in electrical engineering.

Table 17

PERCENTAGE OF FIRMS IN SAMPLE AND PERCENTAGE OF INDUSTRIES' TURNOVER

Industry	1973 %F	1973 %T	1975 %F	1975 %T	1977 %F	1977 %T
Food	0.7	40	0.8	46	0.8	43
Chemicals	0.8	70	0.9	83	0.8	67
Electrical eng.	1.1	72	1.1	74	1.0	74
Mechanical eng.	0.4	27	0.5	34	0.4	35
Metal industries	0.3	48	0.4	66	0.3	55
Transport equip.	1.3	74	1.3	68	1.4	72
Paper	0.2	24	0.2	30	0.2	20
Textiles	0.1	13	0.1	14	0.1	13
Total	0.3	49	0.4	56	0.4	52

Source: EEC, 1982, p. 165.

Using the same European-wide sample, CR4 and CR12 can be worked out for just the firms in the sample. These are labelled (S) in Table 18. In addition, for years when information was available about the total number of firms in each sector and total turnover, it was possible to work out equivalent, overall CRs. These are labelled (T) in Table 18 but are not available for years after 1977. Again, the ratios highlight the inter-industry differences in the degree of concentration. In 1977, for example, the top four firms in textiles accounted for 6 per cent of the total turnover of the industry. In the same year, the top four firms accounted for 31 per cent of total turnover in the electrical engineering industry. Other information provided indicates that concentration appears to be increasing in transport equipment, electrical and electronic engineering and chemicals, but decreasing in agri-foodstuffs and textiles. However, it is the differences in concentration between sectors which are most marked, rather their variation over time (at least over the relatively short period of time for which the data are available).

The same report claims that the enlarged Herfindahl and Linda indices give a good indication of situations in which an oligopolistic nucleus exists, in which one or two firms hold a dominant position (EEC, ibid., pp. 172-175). The results of these calculations are shown in Table 19. They indicate that, throughout the period a single firm was in a dominant postion in the food and the textile industries; two firms held a dominant position in the paper industry. In other industries, the oligopolistic nucleus was both larger and more variable.

3. International Comparisons of Concentration: Europe

The up-to-date information about the European-wide level of industrial concentration treats the EEC as a single market. This may be misleading if the activities of certain major producers are located in more limited geographical areas (others may be spread more evenly over the region). If this is the case, two possibilities might arise. First, there might be considerable differences in industry CRs, with a moderately high EEC measure formed from a number of low CRs in some countries, but a high ratio in one or two others. Second, a similarity of CRs across countries might mean a fairly large number of moderately sized firms resulting in a modest EEC CR; nevertheless, in each country, a relatively small number of firms might dominate the domestic market.

An early comparative country study of concentration in the EEC provides some limited (and somewhat dated) information about this problem (Phlips, 1971). According to the author, "Comparing CRs industry by industry, for a pair of countries, it is immediately apparent ... that an industry with high concentration in one country will have high concentration in the other country" (ibid., p. 146). Ignoring the inter-industry comparisons for a moment, taken at face value, the results suggest the following ordering of economies in terms of concentration (from high to low): Luxembourg, Belgium, Netherlands, France and Italy (ibid., p. 149). However, the author argues that a more meaningful comparison would be possible after normalising for differences in the size of markets. The result of this appears to be that the ordering is changed to (from high to low): France, Netherlands and Belgium and Italy at a comparably low level of concentration (ibid., pp. 159-160).

Information from Phlips is used to construct the distribution of CRs for Belgium, France, Italy and the Netherlands, shown in Table 20. The results do seem to indicate certain similarities between industrial groups: chemicals appears to be relatively highly concentrated, while both textiles and other manufacturing lie at the other end of the spectrum. While such similarities are important, at the same time, the table serves to indicate that there seem to be a number of important differences between countries. Metal manufacturing, for example, appears to exhibit a significantly higher number of more concentrated industry sub-groups in some countries compared with others.

Data from the UK Report on the Census of Production has been added into

Table 18

INDUSTRIAL CONCENTRATION IN THE EEC

Sector		1973 CR4	1973 CR12	1975 CR4	1975 CR12	1977 CR4	1977 CR12	1979 CR4	1979 CR12	1981 CR4	1981 CR12
Food	S	33	54	34	52	31	49	29	46	25	53
	T	(13)	(21)	(15)	(24)	(13)	(21)	(-)	(-)	(-)	(-)
Chemicals	S	25	57	27	58	33	61	34	62	31	56
	T	(18)	(40)	(23)	(48)	(22)	(41)	(-)	(-)	(-)	(-)
Electrical	S	38	66	44	67	42	69	46	68	43	68
engineering	T	(27)	(47)	(32)	(49)	(31)	(51)	(-)	(-)	(-)	(-)
Mechanical	S	33	52	31	49	34	54	33	58	33	55
engineering	T	(9)	(14)	(10)	(16)	(12)	(19)	(-)	(-)	(-)	(-)
Metal	S	24	55	28	57	28	58	28	58	26	53
industries	T	(12)	(26)	(18)	(37)	(15)	(32)	(-)	(-)	(-)	(-)
Transport	S	34	69	38	68	39	69	41	74	44	75
equipment	T	(25)	(51)	(26)	(46)	(28)	(50)	(-)	(-)	(-)	(-)
Paper	S	47	73	46	71	53	77	50	74	45	75
	T	(11)	(17)	(14)	(22)	(11)	(16)	(-)	(-)	(-)	(-)
Textiles	S	53	80	50	79	45	74	49	78	42	70
	T	(7)	(11)	(7)	(11)	(6)	(10)	(-)	(-)	(-)	(-)

Source: EEC, ibid., p. 169.

Table 19

DETERMINATION OF THE NUMBER OF FIRMS FORMING AN OLIGOPOLISTIC NUCLEUS

Industry	1973 EH	1973 L	1975 EH	1975 L	1977 EH	1977 L	1979 EH	1979 L	1981 EH	1981 L
Food	1	-	1	-	1	-	1.	-	1	-
Chemicals	10	10	10	10	6	11	6	10	9	12
Electrical eng.	6	19	4	-	5	8	4	2	5	-
Mechanical eng.	2	2	3	-	3	3	5	5	5	4
Metal industries	15	20	10	34	13	13	11	25	12	23
Transport equip.	5	5	7	12	6	10	5	5	5	5
Paper	2	2	2	2	2	2	2	2	2	2
Textiles	1	-	1	-	1	-	1	-	1	-

Source: EEC, ibid., p.174.

Table 20. It should be pointed out that the data are different in two important respects. First, they relate to a later year, although earlier information based on the distribution of CRs for product groups (rather than MLHs) gave very similar results. Second, the level of industrial detail is greater and we would anticipate that the degree of concentration will generally rise the more detailed the level of disaggregation adopted. Nevertheless, despite these differences, the data for the United Kingdom does appear to show a considerably higher degree of concentration overall. The proportion of industries appearing in the 0-30 per cent category is remarkably small in the case of the United Kingdom.

A number of points can be made about these findings. First, casual observation of the data (op. cit. Table A1 or the scattergrams, p.147), appear to support the hypothesis that, while there is an underlying cross-sectional relationship between the CRs in different European countries, the link is far from perfect. It is difficult to show the differences in any detail without repeating all of the published data. Table 21, however, gives some indication of the heterogeneity amongst the industry results for the four countries by reporting on the differences between the CRs for each NICE within the broader industry groups.

The range of CRs is denoted by the difference between the lowest and highest reported CR for each of the NICEs (to the nearest 10 per cent band). Thus, the figures reported in the table indicate the number of NICEs with differences of 0, 1, ..., 9 bands of 10 per cent. This tends to overemphasize differences in the sample, as a situation in which three countries had an identical CR value, but differed from the fourth country by 30 per cent, would be recorded as a difference of 3. On the other hand, it does tend to emphasize that countries might differ in the extent to which they might pass on the benefits of a cost reducing innovation. The modal difference was over 20, although there were 22 industries in which the difference was over 50 and 2 in which it was over 80. It should be noted that this data excluded the more limited information for Luxembourg, which, when it was available, often formed an outlier.

VII. SUMMARY OF RESULTS: WITH SPECIAL REFERENCE TO EMPLOYMENT EFFECTS

The availability of comprehensive evidence of the type outlined in Sections II-VI would not only have enabled something positive to be said about the likely employment effects of IT innovations by product group and country, but also about how these two are connected via the product mixes of each OECD country, and the associated elasticities (E_p, E_y, E_x and E_m) and degrees of monopoly power (CR_n). In practice, what we have managed to piece together is an extremely patchy picture in almost all respects. First, information is not readily available about all these measures for more than a handful of OECD countries. Second, where information is available for different countries, it is often not constructed on a comparable basis. Third, the domestic own price elasticity data tend to relate almost exclusively to final goods, while the concentration measures related to all products.

Table 20

DISTRIBUTION OF "NICE" CONCENTRATION RATIOS

	70-100	30-70	0-30	Total
Belgium (1963)				
Food, drink & tobacco	2	6	6	14
Chemicals & allied	2	3	2	7
Metal manufacture	1	4	2	7
Engineering & allied	9	13	10	32
Textiles & allied	0	2	13	15
Other manufacturing	1	4	15	20
Total	15	32	48	95
France (1963)				
Food, drink & tobacco	1	2	12	15
Chemicals & allied	2	3	3	8
Metal manufacture	1	3	3	7
Engineering & allied	3	13	17	33
Textiles & allied	0	2	13	15
Other manufacturing	0	3	16	19
Total	7	26	64	97
Italy (1963)				
Food, drink & tobacco	1	1	13	15
Chemicals & allied	2	3	3	8
Metal manufacture	0	3	4	7
Engineering & allied	4	13	16	33
Textiles & allied	0	1	14	15
Other manufacturing	0	2	18	20
Total	7	23	68	98
Netherlands (1963)				
Food, drink & tobacco	1	5	8	14
Chemicals & allied	2	4	2	8
Metal manufacture	4	2	1	7
Engineering & allied	5	12	15	32
Textiles & allied	2	2	11	15
Other manufacturing	1	4	15	20
Total	15	29	52	96
United Kingdom (1972)				
Food, drink & tobacco	6	11	0	17
Chemicals & allied	10	10	0	20
Metal manufacture	2	4	0	6
Engineering & allied	19	21	12	52
Textiles & allied	2	15	11	28
Other manufacturing	3	18	9	30
Total	42	79	32	153

1. Domestic Own Price and Income Elasticities

The results of this part of the study indicate that the models of final demands yield results broadly in agreement with a priori expectations. These are perhaps typified by the results for Belgium in Table 5. The table (almost) divides into two: with basic necessities (e.g. food, drink, housing and perhaps clothing) and habit forming goods (e.g. tobacco and perhaps certain types of drink) associated with low Ep and Ey; and luxury items (e.g. durables, services and expenditure abroad) associated with high Ep and Ey.

Table 21

RANGES OF CRs: AN ILLUSTRATION OF HETEROGENEITY

Industry	Range of CRs (0 to 9)									
	0	1	2	3	4	5	6	7	8	9
Food, drink & tobacco	1	4	3	1	1	3	1	1	0	0
Chemical & allied	0	3	0	1	2	2	0	0	0	0
Metal manufacturing	0	0	1	1	3	1	0	0	1	0
Engineering & allied	1	3	8	8	5	2	5	0	1	0
Textiles & allied	1	5	3	3	1	1	1	0	0	0
Other manufacturing	1	6	7	3	0	2	1	0	0	0
Total	4	21	22	17	12	11	8	1	2	0

Source: Constructed from data contained in Table A1, Phlips, 1971, pp. 184-194.

The main exception to this simple categorisation appears to be recreation (with a relatively low Ep but high Ey). With certain differences, similar results are apparent for the United Kingdom and United States. It seems fairly certain that consumer tastes and behaviour are sufficiently alike across industrialised countries to lead to similar results in other countries.

Whilst bearing this conclusion in mind, a number of more tentative suggestions may be gleaned from the results, although data differences and variations in modelling make it impossible to draw any hard and fast conclusions. First, despite probable similarities in the ranking of broad classes of goods, there seem certain to be inter-country differences in the values of the elasticities. If the results reported in Section II can be taken at face value, Italy appears to have the highest income and own price elasticities; the United States appears to have relatively low income elasticities by international standards, but relatively high own price elasticities; the United Kingdom appears to be in the middle range in terms of income and own price elasticities (but it is very difficult to disentangle the relative position of the United Kingdom, Belgium and France in terms of their own price elasticities). While France appears to have a relatively high comparative income elasticity, its price elasticities are relatively low;

Belgium appears to have relatively low income and price elasticities.

A number of caveats ought to be stated. First the results are not entirely consistent from model to model and this gives rise to considerable concern about drawing hard and fast conclusions about the relative positions of different countries and different products. Second, where the results are based on broad product groups, it should be recognised that these often contain a wide variety of products (e.g. see Tables 1 and 3), where the elasticities will generally be much higher (because of the availability of close substitutes within the group, but a lower degree of substitutability between groups), and where there may be a great deal more variability across countries. Third, tastes and, hence, the pattern of final consumer demands are generally recognised to vary less than the pattern of all demands including intermediate products (because of differences in input-output matrices across countries). Thus, similarities in final goods consumption may mask important differences in employment effects when intermediate goods are also taken into account.

2. International Trade Price Elasticities

Import and Export Elasticities

The discussion of Section III provided more comprehensive information about price elasticities, in this case in international trade. Import price elasticities are available by product area and country, although equivalent export price elasticities are generally only available by country for all goods combined. The aggregate (absolute) import elasticities of the United Kingdom, Netherlands, Finland and Australia all lie below 0.70; those of the United States, Canada, Ireland and Austria all lie above 1.30. The aggregate (absolute) export elasticities of Canada, the United Kingdom, Finland, Australia and New Zealand all lie below 0.80; those of the United States, France and Sweden lie above 1.30.

Comparison of Import and Export Elasticities

Cross country comparisons reveal important differences between Em and Ex for each country (see Table 12 and Figure 1). The majority of countries have relatively price elastic trade on either the import or the export side. It was argued above that high elasticities are associated with the potentially most important employment effects. In this sense, however, Em and Ex are double edged weapons: those countries with high values have the least to fear from early and successful innovation and the most to fear from allowing other countries to "steal a march" on them. According to this criteria, the United States, France, Denmark and Switzerland appear to be favourably placed to take advantage of process innovation without significant negative employment effects; the United Kingdom, Netherlands, Finland and Australia, on the other hand, appear to be in potentially the most unfavourable positions to innovate.

Comparisons of Domestic and Trade Elasticities

The food, drink and tobacco groups, which have one of the lowest domestic own price elasticities, also have a relatively low import elasticity (e.g. as shown by the cross country average for SITC 0+1 in Table 12 and industries 14, 20 and 21 in Table 13). Other comparisons are more tentative. Nevertheless, manufactured (final) goods tend to have somewhat higher domestic own price elasticities (e.g. clothing, parts of transport and communication and other goods in Table 2); clothing and durable goods in Table 4; furniture, household goods, automobiles and other durable goods in Table 5) and form the group with the highest import elasticity (see the SITC 5-9 column average in Table 12). As far as comparisons can be made between the more detailed product groups, Tables 3 and 13 (which is not very far, as they relate to different countries and use somewhat different product categories), they do indicate that there may be specific products with both low Ep and Em (e.g. food, drink and tobacco). However, at this stage, we would wish to refrain from any further comparisons until more compatible data sets become available.

Of the countries that we considered in some detail with regard to Ep, Italy appears to lie in the middle ground with respect to Em and Ex: it has an absolute Em somewhat greater than unity, but an Ex slightly less than unity. If the relatively high value of Ep can be taken at face value, Italy's middle range values of Em and Ex should still place it in a fairly favourable overall position to innovate. The cases of the United Kingdom and United States are perhaps more clear cut. Although the United States has somewhat lower short-run Eps, the evidence of higher longer-run Eps is more favourable. This result should be seen in conjunction with the fact that the United States has potentially the most advantageous Ex and Em for early innovation. On the other hand, a failure to innovate could place the United States in a difficult position with regard to job losses because of foreign competition. In contrast to the United States, the United Kingdom not only appears to have lower Eps than, for example, Italy, but these seem to be coupled with one of the least favourable Em and Ex combinations for early innovation.

3. Quality and Performance

The discussion of Sections IV and V served to emphasize that simple elasticities, while useful, only gave a part of the picture necessary to the understanding of the employment consequences of technological change. In effect, the elasticity data is most useful in understanding the consequences of process changes; information about technical characteristics is essential to understanding the role of product innovation in employment creation and destruction. However, if anything, the evidence is even more piecemeal than in the case of technical characteristics (hedonic regression work), than it was for elasticities. There is, at this stage, no hope of undertaking systematic comparisons between product groups and between countries. Nevertheless, of all areas this is probably the one with the greatest research potential. Even the rather disjointed results currently available appear to point to the central role played by quality change both in influencing domestic demand (e.g. the growth performance of particular products, firms and industries) and patterns of international trade (e.g. the growth performance of imports and exports, and thereby of particular economies).

4. Monopoly Power

Again the evidence relating to the degree of monopoly power is only patchy: there is lack of detail outside of the manufacturing sector and very few countries have comparable information. From a theoretical point of view, there are grounds for believing that the degree of monopoly power may be inversely correlated with the absolute Ep. If this is the case, the two effects would, to some degree off-set one another with regard to the employment effects of an IT innovation. This hypothesis is impossible to test, however, given the incompatibility of the two data sets. From the information to hand, it seems likely that many components of the food, drink and tobacco group have relatively low Eps and, at most exhibit a modest concentration ratio (see Tables 18, 19 and 20). Chemical goods appear to have relatively high own price elasticities of both domestic and import demands, but are associated with moderate to highly concentrated industries. Without further information, or some new way of resolving the incompatibility of the Ep and CR data bases, it seems unlikely that we will be able to do anything other than consider the broadest links between the two sets of measures.

Cross country comparisons again look more promising, despite the fact that there is still a lack of comparable information. There may also be hidden problems of measurement that require more detailed consideration. Nevertheless, whatever the precise outcome of the debate about the relative levels of concentration in Belgium, France, Italy, and the Netherlands, comparison of all four with the United Kingdom appears to reveal their relatively low level of concentration compared with the United Kingdom. If this result is in fact true, it should be seen in the light of the already unfavourable omens for the employment consequences of IT innovation in the United Kingdom that became apparent from consideration of Ep, Ey, Em and Ex.

VIII. CONCLUSIONS AND SUGGESTIONS FOR FUTURE RESEARCH

From a theoretical point of view, the approach adopted in this paper appears potentially rewarding; from a practical point of view its promise was never wholly fulfilled because of a lack of readily available, compatible data. Nevertheless, the initial foray served to highlight the nature of the data that are required. Certainly further information about elasticities appears to be essential. The preceeding discussion reveals that this has two dimensions. First, to build up information about the domestic elasticities of demand for all product groups, and not just for final goods. Second, there is a need to expand the number of countries for which results are reported.

Of all the areas of research, the work on technical characteristics (hedonic prices) appears potentially the most rewarding. The early indications are that product quality is a dominant force in determining firm and industry growth, as well as trade performance. At a micro level, much could be done to systematise the results of existing studies. The large and growing volume of work by the World Bank, which provides comparable international quality adjusted price indices, could be utilised in detailed studies of international trade. Finally, patent and other innovation information could be used to try and categorise countries according to the threefold breakdown (innovators, imitators and non-innovator/non-imitator) suggested by Cooper and Clark (1982).

In a similar way, there are currently gaps in the area of concentration and other measures of market structure. One omission is the absence of US data on concentration from the current report. The European data could probably also be extended by reference to the product area reports of the Commission for European Communities. These reports often deal with the same product group in a number of different European Member States. Nevertheless, it would be difficult, if not impossible to build up a completely comprehensive picture in this way. On the other hand, it would give some insights about which product areas and countries are most or least favourably placed with regard to the potential employment consequences of technological change.

The results of the present study did help to emphasize a number of other points. First, they clearly highlighted the heterogeneity within certain broad industrial groups designated to be of particular interest. Thus, the implications of IT innovations within a group might well differ substantially depending on whether they are concentrated in particular product areas or spread evenly across the group. Second, greater understanding about the overall, economy-wide employment consequences seems to depend on a knowledge of the inter-industry flows of each country and the elasticity of demand and degree of concentration in each cell of the input-output matrix. Third, the information about import and export elasticities, while of interest in their own right, should ideally be coupled with knowledge of the level of such activities in each product group and each economy. Finally, a complete understanding of the employment consequences of IT almost certainly also depends not only on knowledge about the implications of new technologies for product quality, but also on the possible invention and introduction of entirely new products and processes.

NOTES

1. I wish to thank the participants at the OECD Workshop for helpful comments on an earlier draft of this paper, particularly to Paul Stoneman and Robert Wilson for references to sources giving estimates of elasticities.

2. Mike Fleming kindly provided an extensive list of publications on technical characteristics and hedonic regressions, from a project on house price indices being undertaken at Loughborough University.

BIBLIOGRAPHY

P.W. Abelson, "A Study of Property Valuations in Relation to Market Prices and the Characteristics of Properties", The Economic Record, December 1979a, pp.328-334.

P.W. Abelson, "Property Prices and the Value of Amenities", Journal of Environmental Economics and Management, Vol. 6, 1979b, pp.11-28.

I. Adelman and Z. Griliches, "On an Index of Quality Change", American Statistical Association Journal, Vol. 56, 1961, pp.535-548.

M.J. Bailey, and R.F. Muth, "A Regression Method for Real Estate Price Index Construction", Journal of the American Statistical Association, Vol. 58, December 1963, pp. 933-942.

T.S. Barker, Economic Structure and Policy, Cambridge Studies in Applied Econometrics 2, Chapman and Hall, London, 1976.

D.L. Bosworth, "Price and Quality Changes in Metal Working Machine Tools", Applied Economics, Vol. 8, 1976, pp.283-288.

S.E. Boyle and T.F. Hogarty, "Pricing Behaviour in the American Automobile Industry, 1957-71", Journal of Industrial Economics, December 1975.

G.W. Brook, "A Study of Prices and Market Shares in the Computer Mainframe Industry: Comment", Journal of Business, 1980.

J.K. Brueckner and P.F. Colwell, "A Model of Housing Attributes: Theory and Evidence", BEBR Faculty Working Paper No. 786, College of Commerce and Business Administration, University of Illinois, Urbana-Champaign, June 1981.

Business Statistics Office, "Statistics of Product Concentration of UK Manufacturers for 1963, 1968 and 1975", Business Monitor Quarterly Statistics, Government Statistical Service, HMSO, London, 1978.

P. Cagan, "Measuring Quality Changes and the Purchasing Power of Money: An Exploratory Study of Automobiles", National Banking Review, Vol. 3, December 1965.

G.C. Chow, "Technological Change and the Demand for Computers", American Economic Review, December 1967.

S.A. Cobb, "Site Rent, Air Quality and the Demand for Amenities", Journal of Environmental Economics and Management, Vol. 4, 1977, pp.214-218.

A.T. Court, "Hedonic Prices with Automobile Examples", The Dynamics of Automobile Demand, G.M. Corporation, New York, 1939.

K. Cowling and J. Cubbin, "Price, Quality and Advertising Competition: An Econometric Investigation of the UK Car Market", Economica, November 1971.

K. Cowling and J. Cubbin, "Hedonic Price Indices for UK Cars", Economic Journal, Vol. 82, September 1972, pp.963-978.

K. Cowling, D. Metcalf and A.J. Rayner, Resource Structure of Agriculture: An Economic Analysis, Pergamon Press, Oxford, 1970.

K. Cowling and A.J. Rayner, "Price, Quality and Market Share", Journal of Political Economy, November-December 1970.

J. Cubbin, "A Hedonic Approach to Some Aspects of the Coventry Housing Market", Discussion Paper No. 14, Department of Economics, University of Warwick, Coventry, August 1970.

J. Cubbin, "Quality Change and Pricing Behaviour in the UK Car Industry 1956-68", Economica, February 1975.

D. Dale-Johnson, "An Alternative Approach to Housing Market Segmentation Using Hedonic Price Data", Journal of Urban Economics, Vol. 11, 1982, pp.311-332.

A. Dawson, "Quality Characteristics of 35mm Slide Projectors", Wolverhampton Economics Discussion Papers, Department of Economics and Social Sciences, September 1977.

A. Deaton, "The Analysis of Consumer Demand in the UK", Econometrica, Vol. 42, 1974, pp.341-368.

A. Deaton, Models and Projections of Demand in Post-War Britain, Chapman and Hall, London, 1975.

P.J. Dhrymes, "On the Measurement of Price and Quality Changes in Some Consumer Capital Goods", American Economic Association Papers and Proceedings, May 1967.

B. Ellickson, "An Alternative Test of the Hedonic Theory of Housing Markets", Journal of Housing Economics, Vol. 9, 1981, pp.56-79.

R.F. Engle, D.M. Lilien and M.W. Watson, "A Dynamic Model of Housing Price Determination", Discussion Paper No. 922, Harvard Institute of Economic Research, Cambridge, Massachusetts, October 1982.

European Commission, Competition Report of the European Communities, 1982, EC, Brussels, 1982.

L.P. Fettig, "Adjusting Farm Tractor Prices for Quality Changes, 1950-62", Journal of Farm Economics, Vol. 3, 1963, pp.17-22.

F.M. Fisher, Z. Griliches and C. Kaysen, "The Costs of Automobile Changes Since 1949", Journal of Political Economy, October 1962.

A.M. Freeman, "Hedonic Prices, Property Values and Measuring Environmental Benefits: A Survey of the Issues", Scandinavian Journal of Economics, December 1979, pp.154-173.

M. Gibbons, R. Coombs, P. Saviotti and P.C. Stubbs, "Innovation and Technical Change: A Case Study of the UK Tractor Industry, 1957-77", Discussion Paper, University of Manchester, June 1981.

R. Gillingham and J.S. Greenlees, "Estimating Inter-city Differences in the Price of Housing Services: Further Evidence", Urban Studies, Vol. 18, 1981, pp.365-369.

R. Gillingham, "Measuring the Cost of Shelter for Homeowners: Theoretical and Empirical Considerations", Discussion Paper of the Division of Price and Index Number Research, Office of Prices and Living Conditions, Bureau of Labour Statistics, 1982.

A. Goldberger and T. Gamaletsos, "A Cross Country Comparison of Consumer Expenditure Patterns", European Economic Review, 1970, pp.357-400.

A.C. Goodman, "Hedonic Prices, Price Indices and Housing Markets", Journal of Urban Economics, Vol. 5, 1978, pp.471-484.

A.C. Goodman and M. Kawai, "Permanent Income, Hedonic Prices and Demand for Housing: New Evidence", Working Papers in Economics No. 61, John Hopkins University, June 1980.

A.C. Goodman, "Willingness to Pay for Car Efficiency: a Hedonic Price Approach", Working Papers in Economics No. 93, John Hopkins University, Department of Political Economy, March 1982.

Z. Griliches, "The Demand for a Durable Input: Fram Tractors in the US 1921-57", in The Demand for Durable Goods, A.C. Harberger (ed.), University of Chicago Press, 1960, pp.181-207.

Z. Griliches, "Notes on the Measurement of Price and Quality Changes", Models of Income Determination, Studies in Income and Wealth, NBER, Vol. 28, 1964, pp.381-418.

W. Gruber, D. Mehta and R. Vernon, "The R&D Factor in International Trade and International Investment of United States Industries", Journal of Political Economy, Vol. 75, February 1967, pp.20-37.

R.E. Hall, "The Measurement of Quality Change from Vintage Price Data", Z. Griliches (ed.), Price Indices and Quality Change: Studies in New Methods of Measurement, Harvard UP, 1971.

D. Harrison and D.L. Rubenfeld, "Hedonic Housing Prices and the Demand for Clean Air", Journal of Environmental Economics and Management, Vol. 5, 1978, pp.81-102.

L. Hesselman, "Non-Price Factors in the UK Washing Machine Market: A Hedonic Approach", Economic Working Paper No. 1, April 1981.

H.S. Houthakker and L.D. Taylor, Consumer Demand in the United States, 1929-70: Analyses and Projections, Harvard UP, Cambridge, Massachusetts, 1966.

A.T. King, "The Demand for Housing: A Lancastrian Approach", Southern Economic Journal, Vol. 43, 1976/1977, pp.1077-87.

I.B. Kravis and R.E. Lipsey, <u>Price Competitiveness in World Trade</u>, National Bureau of Economic Research, New York, 1971.

I.B. Kravis, Z. Kenessey, A. Heston and R. Summers, <u>A System of International Comparisons of Gross Product and Purchasing Power</u>, John Hopkins UP, Baltimore, 1975.

I.B. Kravis, A. Heston and R. Summers, <u>International Comparisons of Real Purchasing Power</u>, John Hopkins UP, Baltimore, 1978.

P. Krugman, "A Model of Innovation, Technology Transfer and the World Distribution of Income", <u>Journal of Political Economy</u>, Vol. 87, pp.253-66, 1979.

K. Lancaster, "A New Approach to Consumer Theory", <u>Journal of Political Economy</u>, Vol. 74, April 1966, pp.132-157.

J.R. Lang and W.H. Jones, "Hedonic Property Valuations Models: Are Subjective Measures of Neighborhood Amenities Needed?", <u>American Real Estate and Urban Economics Association</u>, Vol. 7, 1979, pp.451-465.

D. Leech and J. Cubbin, "Import Penetration in the UK Passenger Car Market: A Cross Section Study", <u>Applied Economics</u>, October 1978.

M.M. Li and H.J. Brown, "Micro-Neighborhood Externalities and Hedonic Housing Prices", <u>Land Economics</u>, Vol. 56, May 1980.

P. Linneman, "Some Empirical Results on the Nature of the Hedonic Price Function for the Urban Housing Market", <u>Journal of Urban Economics</u>, Vol. 8, 1980, pp.47-68.

D.G. Mayes, <u>Applications of Econometrics</u>, Prentice Hall, London, 1981.

R. Michaels, "Hedonic Prices and the Structure of the Digital Computer Industry", <u>Journal of Industrial Economics</u>, Vol. 27, March 1979, pp.263-275.

D. Morris, "Household Production Theory: The Lancaster Hypothesis and the Price Quality Relationship", <u>Bulletin of Economic Research</u>, Vol. 30, May 1978, pp.14-24.

J. Muellbauer, "Testing the Cagan-Hall and the Hedonic Hypothesis", Warwick Economic Research Papers No 19, September 1971.

J.C. Musgrave, "The Measurement of Price Changes in Construction", <u>Journal of the American Statistical Society</u>, 1969, pp.771-786.

J.G. Nellis and M.C. Fleming, "Hedonic House Prices for Scotland", Occasional Paper No. 55, Department of Economics, Loughborough University of Technology, December 1980.

C.W. Nolan, "Assessing Hedonic Indexes for Housing", <u>Journal of Financial and Quantitative Analysis</u>, Proceedings Issue, Vol. 14, November 1979, pp.783-803.

M. Ohta and Z. Griliches, "Automobile Prices Revisited: Extensions of the Hedonic Hypothesis", Discussion Paper No 325, Harvard Institute of Economic Research, October 1973.

R.B. Palmquist, "Alternative Techniques for Developing Real Estate Price Indices", Review of Economics and Statistics, Vol. 62, August 1980, pp. 442-448, .

K. Pavitt and L. Soete, "Innovative Activities and Export Shares: Some Comparisons Between Industries and Countries", K. Pavitt (ed.), Technical Innovation and British Economic Performance, Macmillan, London, 1981.

L. Phlips, Effects of Industrial Concentration: A Cross-Sectional Analysis for the Common Market, North Holland Publishing Co., Amsterdam, 1971.

L. Phlips, Applied Consumption Analysis, North Holland Publishing Co., Amsterdam, 1974.

J.M. Quigley, "Non-linear Budget Constraints and Consumer Demand: An Application to Public Programs for Residential Housing", Journal of Housing Economics, Vol. 12, 1982, pp.177-201.

B.T. Ratchford and G.T. Ford, "A Study of Prices and Market Shares in the Computer Mainframe Industry", Journal of Business, April 1976.

B.T. Ratchford and G.T. Ford, "A Study of Prices and Market Shares in the Computer Mainframe Industry: Reply", Journal of Business, 1980.

A.J. Rayner, "An Econometric Analysis of the Demand for Farm Tractors", Bulletin No. 113, Department of Agricultural Economics, University of Manchester, October 1966.

A.J. Rayner and K. Cowling, "Demand for a Durable Input: An Analysis of the UK Market for Farm Tractors", Review of Economics and Statistics, Vol. 49, November 1967, pp.590-598.

A.J. Rayner and K. Cowling, "Demand for Farm Tractors in the US and the UK", American Journal of Agricultural Economics, Vol. 50, November 1968, pp.896-912.

A. Rees, The Economics of Work and Pay, Harper and Row, New York, 1979.

S. Rosen, "Hedonic Prices and Implicit Markets: Product Differentiation in Pure Competition", Journal of Political Economy, Vol. 82, 1974, pp.34-55.

C. Rowley, Antitrust and Economic Efficiency, Macmillan Studies in Economics, Macmillan, London, 1973.

R. Sanz-Ferrer, "Prévisions de la consommation privée en Belgique", Recherches économiques de Louvain, Vol. 38, 1972, pp.17-37.

L. Soete, "A General Test of Technological Gap Trade Theory", Weltwirtshaftliches Archiv, Vol. 117, 1981, pp.638-666.

R.M. Stern, J. Francis and B. Schumacher, Price Elasticities in International Trade, Macmillan, London, 1976.

P. Stoneman, The Economic Analysis of Technological Change, Oxford UP, Oxford, 1983.

L. Sveikauskas, "Science and Technology in United States Foreign Trade", Economic Journal, Vol. 93, September 1983, pp.542-554.

J.E. Triplett, "Automobiles and Hedonic Quality Measurement", Journal of Political Economy, Vol. 77, May-June 1969, pp.408-417.

J.E. Triplett and R.J. McDonald, "Assessing the Quality Error in Output Measures: The Case of Refrigerators", Review of Income and Wealth, Vol. 23, 1977, pp.137-156.

J.S. Wabe, "A Study of House Prices as a Means of Establishing the Value of Journey Time, the Time Rate of Preference and the Valuation of Some Aspects of Environment in the London Metropolitan Area", Applied Economics, Vol. 3, 1971, pp.247-255.

D. Weiserbs, "Contribution à une analyse dynamique des choix du consommateur", Doctoral Dissertation, Anec, Louvain, 1972.

D. Weiserbs, "More About Dynamic Demand Systems", Working Paper No. 7312, Institut des sciences économiques, Louvain, 1973 (mimeo).

A.D. Witte, H.J. Sumka and H. Erekson, "An Estimate of a Structural Hedonic Price Model of the Housing Market: An Application of Rosen's Theory of Implicit Markets", Econometrica, Vol. 47, September 1979, pp.1151-1173.

IV. MICRO-MACRO ANALYSIS

1

DYNAMIC MICRO-MACRO MARKET CO-ORDINATION AND TECHNICAL CHANGE

by

Gunnar Eliasson
The Industrial Institute
for Economic and Social Research
(Sweden)

SUMMARY

This paper discusses the nature of macro productivity change from the perspective of a Schumpetarian micro-to-macro (M-M) model. It emphasizes the dynamics of resource allocation through markets (firms) where agents are both price and quantity setters. The organisation of market processes (the market regime) proves to be important for the rate of total factor productivity change at aggregate levels. This is especially so when relative prices shift as a consequence of the ongoing market process, and markets, notably the capital markets, are in disequilibrium.

Illustrative simulations on the M-M model of the Swedish economy are presented. The effects of shifts in the nature of technical change from a labour saving toward a capital saving bias are investigated in a semi-closed economy and in a fully open economy. In the latter exports adjust to the relative profitability of foreign and domestic deliveries and price transmission across borders occurs. The allocation effects of effective exploitation of technical change through international specialisation matter significantly for productivity growth. If the economy is kept semi-closed the same (exogenous) technical advance generates significantly smaller productivity expansion. The analysis suggests that the "mystic" residual shift factor in macro production function analysis that persisted for such a long time and then disappeared in a "mystic" way may partly or wholly be explained by a shift into a different "market regime" in the 70s.

In all scenarios of the model, reasonable price and quantity flexibility prevent long-term technological unemployment from occurring. A change in the bias of technical change (labour saving/capital using) makes little difference in the medium term.

In the M-M-model applied, the relevant factor and product prices are endogenised and depend on the factor and investment allocation process itself.

Three aspects of the macro-economic process have been made explicitly to demonstrate the nature of dynamic resource allocation and the economic growth process:

1. Technology;

2. Market regime;

3. Macro demand management and the role of government.

2

QUANTIFYING THE IMPACT OF INFORMATION TECHNOLOGY ON EMPLOYMENT USING A MACROECONOMIC MODEL OF THE UNITED KINGDOM ECONOMY

by

J.D. Whitley and R.A. Wilson
University of Warwick,
(United Kingdom)

1. INTRODUCTION

Economists have debated the question of whether technological change benefits the labouring classes since the very beginnings of the subject as a separate discipline. Ricardo was not the first of the "classical" economists to address this question but he probably paid it more attention than most other economists of that time. In his earlier works he concluded that the introduction of new machinery would benefit the workforce. However, in later years he extensively revised his views and concluded that the replacement of labour by machines is "often very injurious to the interests of the class of labourers". This conflict in views about the effects of technological change on employment still remains, to a large extent, unresolved to this day.

The kernel of the debate concerns the extent to which the initial impact of technical change in terms of job displacement may be compensated for by endogenous and exogenous factors which tend to increase employment in other ways. The results of over 250 years of scholarly effort and research have greatly improved our understanding of the nature of this balance, but the complexity of the political-economic-social interrelationships involved has defeated all attempts at providing a final answer to this question.

On the one hand, the so-called neo-classical economists argue that, in what they term a "perfect" world of complete information, freely operating markets, and absence of market power, full employment of all resources is guaranteed. They might agree that, in the short term, adjustment lags and frictions in the operation of markets may result in the existence of less than full employment, but this, it is argued, is only a temporary phenomenon and any exogenous shock to the economy such as a new technological development will eventually be accommodated without any permanent loss of jobs. This is of course an extreme position, and most economists would not wish to defend it too seriously. They would, to a greater or lesser degree, accept the weight of various criticisms made of this view of the world over the years, which recognise the importance of imperfect information, market imperfections and other characteristics of the real world which distinguish it from the neo-classical model of the perfect economy. Nevertheless, a large number of economists would argue that there are important equilibrating forces which do operate within an economy in such a way as to restore to employment any resources, such as labour, that may have been made idle as a result of technological progress, even though this process may not be perfect. The view that a major technological advance such as that represented by the overall terms "microelectronics" or "Information Technology" (IT) might lead to massive technological unemployment is held by only a small minority of economists. However, this point of view has been quite widely expressed by various commentators during the late 1970s (and indeed was popular much earlier, with regard to the initial introduction of computers on a wide scale in the early 1960s).

II. THE MAIN ELEMENTS OF THE DEBATE

Many of the early studies of the effects of microelectronics upon employment predicted a massive impact on United Kingdom employment levels. Barron and Curnow (1979) in a study carried out between 1976 and 1977 predicted a 16 per cent loss of jobs in the United Kingdom over the following 15 years (op. cit., p.191). Although they emphasized that these effects would be cumulative rather than sudden, it was implied that the major impact would be felt within 5-10 years. Clive Jenkins and Barry Sherman (1979) painted an equally gloomy picture and estimated that there could be 1 million jobs lost by 1983, 3.8 million by 1993 and over 5 million by the year 2003 as a direct result of microelectronics. A study by ASTMS (1979) suggested a loss of 2.6 million office jobs by 1985 whilst APEX (1979) predicted a more modest figure of about 250 thousand jobs lost by 1983. In the light of recent experience, most of these estimates of net job loss appear to be exaggerated. We are now some seven to eight years into Barron and Curnow's future and, although employment in the United Kingdom has fallen sharply, this has much more to do with the world recession than with the implementation of new technology. Indeed, until very recently, productivity growth has slowed in most industries, precisely the opposite of what one would expect from an acceleration in the pace of technological change. Even when dramatic increases in productivity have occurred in recent years the general consensus amongst those who have analysed these changes is that they represent the combination of a lagged response of employers to the changing environment they face, with labour hoarded in anticipation of recovery being discarded during 1981 and 1982 as the prospects of such a recovery faded, together with the effects of the scrapping of obsolete plant and equipment.

It is possible to identify four main factors which have contributed to potential over-estimation of the adverse effects on employment of new technology in general, and microelectronics in particular. It will become clear from the discussion that these four factors are interrelated.

Inappropriate generalisation

The first reason for over-estimation of the impact of new technology is due to the inappropriate generalisation of results from particular case studies to the economy at large. For example, it is clear that the potential job displacement effects of microelectronics are very large in the context of the office environment. Barras (1984, p.22), Swords-Isherwood and Senker (1980, p.164) and Sleigh et al (1979, p.61) quote various examples of dramatic gains in productivity from the use of word processors. One management consultancy firm, for example, reported that such innovations could allow 39 people doing routine typing and clerical work to do 25 per cent more work than over 80 people had done previously. It is this sort of example, together with the fact that large numbers of people are engaged in routine clerical and typing jobs, that has led some commentators to predict job displacement in the service sector on a massive scale. Arnold (1980), however, points out that only where typing, etc., is pooled are such very large improvements in productivity possible. Most offices are small and the consequent potential for improvement is very limited without a considerable re-organisation of the typical office. In addition, most secretaries spend only a relatively small part of their time doing typing and other tasks that could potentially be taken over by the word processor. This highlights the danger in applying displacement effects from particular examples to the economy as a whole. Crudely applying displacement rates based on particular studies to broad groups of workers, as some of these studies have done, ignores the presence of the many barriers to such a wholescale adoption of the technology. Thus, in the case of clerical workers, huge productivity gains can often only be achieved in large centralised office systems and, since these are the exception rather than the rule, the overall displacement effect in the short to medium term is likely to be on a relatively small scale. Richard Barras (1984) concludes that in the short to medium term labour productivity in office-based services is only likely to grow modestly although the longer-term gains may be more substantial.

The study by Green et al (1980) gives some indication of other examples of a gap between the potential improvement in output per person and that which might actually be achieved in the medium term, given the particular circumstances in which individual firms find themselves. They suggest that the potential for job displacement as a result of the introduction of microelectronics in the clothing industries over a period of ten years is of the order of 10 per cent. Yet, taking into account the composition of individual firms in their survey and their historical pattern of investment, they conclude that the actual displacement effect might only be 1 per cent, or one-tenth of the potential effect. This sort of result is repeated in all the industrial orders that they investigate.

The rate of diffusion

A second reason for overestimating the effects of microelectronics on employment seems to have been over-optimism regarding the rate of diffusion of the new technology. Much of the early literature appeared to take into account only the marginal costs of the chip itself rather than including the costs of applying the technology in terms of new capital equipment, etc. Thus some authors [e.g. Johns, (1979)] regard the new technology as almost costless. While the cost of chips has fallen dramatically the cost of equipment embodying the new technology often remains extremely expensive. Innovation does not usually take place just because new and superior technologies exist but rather because the new technology is feasible on economic grounds. More recent studies including other papers prepared for the present project have recognised the importance of these issues. The work of Sleigh et al (1979) and Swords-Isherwood and Senker (1980) in noting the economic problems in applying the microprocessor to manufacturing processes is still highly relevant. In particular, it is important to recognise that the potential benefits cannot be reaped without prior investment in both physical capital (new machines) and human capital (both requisite skills and necessary research and development into new products and processes). These economic constraints tend to slow down the rate of diffusion. To the costs of developing new applications we might also add the general effects of the recent recession which have led to a substantial decline in the level of investment in new plant and machinery in many OECD countries.

Revolutionary versus evolutionary change

Most of the studies previously referred to have regarded microelectronics as revolutionary. In the United Kingdom, output per man has risen by about 2.5 per cent per annum in manufacturing since the Second World War, although this rate has fallen somewhat during the recent recession. Were this rate to continue for fifteen years, it would imply an improvement of more than 40 per cent in output per person (1). The question is whether the 16 per cent improvement envisaged by Barron and Curnow, for example, is a continuation of previous trends and can therefore be regarded as an evolutionary change subsumed within this 2.5 per cent per annum improvement or whether it is a revolutionary change in addition to the long-term trend rate of increase in productivity.

Few, if any, of the studies to date have really considered this question, yet it is crucial to an assessment of the overall impact of this new technology on employment. Even if microelectronics represents the major source of technological change likely to occur during the 1980s and 1990s, it will need to result in a marked acceleration in the pace of improvement in productivity for it to have an impact in terms of the direct displacement of labour that is noticeably different from previous generations of technological change. A number of the studies in the present project, notably those by Barras, Rush and Hoffman, and Wilson, have concluded that the immediate prospects for productivity growth are not very different from the post-war period as a whole. This confirms earlier work by the Science Policy Research Unit [e.g. Swords-Isherwood and Senker, (1980)] whose position is usefully summarised by Sleigh et al (1979, p.14):

> "The general conclusion which emerges from this analysis, with exceptions in particular areas, is that over the next five to ten years the effects of microelectronic technology in reducing industry's demand for labour are unlikely to be any more dramatic than those of many previous examples of technological improvement."

In an analysis of the impact of robotics in the United States, Hunt and Hunt (1983, p.165) reach very similar conclusions:

> "The robots are coming; not as rapidly as anticipated by some nor with the devastating impact predicted by others but they are coming... We have argued throughout this monograph that robots should be regarded simply as another labour-saving technology, one more step in a process that has been going on for some 200 years."

The new technology is therefore best regarded as a development from previous technologies (e.g. hard wire controlled systems in manufacturing and computers in services, etc.) rather than as a revolutionary change. In manufacturing the effect on process innovations is primarily expected to affect the structure of the demand for labour rather than its overall level. In the instance of services (and the office functions within manufacturing) the position is less clear but, for the reasons already noted above, the potential for dramatic job displacement may be less than has generally been feared.

The assumption of unchanged output levels

This is perhaps the most important of the four factors that are identified here. Most of the alarmist predictions referred to above concentrate upon what one might term the direct displacement effect of technological change on employment, holding output levels constant. They fail to recognise the importance of a number of compensatory factors which will tend to offset the initial displacement effect on employment by causing output levels to increase. Some of the authors have recognised the possibility of such compensating factors but have been unwilling or unable to quantify them. In principle, compensation factors may be identified at both microeconomic and macroeconomic levels, although in practice the latter are probably more important.

An example taken from the area of office employment illustrates the possible type of microeconomic effect. Sleigh et al (1979, p.62) quote the case of government administration where the introduction of a word processor may increase the productivity of those in the typing pool. However, rather than resulting in a loss of jobs, this may be reflected instead by a draft White Paper going through additional drafts. In some sense output may have increased in qualitative rather than quantitative terms, although the final result could still be one White Paper. If new and improved information is generated by the new technology, this may suggest new avenues for using this data and thus the creation of new tasks. In some cases this will result in an increase in the measure of output, but in cases such as the one above, it may not be reflected in the conventional measures of output which do not allow for improvements in the quality of the product.

At the macroeconomic level the assumption of unchanged output is even more debatable. Typically, over the post-war period the residual of the annual rate of growth of output that is not accounted for by increases in factor inputs in the United Kingdom has been some 2 per cent. This residual has been loosely attributed to technological change. Had this 2 per cent improvement in total factor productivity occurred while output levels remained unchanged it would have implied a 35 per cent decline in the level of factor inputs required over a fifteen-year period. In practice, the growth in productivity has been accompanied by a growth in output and real incomes, so that broadly speaking, employment displaced by technological improvements has been offset by compensatory increases due to the rise in aggregate demand (2).

The direct job displacement effect of new technology is just one aspect of its impact. In order to properly consider the full impact, the extent to which new jobs are created by the new technology both directly and indirectly also needs to be assessed. To do this properly the country in question must be considered as part of the world economy rather than regarded in isolation.

In order to clarify the issues involved it is necessary to consider the effects of a change in technology on employment within a macroeconomic framework.

III. A MACROECONOMIC FRAMEWORK

A general theoretical framework has been provided in the Introduction of this Part III. In this chapter an alternative framework is presented based upon an existing computerised model of the United Kingdom economy. In an earlier paper [Whitley and Wilson (1982)], we attempted to quantify some of the compensatory effects on employment that have already been outlined. The study used simulation techniques with a detailed macroeconomic model of the United Kingdom economy to assess the potential importance of these different effects in comparison to the initial employment displacement effect. The remainder of this paper summarises the results of an extension to this work which attempts to throw further light on the orders of magnitude of these various compensatory effects using the IER's macroeconomic model of the United Kingdom economy as a guide.

As noted in the introduction, neo-classical theory regards technological unemployment as a theoretical impossibility. Any technological change will simply result in falling costs and prices. This in turn will lead to an expansion of demand at home and abroad, either for the product concerned or for other products. As real incomes rise, any workers displaced will therefore find new jobs producing this additional output. Even if this does not immediately clear the labour market, there will be an adjustment of wage levels until full employment is achieved. Technological unemployment can only be created as a result of lags in adjustment to this new position or by the failure of markets to adjust. [For an exposition of this view see Beenstock, (1979)]. Criticisms of the neo-classical view centre upon two issues: first, whether in practice wages and prices are sufficiently flexible to achieve the speedy return to equilibrium envisaged in the neo-classical model; and second, whether wage and price flexibility is in fact a sufficient condition for full employment [many authors have argued that it is not, see Malinvaud (1977) and Freeman (1978a, b)].

Freeman, for example, has emphasized the independence of the forces resulting in the displacement of workers and those leading to compensatory increases in demand. The rate of technological change, together with the growth of the labour supply, determines the natural or warranted rate of output in the economy. An acceleration in the pace of change implies an equal acceleration in the actual growth rate is required if full employment is to be maintained. Unless the actual rate of growth automatically responds to changes in the warranted rate, technological unemployment may emerge. It is clearly inappropriate to consider each and any acceleration in the warranted rate of growth as due to technological change since it may also alter as a result of demographic rather than technological factors. To attribute the consequent rise in unemployment to technology would be grossly misleading. The main importance of viewing the effects of technological change in this fashion, however, is that it emphasizes the fact that the forces displacing employment on the one hand and those resulting in increased employment on the other are theoretically and practically distinct and that the normal price mechanism may fail to restore full employment, especially in the short to medium term.

Nevertheless, despite scepticism regarding the automatic tendency to return to full employment there are various compensatory factors resulting in higher output levels which are worthy of consideration and which will tend to offset some, if not all, of the direct employment displacement effects. In particular, the links between different industries, the implications for trade and competitiveness, and changes in real incomes resulting from changes in costs and employment levels must all be taken into account.

As an example, consider a labour displacing technological change involving a change in labour requirements per unit of output. If this improvement is translated via lower unit costs into lower prices, this will stimulate demand at home and abroad, as real incomes rise and domestic prices fall relative to those abroad. There will, however, be some leakage to this process as some of the extra demand is met from imports rather than from domestic production.

A second important set of compensatory effects comes from the need to make a considerable injection of physical investment in order to achieve the benefits from new technology. The motor industry's adoption of robotics is a case in point. We have already noted how the high costs involved may slow down the rate of diffusion. The relevant point here is that any such increase in capital formation that does take place will provide a further offset to the direct displacement effect through its impact on aggregate demand. Not that all of this extra demand will come from domestic production. The extent to which producers turn to foreign sources of supply of capital equipment will determine the strength of this extra injection of demand and therefore its potential in offsetting the direct displacement effect.

A third set of compensating feedbacks may come from the equilibrating mechanism of the labour market as displaced workers bid down wage levels although, as noted above, many economists would not necessarily expect the magnitude of this compensation effect to ensure the maintenance of full employment as the neo-classical position would predict.

In discussing compensation effects it is also important to distinguish between products and processes. In their study of the engineering industry Swords-Isherwood and Senker (1980, p.8) conclude that long before dramatic process innovations result in significant direct displacement effects:

> "the extensive redesign of products to incorporate microelectronic components will have more significant effects on manpower and skill requirements (3)".

They argue that the redesign of products and the development of new products will dramatically alter the demands for different industries' output, directly via the impact on aggregate demand and indirectly via changes in intermediate demands and through international competition. The various sectoral studies conducted as part of the present project also highlight the importance of new products in both services and manufacturing industries. The emphasis on changes in products rather than processes implies that the effects on employment of factors other than the direct displacement effects are potentially of greater significance. For firms producing for final demand, such as consumption and investment, the trend in favour of non-price competition will accelerate and improvements of the product and the introduction of new products will become increasingly important in terms of competing in world markets. Firms which adopt the new technology most successfully in terms of introducing such improvements will survive while others will lose market shares. An obvious example here is the Swiss watch industry. The direct displacement effect of the new technology on employment in conventional watch production has probably been insignificant. Nevertheless, the overall impact on employment in this industry has been devastating since output levels have been drastically reduced as consumers have switched to electronic substitutes. The changeover from mechanical to electronic cash registers provides a further example.

In addition to any extra investment resulting from the introduction of the new technology, there may also be significant changes in the demand for certain commodities and products used in the production of other goods (intermediate demand). A good example is the substitution of electronic control and switching devices for electro-mechanical ones. Even if the direct displacement effect is zero in the industry concerned, the employment effects may be large due to the effect on the demand for the industry's output.

To summarise the possible impacts of the various compensatory factors that we have discussed we group them under the following headings:

i) Increased domestic demand resulting from higher real incomes;

ii) Increased foreign demand resulting from improved price and non-price competitiveness;

iii) Increased demand for investment goods in order to implement the new technology;

iv) Dynamic effects such as the multiplier effects on real incomes following increases in autonomous expenditures;

v) Equilibrating effects in the labour market.

In order to quantify the possible impact of microelectronic technology it is therefore necessary to consider not only its direct impact but also its effects on intermediate demands and the various components of final demand. In addition, a key issue is the rate at which the new technology is introduced in a particular country relative to the rate of introduction of its main competitors. The outcome of this will impinge on trade performance, not just through the obvious impact on relative costs and prices, but also through changes in the non-price aspects such as quality, versatility, and the introduction of new products. Indeed, once one takes a more comprehensive view it becomes clear that (at least over the next 10-15 years) the major impact on employment levels may result from the differences in the rate of adoption of microelectronic technology which thereby affect the international distribution of employment rather than from any direct impact within the country concerned.

IV. THE MACROECONOMIC MODEL

The macroeconomic model used is a development of the static one constructed by the Cambridge Growth Project and described in Barker (1976). The present model is a dynamic version of this and is described in Barker (1980 and 1981) (4). It has a keynesian structure incorporating an input-output system and concentrating on the determination of changes in the real sector of the economy. The level of disaggregation of commodities and industries is considerable by the standards of other models of the United Kingdom economy. Primarily because of the degree of disaggregation, the model is a large one and comprises over 1 400 behavioural and technical relationships (excluding accounting identities). Its main components are equations explaining consumption, investment, employment, exports, imports, prices and an input-output sector which deals with the flows of goods and services between industries and determines total industrial outputs. These equations are all solved together so that the final results are consistent with the various identities required by the national accounts. There are 49 employing activities distinguished, and these are listed in Appendix A together with the 16 aggregate groups normally used for the presentation of results. Various developments have been made to the model at Warwick. These include the addition of a monetary sector, which endogenises the exchange rate, and a wage model as well as sub-models to disaggregate employment by occupation and region.

The advantages of disaggregation accrue not only from the greater accuracy achieved in the simulation of aggregate economic quantities, such as GDP and its main components, but also through the value of the additional detail itself. Thus, if the industrial groups are chosen so that nationalised industries and other industries particularly affected by government policy (for example, agriculture and construction) are identified separately, this makes it possible to distinguish the effects of different policies upon these specific industries. Moreover the peculiar circumstances of industries can be recognised, incorporating exogenous information which otherwise would be of little use. One of the great strengths of a disaggregated model is its ability to simulate interaction between different industries and between them and the rest of the economy. The possibility for detailed feedback from industrial experts about the performance of their own industries also allows for the incorporation of much additional information that might not be easily included within the national accounts.

The disadvantages of disaggregation relate not only to the increase in the amount of data preparation and estimation required, but also to the fact that this involves pushing disaggregated analysis to the limits of the reliability of the data. A second main practical disadvantage of disaggreation is that it normally increases the number of exogenous inputs required to run the model. For example, if exports and imports are disaggregated in some detail then so must, to some extent, the exogenous projections of world prices in order to prove the disaggregated equations with values of the relative price variables which help to determine these trade flows. Not only are there difficulties in obtaining recent past estimates of these variables but also a greater degree of judgement must be exercised in projecting values for the future.

When developing a disaggregated model for medium-term analysis it is almost inevitable with presently available data that the model-builder should concentrate upon annual data. This means that the estimation of lag structures, which are usually difficult to identify properly, does not assume the importance applicable to short-run macroeconomic modelling. Nonetheless many important lag effects remain, for example in the determination of consumption, and do need to be modelled explicitly. A consequence of working with annual data is that the timing of policies and their effects will be less precise and residual adjustments to the early part of the projection period cannot be made as conveniently as in the case of short-run models. The results of a medium-term dynamic model are only generally indicative therefore of the profiles of economic change under alternative policies.

A consequence of attempting to model the development of the economy in the medium term is that certain types of estimated equation which appear to track short-term changes quite successfully begin to break down. The ubiquitous time trend is often at the root of the trouble, and when included in equations embodying simple autoregressive lags (for example the Koyck adjustment mechanism), forecasting can be more than usually hazardous. Moreover, whilst over the short term it may be reasonable to capture the growth of technical progress or even capital stock by such devices, this becomes increasingly unsatisfactory with the extension of the forecasting horizon.

The above comments apply with particular force to the projection of labour demand. Attempts to move closer to reality through the use of vintage production functions have yielded employment functions of the kind estimated by Wigley (1970) and Peterson (1976) in which employment is related to both output and the ratio of gross investment to output. These introduce the time trend implicity but at one remove from its direct inclusion in the neo-classical short-term employment function. In vintage models it proxies the pace of productivity growth associated with successive vintages of capital. At the same time these vintage employment functions are somewhat awkward to evaluate because their rationale is directed basically at the explanation of productivity changes abstracting from cyclical fluctuations. The typical short-term employment function on the contrary is clearly mainly designed to explain these cyclical fluctuations about some trend.

An alternative approach has been suggested by Hazledine (1978). In this model the adjustment of actual employment to short-run desired employment is distinguished explicitly from the adjustment of short-run desired employment to the "technically optimal" level of employment. With the capital stock available it is argued that there is some optimal level of output which it was designed to produce and associated with this output level is an optimal level of man-hours of labour input which maximises productivity and minimises labour costs (per man-hour). Should demand be such that firms wish to produce more or less than their capital was designed to produce then desired employment in the short-run will differ from the technical optimal. Moreover the firm has then to adjust to this desired level.

Wilson (1980) provided a detailed comparison of the Hazeldine approach with alternative models, including those discussed above, and this revealed that the Hazeldine model provides a better explanation of past changes in employment and, more importantly, would seem to provide the best <u>ex ante</u> forecasts of employment change. However, incorporating such equations within a macroeconomic forecasting model involves projecting optimal levels of output, employment and hours as well as defining the degree of technical optimality achieved in the future. This proved very problematic in the context of the dynamic version of the macroeconomic model and so a further development of the Hazledine approach has been adopted. This new model is a synthesis of the Hazledine and conventional short-term employment functions which replaces the time trend in the latter by an exogenously determined growth of optimal productivity. The latter is obtained by observation of the growth in productivity between peaks in the economic cycle in each industry. It therefore grows discontinuously and at different rates in each sector. This is combined with a conventional partial adjustment mechanism to take into account the cost to firms of adjusting employment towards the desired levels implied by the underlying changes in optimal productivity.

The use of the model for forecasting therefore requires an exogenous projection of the underlying growth in optimal productivity. Together with output levels, which are determined endogenously, this employment model generates a project of realised productivity growth. The model is applied to all the employing activities except for non-profit-making bodies and the public sector services. The treatment of these groups involves the estimation of a set of relatively straightforward expenditure-employment functions. Adjustments to the exogenous assumption about the underlying growth in optimal productivity provides the main means of characterising a scenario of accelerated technical change. The details of these adjustments are described in Section V.

Obviously the macroeconomic model does not explain every aspect of behaviour which affects the progress of the economy. Changes in the economy are viewed through changes in a large selection of economic variables. The model brings together the results of attempting to establish the relationships between these variables. However some are determined by what happens not just in the British economy but in many other economies (e.g. world commodity prices). Others are determined by complex social and political processes within the United Kingdom whose evolution economists cannot pretend to be able to forecast (e.g. government expenditure on health services; the structure of taxation). These two types of variables are treated exogenously. Exogenous variables can be classified into four main groups concerned with:

    i) the world environment;

    ii) public expenditure,

    iii) taxation and transfers of income, and

    iv) the labour market (including optimal productivity).

The main exogenous and endogenous variables are listed in Tables A2 and A3 in Appendix A.

V. THE BASE RUN SIMULATION: BACKGROUND ASSUMPTIONS

In order to quantify the economic impact of microelectronics a series of simulations were conducted using the macroeconomic model described above.

The starting point or base run simulation is a projection which is intended to characterise a likely outcome, with a large margin of error. This is based on our reading of the literature, including the results from the present OECD project, on the way in which microelectronics is likely to affect the economy compared to previous generations of technical change. Essentially this involves an assessment about how the various long-term trends embodied into the model will be affected by microelectronics and IT in general. It necessarily involves a considerable amount of judgement. However disagreement regarding the most likely outcome should have very little bearing on the results of the other simulations carried out around this base run.

The main assumptions underlying this base run are as described in Whitley and Wilson (1982). However, these have been revised in the light of more recent information including in particular other papers prepared as part of the present project. The nature of these assumptions is summarised in Table 1.

The first basic assumption is that in terms of its impact on the underlying trends in productivity growth (i.e. primarily the effect on process innovation) microelectronics will result in a return to the long-run trend rate of increase in productivity observed in the immediate post-war period. In certain industries, as indicated in the table, an acceleration relative to this trend is anticipated. This improvement in productivity growth is assumed to have further ramifications for investment, trade performance, etc., as outlined in Whitley and Wilson (1982). These are illustrated in Table 2.

The second basic assumption relates to the impact on demand for each sector's output other than effects arising from reductions in costs associated with productivity gains. Here it is product innovation that is the main focus. In the table the industries in which significant changes in products are likely to affect aggregate demand for their outputs are highlighted. The most obvious example here is the electronics industry (part of electrical engineering) where product innovation is expected to result in a shift in consumer, investment and intermediate demands towards this industry's output. This industry is not unique however and other sectors are also expected to benefit from favourable shifts in demand (e.g. communications and certain services). In contrast other sectors such as mechanical engineering are expected to suffer a loss of output relative to trend because of such shifts in the pattern of final demands.

For those industries where microelectronics is expected to result in a divergence from past trends, exogenous assumptions (such as optimal productivity), parameters (such as those in the export functions) and some endogenous variables (such as investment levels) have been adjusted for the base run, along the lines described in Whitley and Wilson (1982). These modifications are summarised in Table 2. In industries not specified in the table the rate of growth in optimal productivity is assumed to return to the long-run trend value. Other parameters are assumed to be maintained at the values observed for the post-war period. The precise values adopted for these assumptions are based on a review of the case study evidence from the present project and other studies. This information also provides the basis for the simulations conducted around the Base Run.

It is clear, from much of the case study evidence for manufacturing industries, that there are many exogenous factors operating which are likely

Table 1

IMPACT OF INFORMATION TECHNOLOGY RELATIVE TO TREND (a)

	Productivity Growth (b)	Product demand (c)
Agriculture		
Coal mining		
Oil & natural gas		
Mining nes		
Cereal processing		
Food processing n.e.s.	+	
Drink	+	
Tobacco		
Coke ovens		
Mineral oil refining		
Chemicals		
Iron & steel		
Non-ferrous metals		
Mechanical engineering	++	-
Instrument engineering	++	+
Electrical engineering	++	++
Shipbuilding		
Motor vehicles	++	+
Aerospace equipment	+	+
Vehicles n.e.s.	++	+
Metal goods	++	
Textile fibres	++	+
Textiles	+	+
Leather, clothing, etc.		+
Bricks		
Timber & furniture		
Paper & board	+	
Printing & publishing	++	+
Rubber	++	
Manufactures n.e.s.	++	+
Construction		
Gas		
Electricity		
Water		
Transport		
Communications	+++	++
Distribution	+	
Insurance	++	+
Professional services	++	+
Miscellaneous services	+	

a) Effects compared with trend rates of increase observed in the post-war period.
b) Labour productivity growth.
c) Consumer, investment and intermediate demand.

to continue to slow the rate of diffusion of IT, and thus moderate the size of any increase in productivity growth. This is especially true of the more extreme forms, such as the flexible manufacturing systems and the unmanned factories foreseen by some commentators. The factors slowing down the rate of diffusion include: problems of standardization, both in terms of hardware and software; the need for significant organisational and institutional change in order to facilitate the full-scale implementation of such systems; the need for substantial investments to be made in human capital, both in terms of conventional skills and the software itself; and finally, the sheer scale of the investment in physical capital required and the concommitant risks involved. All these problems are bound to take many years to overcome no matter how fast the hardware itself may be developed and the price of the chips themselves may continue to decline.

On the other hand it is apparent that in the engineering sector, and in manufacturing in general, IT will impinge on all aspects of the production process. In particular, and in contrast with the bulk of post-war experience, the processing and handling of information is likely to be affected at least as much as the processing and handling of materials. The importance of white collar employment within manufacturing is not generally appreciated. Over 30 per cent of employment in the United Kingdom engineering industry now falls into this category. Within the economy as a whole the share is even larger at almost 50 per cent. The potential impact of IT on office employment is very great. But again, problems of the kind already referred to seem likely to slow the rate of diffusion of the new technology and moderate its impact in employment. However, some acceleration in the underlying rate of productivity growth as a result of office mechanisation seems likely. On balance, the evidence suggests that in the immediate future IT is unlikely to result in a marked increase in productivity growth compared with the impact of the technological improvements observed over the post-war period as a whole, although some improvement in the rate of productivity growth observed since the mid-1970s seems likely.

Case studies of other manufacturing industries have reached broadly similar conclusions. The recent study by Northcott and Rogers (1984) provides a good overview of the current state of play as far as the application of microelectronics in both products and processes in United Kingdom manufacturing is concerned. Their overall assessment of the impact on employment for users of the technology suggests that the direct displacement effect between 1981 and 1983 amounted to only about half a per cent of United Kingdom manufacturing employment or 34 000 jobs, this during a period when employment as a whole in this sector fell by over 1.2 million. The change expected by respondents to the survey for the period 1983 to 1985, is even smaller. These estimates do not include indirect effects, particularly those on non-users, which may result from a failure to remain competitive. Equally however, these estimates cannot be regarded as a pure direct displacement effect, since employment losses may have been even greater had users not innovated, and thereby maintained their competitive positions.

In addition this estimate does not include the impact of IT on office employment within manufacturing. The definition of microelectronics used by Northcott and Rogers excludes the more general applications to information technology. Their use of the term is restricted to the use of microelectronics in products and its applications for the direct control of manufacturing process and materials handling generally. It does not encompass

Table 2

ASSUMED DIVERGENCE FROM TREND IN THE BASE RUN
SIMULATION IN 1995

	Optimal productivity (a)	Investment in plant and machinery (a)	Investment output ratio (a)	Export Elasticity of demand (a)	Import Share (a)
Agriculture	0.1	3	1	0.000	0.009
Coal mining	0.2	4	2	0.001	0.035
Oil & natural gas	-	-	-	-	-
Mining n.e.s.	0.4	2	3	0.001	0.038
Cereal processing	0.3	3	4	0.002	0.056
Food processing n.e.s.	5.3	72	49	0.024	0.742
Drink	5.5	51	34	0.048	0.505
Tobacco	0.5	1	7	0.002	0.109
Coke ovens	0.2	1	10	0.006	0.156
Mineral oil refining	0.5	4	4	0.003	0.058
Chemicals	0.5	18	3	0.001	0.043
Iron & steel	0.3	9	12	0.009	0.184
Non-ferrous metals	0.3	2	4	0.002	0.054
Mechanical engineering	5.4	101	28	0.025	0.427
Instrument engineering	5.5	15	28	0.012	0.414
Electrical engineering	5.4	83	25	0.019	0.375
Shipbuilding	0.2	1	2	0.001	0.030
Motor vehicles	5.3	98	29	0.016	0.433
Aerospace equipment	2.5	9	18	0.012	0.274
Vehicles n.e.s.	5.3	5	116	0.074	1.740
Metal goods	5.4	54	24	0.022	0.357
Textile fibres	5.2	17	39	0.014	0.590
Textiles	2.3	27	18	0.025	0.274
Leather, clothing, etc.	0.2	1	1	0.002	0.020
Bricks	0.3	4	3	0.002	0.041
Timber & furniture	0.3	1	2	0.001	0.032
Paper & board	5.3	24	15	0.009	0.220
Printing & publishing	5.5	58	44	0.028	0.662
Rubber	5.4	34	56	0.037	0.834
Manufactures n.e.s.	5.3	24	17	0.011	0.255
Construction	0.2	5	1	0.001	0.020
Gas	0.9	23	18	0.012	0.275
Electricity	0.6	46	12	0.008	0.181
Water	0.7	19	36	0.023	0.539
Transport	0.5	47	6	0.004	0.083
Communications	8.8	117	21	0.013	0.311
Distribution	3.5	54	6	0.004	0.086
Insurance	4.6	55	4	0.002	0.057
Professional services	4.2	44	20	0.013	0.301
Miscellaneous services	3.4	44	7	0.005	0.111

a) Percentage points.
b) £m 1970 prices.

the processing and handling of information. (Although in practice it is quite difficult to draw a clear dividing line between the former and the latter when one starts to consider the more sophisticated flexible manufacturing systems.) Northcott and Rogers do show however that the use of microelectronics, directly in products or in processes (47 per cent of United Kingdom factories in 1983) is not as widespread as the use of computers (66 per cent of factories), but is three times as common as the use of word processors. However recent evidence (see for example, IER, Review, 1985, Part 2) suggests that for the first time, the number of lower grade clerical jobs may be showing signs of declining in the United Kingdom. This occupational category was one of the fastest growing during the 1950s and 1960s. Between 1981 and 1984 the number of clerical jobs fell by 80 000, although this was a period when total employment fell by a third of a million.

Estimates of the impact of IT in offices, both within manufacturing and more generally in all other industries and services, are not so readily available. In general, while emphasizing the massive potential for the use of IT, most of the case studies have noted the importance of the types of factors already mentioned in slowing the diffusion and moderating the impact on employment of such technology. Barras (1984), in a paper prepared as part of the present project, emphasizes the relatively slow rate of development of the software (as opposed to the hardware) required for large-scale office automation, as well as lack of flexibility and difficulties of use which inhibit operational effectiveness. Organisational inertia, problems of standardization and the very rapid pace of change itself are other important factors. Another key point emphasized by Barras is the need for a massive investment in infrastructure before the full potential of IT can be achieved. The most important development will be the installation of national and international broad bank cable networks, offering interactive services to both domestic and business users. Such developments are likely to bring about dramatic potential savings in labour requirements per unit of output. However, savings in other inputs, including capital services, may be at least as great and there is no clear indication of a labour-saving bias. At the same time the reduction in costs and the new possibilities opened up by this development are likely to act as a catalyst for the development of many types of services, both to consumers and firms. The overall impact on employment is therefore very difficult to gauge. Barras argues however, that while in the short term the effect of process innovations is likely to dominate, and some job displacement may occur, in the longer term the labour-absorbing effects resulting from the development of new services will predominate. These phenomena are discussed in Section VII.

On the basis of this review, the industries where an acceleration in productivity growth, as a consequence of microelectronics, is expected are concentrated in the manufacturing sector and, (at least in terms of employment impact due to their large and growing share of total employment), the service sector. Within manufacturing, some of the largest effects are expected in engineering, but other manufacturing industries are expected to be affected by automation. The impact on the service sector is represented by effects in communications, distribution, insurance, banking and finance, professional services and miscellaneous services. Here, although the potential for use of electronically-based information system and mechanisation of some clerical and sales jobs is high, the direct displacement is expected to be rather modest. In insurance, banking and finance, for example, this new technology probably represents only a continuation of past trends experienced as a result of computerisation and any acceleration in the growth of output per person is therefore likely to be small. In distribution, many people are engaged in transportation activities which is is not so vulnerable to displacement. Further, many retailers are small businesses and any major impact is likely to occur only after a significant change in the structure of the industry which may take many years. Similar remarks apply to other industries such as miscellaneous services. An important point is that non-manual jobs (especially routine clerical work) may be affected within many non-services industries. In considering areas where an acceleration in productivity growth may occur the proportion of such jobs is therefore important. Particularly high employment shares are found in certain industries where bureaucracies have developed such as the public utilities. An additional element, representing a modest rise in the trend rate of increase in productivity for such work is therefore incorporated into Table 2, proportionate to the share of such jobs in total employment. This results in quite substantial effects in certain sectors such as those mentioned above.

If these productivity gains are to be achieved, an increase in investment in each of the industries concerned is assumed to be required. The size of this increase (shown in Table 2) is based on coefficients relating investment to improvements in productivity (5). The type of investment required is assumed to be primarily in new electrical and mechanical plant and machinery. In Table 2 substantial increases in investment are assumed for the mechanical and electrical engineering industries, textiles, rubber and manufactures n.e.s. in order to achieve these additional productivity improvements. The total increase in investment rises from £300 million (1970 prices) in 1986 to £1 180 million in 1995. In order to capture more fully the impact of a faster rate of technological change, it is assumed that the existing trend, whereby electrical engineering supplies more of plant and machinery investment, is increased by the order of 1 per cent per annum. Of course, not all of these investment goods will be supplied by domestic producers. This is discussed below.

Other components of domestic demand may also be affected. In particular, the composition of both consumption demand and intermediate demand (of one industry for another's output) is likely to change in favour of particular commodities (e.g. certain types of electrical goods as opposed to electro-mechanical ones). Examination of such effects however suggests that the effect on consumption is not very significant compared with the effects of changes in investment, whilst information on the effect on intermediate demands is very difficult to acquire. However, some changes along these lines are incorporated.

More sophisticated technology embodied in new investment may improve non-price competitiveness in international trade as the extra investment is assumed to be of higher quality and therefore enables potential exporters to compete in more income-elastic world markets. Whitley et al (1980) reported some evidence of a relationship between investment-output ratios and export demand elasticities using international cross-section data, finding a unit elasticity between differences in investment-output ratios and differences in export demand elasticities (6). Applying such an elasticity to the changes in investment-output ratios in Table 2 would imply some very large increases in export demand elasticities. Instead we have assumed that this unit elasticity only applies at the margin in the sense that only demand for new products becomes more income-elastic. On the rather crude assumption that new products will represent some 10 per cent of the total trade market, we obtain the increases in export demand elasticities shown in Table 2 (7).

The potential import response to faster technological change embodied in new investment is more contentious. We have not found the same degree of empirical support for relationships between import demand elasticities and investment-output ratios as for exports. The elasticity we obtain here is 0.15 and we have used this, not to adjust the demand elasticity as we have done for exports, but to reduce the import share <u>ex ante</u>. These adjustments are shown in Table 2. It should be noted however, that these adjustments do not imply that the <u>ex post</u> level or share of imports will necessarily be lower under the simulation of more rapid technological change.

Some specific adjustments to imports have also been made to allow for domestic producers being unable to supply the same proportion of the new investment goods as they have on average in the past. The bulk of the extra investment is supplied by the mechanical and electrical engineering industries and we assume that the proportion of the extra investment coming from imports will be 60 per cent in 1986 falling to 40 per cent in 1995 for mechanical engineering, compared with an average share of some 31 per cent in the benchmark simulation. For electrical engineering, we assume that the marginal share is 80 per cent in 1986, declining to 50 per cent in 1995 -- as against an average underlying share of 39 per cent in the benchmark simulation.

Obviously, even with the very detailed macroeconomic model at our disposal, it is not possible to capture every aspect of the impact of microelectronics. A particularly important aspect which comes across from much of the case study work is the capital savings effects of IT. This is very difficult to quantify and to build into the model given available evidence and no attempt is made to allow for it here. This could have both positive and negative effects on the final outcome as far as employment is concerned. On the one hand, if one of the effects of microelectronics is to reduce the size of the necessary capital input, then the positive impact on demand through additional investment in new capital equipment may be less than we have assumed. On the other hand, the effects on capital productivity may be such as to reverse the historical rise in capital-output ratios. This in turn may ease the capital constraint that some regard as being of particular importance at the current time (see Patel and Soete). Employment prospects may thereby be improved by the introduction of IT easing any capital constraint on job creation.

VI. THE BASE RUN SIMULATION: RESULTS

We begin by describing a projection for the United Kingdom economy over the period 1985-1995 which is intended to provide the basic reference point for all the other simulations. It should be stressed that this is only intended to represent a probable outcome of the effects of IT (with a large margin of error), for a particular economy. Nevertheless it is hoped that the simulations around this base view will result in more general insights applicable to all OECD countries.

The main features of the base run simulation are summarised in

Table 3 (8). In this view United Kingdom GDP is expected to grow by about 2 per cent per annum from 1985 to 1995. This is approximately equal to its long run trend rate of increase as observed in the 1950s and 1960s. The contributions of the main components of aggregate demand to the growth of GDP are also shown in Table 5. Exports are projected to provide the most buoyant elements of demand, with average growth between 1985 and 1995 of 6 per cent per annum. However the trend towards an increasingly open economy, that has been observed in the United Kingdom for many years, is expected to continue and imports are projected to grow at a similar rate. Consumers' expenditure grows at a rate of 1.7 per cent per annum, roughly matching the rise in real disposable income. Gross fixed capital formation, stockbuilding and general government final consumption are all expected to rise between 1985 and 1995, but by less than the rate of increase in GDP.

Productivity growth is expected to be around 2 per cent per annum (as measured by GDP per person). Again this is very much in line with post-war trends. In conjunction with the projected rise in GDP this implies very little change in the level of employment. Unemployment is not therefore expected to fall significantly by 1995, increasing up to the end of the 1980s, before falling again at the beginning of the next decade. On average however it remains stuck at a level of 3 to 3.5 million (about 12 per cent of the labour force). Wage inflation is expected to remain around 6 per cent per annum over the projection period, while consumer prices grow by somewhat less. Real personal disposable income rises by about 1.6 per cent per annum. One of the basic assumptions underlying the base view is a steady depreciaton in the exchange rate of the pound against the dollar. Despite this the balance of payments falls into deficit in the 1990s. A major factor here of course is the run down of North Sea oil production.

Three main factors account for the relatively pessimistic outlook as far as employment is concerned. Firstly, world economic recovery from the recession of the late 1970s and early 1980s is not expected to result in a rapid return to the rates of growth experienced in the 1950s and 1960s. Secondly, domestic policy within the United Kingdom is expected to remain relatively restrictive in the light of the present government's stance towards controlling public expenditure. Thirdly, despite some improvements in competitiveness and the assumed continued depreciation of the pound against the dollar, net trade remains a comparatively restrictive component of aggregate demand.

Essentially in the base run simulation therefore we are projecting that the United Kingdom economy will develop along similar lines to those observed over the post-war period as a whole. Certain underlying trends are expected to "bend", for example the underlying growth rate of optimal productivity in particular sectors as noted in Table 2. The overall impression however is of a continuation of past trends, but with the economy having slipped down to a growth path below, but roughly parallel to, the earlier post-war growth path. It is important to stress however, that this projection is not based upon a simple extrapolation of past trends and patterns of behaviour. It is the result of various assumed deviations from trend in particular industries, as outlined in Section V. These, in combination, result in the projection discussed here.

Turning to the results in greater detail, these are summarised in Table 4. One of the main features of the projection, as far as employment is

Table 3

THE BASE RUN SIMULATION: MACROECONOMIC SUMMARY

per cent per annum (a)

Historical and Projected Macroeconomic Variables, Changes and Levels

	1975-1980	1980-1985	1985-1990	1990-1995	1985-1995
GDP and its components					
GDP at market prices (b)	1.7	1.4	1.8	2.0	1.9
Consumers' expenditure	2.1	1.8	1.6	1.8	1.7
General gov't final consumption	1.2	0.5	1.0	1.0	1.0
Gross fixed capital formation	0.6	2.3	1.7	2.0	1.9
Exports of goods and services	4.4	2.2	6.0	6.2	6.1
Imports of goods and services	4.3	4.1	5.0	5.3	5.2
Labour market, prices and incomes					
Labour force: millions	26.8	26.9	27.2	27.1	27.2
Employment: % p.a.	-0.3	-1.1	0.1	0.4	0.2
millions	25.0	24.0	24.0	24.3	24.2
Registered unemployment: millions	1.4	2.9	3.4	3.0	3.2
% (c)	5.2	12.0	13.7	10.1	11.9
Average earnings	15.0	8.8	6.1	6.8	6.5
Consumer prices	13.8	7.2	5.1	4.8	5.0
Real personal disposable income	2.3	1.5	1.5	1.6	1.6
GDP/person	2.0	2.5	1.8	1.9	1.9
Balance of payments and public sector finance					
Dollar exchange rate	0.9	-10.1	4.3	4.0	4.1
Balance of payments: % of GDP	0.2	1.5	0.2	-0.5	-0.2
PSBR: % of GDP	5.7	3.8	2.0	0.5	1.3

a) Average annual percentage changes. Exceptions to this are labour force, employment and registered unemployment, PSBR and balance of payments, where the figures are average levels over the period.
b) Output measure.
c) Percentage of employees in employment plus unemployed.

195

concerned, is the continued decline in primary and manufacturing industries despite quite substantial output growth. In these sectors productivity advances continue to offset any rise in output. Agriculture and mining are together projected to lose over 200 000 jobs by 1995. Within manufacturing, employment is expected to continue its long-run trend decline in most sectors. Productivity gains are quite rapid in many industries compared with long-run trends. Nevertheless, despite the beneficial effects this has on the United Kingdom's international competitiveness, the consequent growth in demand for domestic output is insufficient to prevent a fall in employment. One hundred thousand jobs are projected to go in food, drink and tobacco. In engineering as a whole, over 450 000 jobs are projected to be lost between 1985 and 1995, of which more than 150 000 are in mechanical engineering. Textiles and clothing are also expected to see a continuation of the decline in both output and employment levels observed in recent years. In contrast, employment in certain service industries is projected to increase as a consequence of strong output growth coupled with relatively modest increases in productivity. Professional and business services and miscellaneous services fall into this category, with over a million and a half jobs being created in these two sectors between 1985 and 1995. Other more mature service industries, such as transport, communications and distribution, as well as the public utilities are expected to experience changes more like those in the manufacturing sector, with productivity gains largely offsetting any growth in output levels, and total employment in these three sectors showing only a very slight increase over the projection period. Finally the public sector, in contrast to the experience of the 1950s, 1960s and 1970s, is not expected to provide any significant employment growth over the 1985 to 1995 period, given current government plans. In the United Kingdom, this latter sector includes the vast bulk of both education and health services which are of course provided by the State.

It is important to note that these kind of structural changes in employment have been a feature of the United Kingdom economy (and others) for many years. This is illustrated in Table 5. From this it is clear that the shift in employment from primary and manufacturing industries to the tertiary sector is very much a continuation of past developments, rather than being particularly associated with microelectronics or information technology. Some indication of the impact of IT at the macroeconomic level can be obtained by considering the effect of the adjustments summarised in Table 2 on the projection. This is done in Tables 6 and 7, which show the effects of the adjustments in the Base Run simulation.

Within the model, optimal productivity represents an average productivity figure for all firms within an industry. It is not a measure of "best practice", but an indicator of maximum productivity, given full capacity utilisation. A speed up in the rate of diffusion of IT can therefore be regarded as being characterised by a situation in which optimal productivity more closely approaches some notional "best practice" level. Actual or realised productivity will still tend to lag behind optimal productivity because of adjustment lags and failure to fully utilise existing capacity. This acceleration in the rate of diffusion of IT is assumed to affect both manufacturing industries and service industries as described in Table 2.

The macroeconomic impacts of these changes are summarised in Table 6. Information is also provided in the table of how the overall effect can be split up into various components related to particular aspects of the

Table 4

OUTPUT, EMPLOYMENT AND PRODUCTIVITY IN GREATER DETAIL, 1985-1995

per cent per annum

Employing Activity	Output	Growth, 1985-1995 Productivity	Employment	Net change in employment 1985-1995
Agriculture	1.5	3.7	-2.3	-126
Mining	-1.2	2.9	-4.0	-103
Food, drink and tobacco	1.5	3.2	-1.7	-96
Chemicals	3.3	4.3	-0.8	-32
Metals	2.0	3.8	-1.8	-44
Engineering	1.7	3.6	-1.8	-467
of which:				
Mechanical engineering	1.0	3.3	-2.4	-166
Electrical engineering	3.6	5.0	-1.4	-90
Motor vehicles	-0.2	2.5	-2.8	-76
Textiles and clothing	-0.9	3.0	-4.2	-205
Other manufacturing	2.3	2.9	-0.4	-44
Construction	1.5	1.0	0.6	91
Public utilities	2.1	4.4	-2.4	-71
Transport and communications	3.9	3.3	0.4	53
Distribution	2.3	2.0	0.2	85
Professional services	3.7	1.5	2.4	669
Miscellaneous services	2.8	0.5	2.3	904
Manufacturing	2.0	3.7	-1.7	-887
Services	3.1	1.9	1.5	1 713
Public services	-	-	-0.0	-10
Whole economy	2.4	2.3	0.2	604

Table 5

EMPLOYMENT BY BROAD INDUSTRY SECTOR 1954-1995

	\multicolumn{7}{c}{Share of total employment (%)}
	1954	1975	1980	1985	1990	1995	
Primary	8.7	4.0	4.0	3.6	3.1	2.6	
Manufacturing	33.9	30.2	27.5	23.5	21.4	19.3	
Construction and public utilities	7.8	8.2	8.2	7.6	7.5	7.5	
Transport, communication and distribution	19.7	19.1	19.2	20.7	20.8	20.8	
Professional and miscellaneous services	12.4	17.0	19.6	23.0	25.8	28.8	
Total	82.5	78.5	78.5	78.4	78.6	79.0	
Social services and public administration	17.5	21.5	21.5	21.6	21.3	21.0	
Whole economy	100.0	100.0	100.0	100.0	100.0	100.0	

	\multicolumn{5}{c}{Net change in employment (000s)}
	1954-75	1975-80	1980-85	1985-90	1990-95	1985-95
Primary	-1 085	1	-152	-120	-109	-229
Manufacturing	-505	659	-1 306	-484	-403	-887
Construction and public utilities	200	-6	-249	-4	24	20
Transport, communication and distribution	104	57	114	58	80	138
Professional and miscellaneous services	1 320	674	567	702	871	1 573
Total	33	68	-1 026	150	463	615
Social services and public administration	1 211	35	-256	-48	38	-10
Whole economy	1 244	104	-1 284	102	502	604

simulation. Column 1 of the table shows the effects of changing the assumed growth rate of optimal productivity without making any other changes. This therefore represents a situation in which the beneficial productivity effects of the new technology falls like "manna from heaven". It also posits that these innovations have no non-price effects on trade performance. These additional considerations are taken into account in column 2 which allows for the fact that any productivity gains achieved will almost certainly require prior capital investment in new equipment, and that such investments, and their concomitant productivity increases, will probably lead to improvements in non-price competitiveness. Column 3 of the table indicates the importance of responses in wages for these results.

The effect of increasing optimal productivity is to raise GDP in 1995 by about 0.5 per cent. The main mechanism by which this is achieved is through the impact of improvements in actual productivity on wage costs and hence international competitiveness. Both wages and domestic prices are reduced by about 4.5 per cent by 1995. As a consequence exports are increased by over 2 per cent. Despite some increase in imports, as a result of the generally higher level of economic activity, the balance of payments improves by around half a per cent of GDP. The overall impact of employment however is negative, the beneficial effects on output being insufficient to offset the initial displacement effects on employment of the productivity gains.

Allowing for the fact that such productivity gains are unlikely to be achieved without cost changes this picture significantly. The implied increases in investment necessary to achieve these productivity gains provide a significant, albeit incomplete, offset to the initial displacement effects (this after allowing for the fact that a much larger proportion than normal of this investment is likely to come from overseas). These beneficial effects are reinforced in column 2 of the table, when the additional beneficial effects of the productivity gains on non-price competitiveness are allowed for. In total the combined effects result in an increase in GDP of just under 2 per cent by 1995. This remains insufficient to offset the initial displacement effect however, so that employment is lower than in the Base Run by about 300 000.

These results are broadly in line with those presented in Whitley and Wilson (1982). The overall impact of IT by 1990 was estimated there to be a net positive employment effect of plus 0.3 per cent compared with the negative impact in the present results. The main reasons for this difference are:

i) revisions to the initial displacement effects assumed (in particular the inclusion of estimated impacts on office based services in all sectors, and in the public sector in particular) in the present analysis; and

ii) the fact that the compensating adjustments to trade performance and investment demands are much less significant for many of the additional sectors considered here, which were not covered in the earlier analysis (again the public sector is the main culprit).

The detailed implications for different industries are summarised in Table 7. This is based on the full simulation, with endogenous wages, as given in column 2 of Table 6. A number of points are apparent from these results. The beneficial employment effects of additional investment demands

Table 6

DIFFERENCES IN THE BASE RUN SIMULATION IN 1995 COMPARED WITH
A PROJECTION INCLUDING NO ADJUSTMENTS TO ACCOUNT FOR THE
IMPACT OF IT

Per cent (a)

Differences attributable to:

	Productivity adjustments (1)	All adjustments connected with the impact of IT (2)	As(2) but holding wages fixed (3)
GDP and its components			
GDP at market prices (b)	0.5	1.9	1.8
Consumers' expenditure	-0.6	1.7	2.2
General gov't final consumption	-	-	-
Gross fixed capital formation	0.0	9.9	10.1
Exports of goods and services	2.1	2.1	1.4
Imports of goods and services	0.6	3.2	3.1
Labour market, prices and incomes			
Employment: %	-2.4	-1.2	-1.3
000s	-568	-288	-314
Registered unemployment: 000s	353	180	268
% (c)	1.2	0.6	0.9
Average earnings	-4.7	-3.3	-
Consumer prices	-4.5	-4.0	-1.9
Real personal disposable income	-1.4	1.6	2.5
GDP/person	2.8	3.1	3.1
Balance of payments and public sector finance			
Dollar exchange rate	-	-	-
Balance of payments: % of GDP	0.5	-1.1	-1.4
PSBR: % of GDP	0.1	-0.1	1.0

a) Percentage differences from a projection with no IT adjustments. Exceptions to this are labour force, employment and registered unemployment expressed as differences in thousands, and the balance of payments and PSBR, which are expressed as a percentage of GDP.
b) Output measure.
c) Percentage of employees in employment plus unemployed.
d) Details of the assumptions are given in the text.

Table 7

OUTPUT, EMPLOYMENT AND PRODUCTIVITY IN GREATER DETAIL:
EFFECTS OF THE IT ADJUSTMENTS

Employing Activity	Difference from a projection excluding IT adjustments, 1995 (%)			Difference in Employment 1995 (000s)
	Output	Productivity	Employment	
Agriculture	1.1	1.2	-0.1	-0.4
Mining	1.9	2.0	-0.2	-0.4
Food, drink and tobacco	0.4	3.7	-3.3	-20.5
Chemicals	0.6	0.6	-0.0	-0.1
Metals	2.5	1.5	1.0	2.6
Engineering	3.8	6.0	-2.3	-61.4
of which:				
Mechanical engineering	4.6	4.5	0.2	2.7
Electrical engineering	6.2	6.8	-0.5	-3.6
Motor vehicles	1.0	3.9	-3.0	-8.3
Textiles and clothing	2.4	3.5	-1.3	-8.2
Other manufacturing	2.6	5.6	-3.1	-39.5
Construction	1.6	0.6	0.9	17.2
Public utilities	1.4	1.3	0.0	0.1
Transport and communications	1.8	2.2	-0.5	-10.0
Distribution	2.4	4.3	-1.9	-40.3
Professional services	2.7	3.7	-0.9	-30.7
Miscellaneous services	2.6	1.1	1.3	47.1
Manufacturing	2.3	4.5	-2.2	-126.9
Services	2.5	2.7	-0.2	-33.9
Public services	-	-	-2.6	-144.0
Whole economy	2.4	3.2	-1.2	-288.3

make themselves felt in certain manufacturing industries such as electrical and, to a lesser extent, mechanical engineering. Output in the former increases by over 6 per cent, although productivity growth is even faster, leaving employment slightly reduced. Other industries which are assumed to be investing in the new technology also see increases in output, especially those subject to fierce international competition, such as textiles and clothing. Overall however the increases in output are insufficient to offset the rise in productivity and employment falls. In manufacturing as a whole over 125 000 jobs are lost. One reason for this is that the service sector, and public services in particular, experience significant job losses as a direct result of the impact of IT. <u>Ceteris paribus</u> this reduces incomes and depresses aggregate demands below what they would have been. The job losses of the public sector are especially significant since, because its output is not traded, there are no compensatory factors to offset the direct displacement effects on employment. Almost 150 000 jobs are lost here. One of the few bright spots, as far as employment is concerned, is in miscellaneous services, where output rises as a result of increases in aggregate consumption. This leads to an additional 50 000 jobs.

The importance of flexibility in wages is illustrated in column 3. In the previously discussed simulations wages are determined endogenously. The results in column 3 demonstrate the effects of rigid wages which do not respond to the changed economic environment. In the previous simulations wages respond to the fall in prices resulting from the productivity gains. Together these result in a significant improvement in competitiveness which raises exports and hence domestic output and employment. Thus although there is not a direct link within the model between employment and wages, the latter do have an impact on the former via the mechanism described. However, if wages do not respond, the impact on the economy as a whole is not that different in aggregate from the case when they are flexible. This is because the deleterious impact on competitiveness and trade performance is, to a large degree, offset by the beneficial impact that higher wages have on incomes and aggregate demand. This is simply a demonstration of the well-known argument about the effects of wage cuts on employment. On the one hand, a reduction in average wages reduces employers costs and encourages expansion of output and hence employment. On the other hand, the reduction in wages reduces incomes of those in employment and thereby their demands for goods and services, which then depresses output and employment levels.

These estimates may undervalue the importance of wage flexibility in achieving a return to full employment following job displacing technical change. To the extent that the labour market clears in response to any exogenous shock that increases unemployment, then lower real wages may result. This may then, in turn, increase labour demand, thus offsetting some of the negative employment effect observed. However, the magnitude of this effect depends on responsiveness of wages to excess supply in the labour market as well as upon the size of the impact of real wages directly on labour demand. In the model used here there is no such direct effect, although an increasing body of evidence suggests some non-zero influence of real wages on labour demand at the aggregate level. For these reasons the estimates discussed above may understate the role of wage flexibility in generating some compensating employment gain. On the other hand the size of understatement is not likely to be great, given existing empirical evidence on labour market adjustment processes.

A related problem is that the indirect responses that do exist within the model which link wages to employment and vice versa are based on the experience of the United Kingdom during the 1950s, 1960s and 1970s. There is some evidence of greater downward flexibility of real wages for the United Kingdom in recent years. Furthermore wages in other countries may be more flexible than in the United Kingdom case. If wages were to fall by more than prices, in response to an increase in unemployment, then this could result in increased demand for labour. However, the point made above with regard to the negative effect of wage reductions on the incomes of those in employment and thereby their demand for goods and services, still holds true.

The simulations described here assume that the exchange rate is held at its base run levels by an appropriate monetary policy. This partly reflects a dissatisfaction with empirical models of exchange rate behaviour. Earlier results with a version of the model which incorporated an exchange rate equation suggest that a 10 per cent permanent reduction in the exchange rate will raise employment by around 100 000 jobs after two years and 70 000 jobs after five years, most of the impact being felt in the manufacturing sector. Given the impact of the full set of IT adjustments on the balance of payments (Table 6, column 2), some depreciation in the exchange rate of aobut this order of magnitude would be likely and this offsetting beneficial impact on output and employment would therefore be unlikely to substantially alter the main conclusions about the overall effects of IT.

Before discussing the other simulations some further general comments should be made regarding the results presented here. The approach has been to take an existing model of the United Kingdom economy and apply it to the problem of quantifying the impact of IT. The United Kingdom economy, like any other has its own peculiarities. Over the post war period as a whole the United Kingdom has performed relatively badly, although this situation may have altered in recent years. One should therefore be cautious in attempting to generalise from the results obtained for the United Kingdom to the OECD economies as a whole. Nevertheless the general methodological approach should be of a more general applicability.

A second point is that all empirical models depend to some extent on historical analysis. The key question is the extent to which historical behaviour is likely to be repeated. This analysis has attempted to identify some of the key relationships which might be expected to alter given the scenario of technical change envisaged. Inevitably however there are many other relationships which are assumed here to remain unaltered that may in practice change significantly. It is to be hoped that the present analysis will provide a useful point of departure for those interested in considering the implications of more radical changes than it has been possible to accommodate with the present framework.

Finally, although the macroeconomic model used is almost certainly the best vehicle for analysing questions of technological change in the United Kingdom economy, inevitably any one empirical model is unlikely to encompass all possible views about the way that economy functions. In particular in the present model the role of expectations is largely ignored (as is the general interaction between real and financial variables, although there is a wealth effect on savings and consumption). To the extent that these omissions are regarded as important, the analysis may be deficient. It is worth noting that the only model of the United Kingdom which does include these influences is the Liverpool one, but this model is market clearing by construction rather than based on empirical evidence, and in any case is not in a form which would enable it to be used for analysing questions of the kind addressed here.

VII. ALTERNATIVE SIMULATIONS

Two alternative simulations have been conducted around the base run to highlight different aspects of the possible effects of IT on a typical economy. These simulations are as follows:

Simulation 1: A general speed up in the rate of diffusion of IT in the Manufacturing Sector

This simulation is characterised by a faster increase in optimal productivity in manufacturing industries as a result of an increase in the rate of diffusion of microelectronic based technologies. The accelerated rate of diffusion is assumed to affect investment, trade performance, etc., in an analogous manner to that described in the main simulation, except that here we concentrate upon the manufacturing sector alone. Details of the assumptions are given in Table 8.

The macroeconomic effects of these assumptions are summarised in Table 9. The improvements in international competitiveness and the increase in investment together result in a significant boost to the economy, with GDP rising by 2.5 per cent. Consumers' demand increases by a similar factor, and this (together with the assumed rise in import shares for new investment), draws in more imports, which rise by over 4 per cent. Consequently, the balance of payments deteriorates slightly. In the absence of significant job displacement effects in other industries, especially in the service sector, a "virtuous circle" is engendered, with multiplier effects benefitting many industries outside manufacturing. Employment is increased by 280 000 in total.

The effects on individual industries are shown in Table 10. Output in the engineering sector increases by almost 6 per cent as a result of higher export and investment demand. Output is also boosted in many other sectors which are assumed to benefit from investment in the new technology. These are especially marked in industries such as textiles and clothing which face strong competition from overseas. Despite increases in productivity averaging over 3 per cent in manufacturing, employment rises in all industries. Sectors such as construction, public utilities and transport and communication, all benefit as a result of the general rise in aggregate demand. Employment increases in the distribution, professional and business, and miscellaneous services are the main sources of extra jobs however. Together these three sectors account for over 150 000 additional jobs. This of course is in the assumed absence of any direct effects of IT on these industries. It is therefore a somewhat artificial result. It does demonstrate very clearly however the potentially beneficial impact upon employment that a speed-up in the rate of diffusion of technological change in manufacturing could have ceteris paribus. The effects of IT on the service sector directly are considered in the next simulation.

Simulation 2: A faster rate of diffusion within the Service Sector

The main objective of this simulation is to characterise the effects of IT on office based services generally, and on the service sector as a whole, as a result of a substantial investment in infrastructure, concentrated in the field of communications. This is intended to complement the previous simulation where the emphasis was on product and process innovation in the production of goods in the manufacturing sector. The main feature of this second simulation therefore is a £5 000 million (in current prices) investment in cabling and associated capital equipment. This is concentrated in the communications industry but impinges directly on other industries (instrument and electrical engineering in particular) as major suppliers of such hardware. This investment in infrastructure is associated with productivity improvements in the communications industry itself, as well as those industries which are major users of the new technology.

Gershuny (1984), amongst others, has emphasized that the future for employment in services depends crucially on high technology innovations in service provision and product innovation. These he argues are likely to take the form of the development of an information infrastructure involving the growth of new markets for self-servicing. The latter is likely to include new markets for computer and communications related hardware as well as markets for software. In Gershuny's view the latter is particularly important. It is important to stress that his definition of software is much broader than simply computer programmes. It includes all kinds of stored intermediate services with which service consumers can interact through computing and telecommunications equipment. Through these means a much larger range of services, which are currently provided directly to consumers, such as education, medical advice and myriad others, can be provided indirectly in an analagous fashion to the manner in which the services of actors and musicians have increasingly been made available in the form of records and videos. It is also interesting to note that the change in the mode of provision of the latter type of services did not, as might have been feared, lead to any reduction in the demand for the more direct mode of provision. On the contrary the numbers of actors and musicians have been stimulated by the growth of the recording and film industries.

It is very problematic to know how to reflect the difficult to predict but highly probable product innovations in this area. Adjustments have been made to consumers' and intermediate demands to reflect the new products and services that are likely to emerge. These adjustments allow for changes in the shares of consumer and intermediate demands impinging on different industries. They do not encompass any absolute increase in the level of these demands compared to the Base Run. However they do also require the purchase of various physical products, by consumers and others, to take advantage of these new services. This implies additional demands on parts of the manufacturing sector, as suppliers of such hardware and other products. The details of the changes in the exogenous assumptions relating to optimal productivity, investment, etc., are shown in Table 11.

The macroeconomic impacts of these changes are summarised in Table 9. While the detailed industrial results are given in Table 12. There is a dramatic contrast with the results of the manufacturing simulation. The productivity gains in service industries, as a result of the assumed acceleration in the rate of diffusion of IT, lead to a large loss of jobs.

Table 8

ASSUMED DIVERGENCE FROM TREND IN THE BASE RUN: SIMULATION 1 (MANUFACTURING) 1995

	Optimal productivity (a)	Investment in plant and machinery (a)	Investment /output ratio (a)	Export elasticity of demand (a)	Import share (a)
Agriculture	0	0	0	0	0
Coal mining	0	0	0	0	0
Oil & natural gas	0	0	0	0	0
Mining n.e.s.	0	0	0	0	0
Cereal processing	0	0	0	0	0
Food processing n.e.s.	5	68	47	0.022	0.700
Drink	5	47	31	0.044	0.459
Tobacco	0	0	0	0	0
Coke ovens	0	0	0	0	0
Mineral oil refining	0	0	0	0	0
Chemicals	0	0	0	0	0
Iron & steel	0	0	0	0	0
Non-ferrous metals	0	0	0	0	0
Mechanical engineering	5	93	26	0.023	0.395
Instrument engineering	5	14	25	0.010	0.376
Electrical engineering	5	76	23	0.018	0.348
Shipbuilding	0	0	0	0	0
Motor vehicles	5	93	27	0.015	0.409
Aerospace equipment	2	7	15	0.009	0.219
Vehicles n.e.s.	5	4	109	0.070	1.641
Metal goods	5	50	22	0.020	0.330
Textile fibres	5	17	38	0.013	0.567
Textiles	2	24	16	0.021	0.238
Leather, clothing, etc.	0	0	0	0	0
Bricks	0	0	0	0	0
Timber & furniture	0	0	0	0	0
Paper & board	5	23	14	0.009	0.207
Printing & publishing	5	53	40	0.025	0.602
Rubber	5	32	51	0.034	0.772
Manufactures n.e.s.	5	23	16	0.010	0.241
Construction	0	0	0	0	0
Gas	0	0	0	0	0
Electricity	0	0	0	0	0
Water	0	0	0	0	0
Transport	0	0	0	0	0
Communications	0	0	0	0	0
Distribution	0	0	0	0	0
Insurance	0	0	0	0	0
Professional services	0	0	0	0	0
Miscellaneous services	0	0	0	0	0

a) Percentage points.
b) £m 1970 prices.

Table 9

DIFFERENCES FROM THE BASE RUN SIMULATION IN 1995

Per cent (a)

	Differences from the Base Run	
	Manufacturing simulation	Services simulation
GDP and its components		
GDP at market prices (b)	2.5	-0.6
Consumers' expenditure	2.3	-0.6
General gov't final consumption	-	-
Gross fixed capital formation	7.0	2.9
Exports of goods and services	2.8	-0.7
Imports of goods and services	4.1	-1.1
Labour market, prices and incomes		
Employment: %	1.1	-2.5
000s	281.0	-521.0
Registered unemployment: 000s	-178.0	360.0
% (c)	-0.6	1.2
Average earnings	-0.7	-2.6
Consumer prices	-1.5	-2.5
Real personal disposable income	3.0	-1.4
GDP/person	1.3	1.8
Balance of payments and public sector finance		
Dollar exchange rate	-	-
Balance of payments: % of GDP	-1.1	0.1
PSBR: % of GDP	-0.2	0.5

a) Percentage differences from the Base Run. Exceptions to this are labour force, employment and registered unemployment expressed in thousands and the balance of payments and PSBR are expressed as differences as a percentage share of GDP.
b) Output measure.
c) Percentage of employees in employment plus unemployed.

Table 10

OUTPUT, EMPLOYMENT AND PRODUCTIVITY IN GREATER DETAIL:
MANUFACTURING SIMULATION
Percentages

Employing Activity	Difference from Base in 1995			Difference in Employment 1995 (000s)
	Output	Productivity	Employment	
Agriculture	1.3	1.3	0.0	0.1
Mining	2.7	1.5	1.2	3.2
Food, drink and tobacco	1.8	1.8	0.0	0.2
Chemicals	1.8	1.4	0.4	1.6
Metals	3.0	2.8	0.3	0.7
Engineering	5.7	5.0	0.8	16.6
of which:				
Mechanical engineering	5.0	4.4	0.6	5.5
Electrical engineering	6.2	5.4	0.9	6.6
Motor vehicles	3.3	2.9	0.5	1.2
Textiles and clothing	5.1	3.1	2.1	13.1
Other manufacturing	4.9	4.1	0.8	10.2
Construction	4.2	1.4	2.8	48.9
Public utilities	2.0	1.6	0.4	1.2
Transport and communications	2.5	1.5	1.0	15.2
Distribution	3.0	1.4	1.6	54.0
Professional services	3.0	1.5	1.5	37.5
Miscellaneous services	3.0	0.9	2.1	77.4
Manufacturing	3.9	3.1	0.8	42.4
Services	2.7	1.1	1.7	171.1
Public services	-	-	-	-
Whole economy	3.2	1.7	1.5	281.6

Table 11

ASSUMED DIVERGENCE FROM BASE RUN:
SIMULATION 2 (SERVICES) -- 1995

	Optimal productivity (a)	Investment in plant and machinery (b)	Investment /output ratio (a)	Export elasticity of demand (a)	Import share (a)
Agriculture	0.1	3	1	0.000	0.009
Coal mining	0.2	4	2	0.001	0.035
Oil & natural gas	-	-	-	-	-
Mining n.e.s.	0.4	2	3	0.001	0.038
Cereal processing	0.3	3	4	0.002	0.056
Food processing n.e.s.	0.3	4	3	0.001	0.042
Drink	0.5	5	3	0.004	0.046
Tobacco	0.5	1	7	0.002	0.109
Coke ovens	0.2	1	10	0.006	0.156
Mineral oil refining	0.5	4	4	0.003	0.058
Chemicals	0.5	18	3	0.001	0.043
Iron & steel	0.3	9	12	0.009	0.184
Non-ferrous metals	0.3	2	4	0.002	0.054
Mechanical engineering	0.4	7	2	0.002	0.032
Instrument engineering	0.5	1	3	0.001	0.038
Electrical engineering	0.4	6	2	0.001	0.028
Shipbuilding	0.2	1	2	0.001	0.030
Motor vehicles	0.3	6	2	0.001	0.025
Aerospace equipment	0.5	2	4	0.002	0.055
Vehicles n.e.s.	0.3	0	7	0.004	0.098
Metal goods	0.4	4	2	0.002	0.026
Textile fibres	0.2	1	2	0.001	0.023
Textiles	0.3	4	2	0.003	0.036
Leather, clothing, etc.	0.2	1	1	0.002	0.020
Bricks	0.3	4	3	0.002	0.041
Timber & furniture	0.3	1	2	0.001	0.032
Paper & board	0.3	1	1	0.001	0.012
Printing & publishing	0.5	5	4	0.003	0.060
Rubber	0.4	3	4	0.003	0.062
Manufactures n.e.s.	0.3	1	1	0.001	0.014
Construction	0.2	5	1	0.001	0.020
Gas	0.9	23	18	0.012	0.275
Electricity	0.6	46	12	0.008	0.181
Water	0.7	19	36	0.023	0.539
Transport	0.5	47	6	0.004	0.083
Communications	8.8	117	21	0.013	0.311
Distribution	3.5	54	6	0.004	0.086
Insurance	4.6	55	4	0.002	0.057
Professional services	4.2	44	20	0.013	0.301
Miscellaneous services	3.4	44	7	0.005	0.111

a) Percentage points.
b) £m 1970 prices.

Table 12

OUTPUT, EMPLOYMENT AND PRODUCTIVITY IN GREATER DETAIL:
SERVICES SIMULATION

Employing Activity	Difference from Base in 1995			Difference in Employment 1995 (000s)
	Output	Per cent Productivity	Employment	
Agriculture	-0.2	-0.1	-0.1	-0.3
Mining	-0.7	0.5	-1.3	-3.2
Food, drink and tobacco	-1.3	1.8	-3.2	-19.3
Chemicals	-1.2	0.4	-1.6	-6.0
Metals	-0.5	-0.3	-0.2	-0.6
Engineering	-1.9	1.0	-2.8	-66.3
of which:				
Mechanical engineering	-0.4	0.9	-1.3	-8.5
Electrical engineering	0.1	1.4	-1.5	-11.3
Motor vehicles	-2.3	1.0	-3.4	-10.4
Textiles and clothing	-2.7	0.4	-3.0	-20.3
Other manufacturing	-2.2	1.4	-3.6	-45.6
Construction	-2.6	-0.8	-1.8	-31.1
Public utilities	-0.7	-0.3	-0.3	-0.9
Transport and communications	-0.7	0.7	-1.5	-24.8
Distribution	-0.6	2.8	-3.4	-93.2
Professional services	-0.3	2.2	-2.5	-72.4
Miscellaneous services	-0.4	0.2	-0.6	-28.7
Manufacturing	-1.6	1.4	-2.9	-158.5
Services	-0.4	1.4	-1.9	-220.1
Public services	-	-	-	-144.0
Whole economy	-1.1	1.5	-2.5	-521.0

210

GDP is reduced by about 0.6 per cent, despite the overall rise in productivity of 1.8 per cent. The reasons for this appear to be:

   i) the initial displacement effects on employment are very large, mainly due to the fact that so many jobs are at risk, both in the service sector and in office based services in other sectors;

  ii) that there are only relatively modest offsets due to investment compared with the manufacturing simulation;

 iii) the fact that much of the impact falls on non-traded services and there is therefore no gain in international competitiveness as in the manufacturing case; and

  iv) that the simulation does not make any allowance for significant changes in the level of aggregate demands for any new services that may emerge as a result of product innovation connected to the so called IT revolution.

As a result of these factors the economy is shocked downwards by the effects of the productivity gains in services. The direct impact on the service industries, and on office based services in other sectors, reduces employment and therefore incomes very sharply. This leads to a general reduction in activity levels. Output is reduced in all sectors but is greater than average in certain manufacturing industries such as textiles and clothing and other manufacturing. Other industries, especially those within engineering do relatively well since they are suppliers of hardware (e.g. electrical engineering). Despite this, employment falls in these industries, albeit by less than the 2.9 per cent decline in manufacturing as a whole. A large part of the total reduction of employment of over 500 000 comes in non-traded services such as the public sector, accounting for 144 000 jobs. Distribution, and professional and business and miscellaneous services, large parts of which are are not traded internationally, account for a further 200 000 jobs.

CONCLUSIONS

This chapter has attempted to demonstrate some of the macroeconomic implications of new information technologies based in particular upon microelectronics. The methodology adopted has been to use a multisectoral macroeconomic model of the United Kingdom economy. The main problem that has been addressed is the way in which information technologies, and microelectronics in particular, are likely to alter the future growth path of a typical developed economy. It is apparent from much of the case study evidence on the impact in individual industries that information technology will to a large degree represent a continuation of many past trends in the development of such economies. The labour saving nature of the technology, and the changes in demand patterns (both final and intermediate) all represent the continuation of well-established patterns of change. It is also clear however that IT may also, in several respects, represent a revolutionary change compared with past experience. This is especially true of its potential effects in the provision of services. Even in its more conventional implications for productivity and flexibility in the production of physical commodities however, it may well result in a number of well-established trends "bending". The Base Run Simulation discussed in this paper attempts to encapsulate some of the more quantifiable ways in which such trends may alter. These include trends in the growth of labour productivity, trends in trade performance and so on.

The results of this simulation suggest that the overall impact of IT compared with past technological developments may be quite modest compared with the doom-laden scenarios painted by some commentators. The detailed analysis of this projection shows that conventional compensation effects, working through the impact of productivity gains on prices, are insufficient to offset the direct displacement effects on employment. Making allowance for the likely effects on non-price competitiveness and for the additional investment that would be necessary to achieve such productivity gains, lead to further compensatory effects on employment. The overall impact remains negative however, with a reduction in employment by 1995 of just over 1 per cent attributable to IT.

An analysis of the effects of a speed-up in the rate of diffusion of IT, firstly in manufacturing industries, and secondly in services generally, throws some further light on how its effects vary between industries. The simulation dealing with the manufacturing sector demonstrates the importance of beneficial effects such as improved international competitiveness and demand for capital equipment and other durables. These offsets to the initial displacement effect are especially important in industries such as electrical engineering. In the absence of job displacement effects in services, the simulation suggests that these factors would result in a virtuous circle with multiplier effects on other industries resulting in a net increase in employment of about 1 per cent.

The services simulation demonstrates quite clearly that the main threat to employment lies in the application of microelectronic technology in services generally (including office based services in other industries). In the absence of any dramatic product innovation in this area which might act so as to expand the overall level of aggregate demand, this simulation suggests that IT in the service sector could result in substantial job loss by 1995. The overall macroeconomic effect of IT in the service sector is estimated to be a job loss of 2.5 per cent after 10 years.

The main thrust of these results is that a very substantial growth in the provision of new service functions based on IT is necessary if unemployment levels in the United Kingdom are to be substantially reduced. This suggests that as far as policy-makers are concerned the main implications are: firstly, the need to encourage new ideas and firms to flourish, especially those based on information; and secondly, (and related to the first point), the need to ensure the right kind of investment in infrastructure to encourage such developments. As Barras and Gershuny have both noted, this latter point means, not simply the need for cabling on a grand scale, but cabling of the correct nature, which is as flexible in operation as possible.

Finally, and on a more negative note, it is important to stress the limitations of the type of analysis presented here. Ideally one would like to endogenise changes in technology and tastes (which are of course not independent). In the analysis presented here, such changes have been modelled by introducing various adjustments to "bend" historical trends and behavioural relationships embedded in the model, based upon the evidence from case studies. In the present state of knowledge, regarding the causes of technological change and changes in tastes, and in particular the absence of any satisfactory models to explain product innovation, such an approach seems to make the most of the available information.

NOTES AND REFERENCES

1. Of this, as much as 2 per cent per annum may be attributable to technological progress, although this is subject to debate.

2. The fact that this has occurred in the past does not of course imply that such compensation is automatic.

3. Process innovations may be more important in other industries which use the products of the engineering sector, e.g. textiles and printing.

4. We would like to express our thanks to the Cambridge Growth Project in general, and to Terence Barker and William Peterson in particular, for their help and advice in setting up this model at Warwick. However, we would emphasize that not only has the model been changed in several important respects but that the Cambridge Growth Project is not to be held responsible for our use of the model and for any of the results presented here.

5. See Whitley, Wilson and Smith (1980) for details.

6. For further evidence on such links see Landesmann (1984).

7. The export and import effects are assumed to lag one year behind the originating increase in investment-output ratios.

8. The results in this and other tables should be regarded as no more precise than the general statements in the text.

Appendix

Table A.1

CLASSIFICATION OF INDUSTRY GROUPS

Industry Group	1968 ISIC
1. Agriculture	001-003
2. Mining	
2.1 Coal mining	101
2.2 Oil and natural gas	104
2.3 Mining n.e.s.	102-3, 109
3. Food, drink and tobacco	
3.1 Cereal processing	211-3, 219
3.2 Food processing n.e.s.	214-229 (except 219) and 232
3.3 Drink	231-9
3.4 Tobacco manufacture	240
4. Chemicals	
4.1 Coke ovens	261
4.2 Mineral oil refining	262-3
4.3 Chemicals	271-9
5. Metals	
5.1 Iron and steel	311-3
5.2 Non-ferrous metals	321-3
6. Engineering	
6.1 Mechanical engineering	331-349
6.2 Instrument engineering	351-354
6.3 Electrical engineering	361-9
6.4 Shipbuilding, etc.	370
6.5 Motor vehicles	380-1
6.6 Aerospace equipment	383
6.7 Vehicles n.e.s.	382, 384, 385
6.8 Metal goods n.e.s.	390-9
7. Textiles and clothing	
7.1 Textile fibres	411
7.2 Textiles n.e.s.	412-429
7.3 Leather, clothing, etc.	431-3, 441-50
8. Other manufacturing	
8.1 Bricks, etc.	461-9
8.2 Timber and furniture	471-9
8.3 Paper and board	481
8.4 Printing and publishing	482-9
8.5 Rubber	491
8.6 Manufactures n.e.s.	492-9
9. Construction	500
10. Public utilities	
10.1 Gas	601
10.2 Electricity	602
10.3 Water	603

11. Transport and communication
    11.1 Transport   701-7, 709
    11.2 Communication   708
12. Distribution   810-832
13. Professional services
    13.1 Insurance, etc.   860-866
    13.2 Professional services   871, 873, 876, 879
14. Miscellaneous services   881-889, 892-9
15. Social services
    15.1 National Health Service   )
    15.2 Private health   ) 874
    15.3 Public education   )
    15.4 Private education   ) 872
    15.5 Religious organisations   875
    15.6 Private domestic service   891
16. Public administration
    16.1 Defence   901 (part)
    16.2 Other central government   901 (remainder)
    16.3 Other local government   906

Table A.2

MAJOR EXOGENOUS VARIABLES

1. Government current expenditure -- 5 categories
2. Government capital expenditure -- 5 categories
3. Investment by nationalised industries
4. Government employment -- 5 categories
5. Employment by non-profit-making bodies and domestic service
6. Total labour supply
7. Total number self-employed
8. Number employed in HM armed forces
9. Wage differentials by industry (40 categories)
10. Normal hours worked by industry (40 categories)
11. Exogenous productivity changes (40 categories)
12. Total population, United Kingdom
13. Export prices of competitors
14. Import prices in foreign currencies (57 categories)
15. Import tariffs (57 categories)
16. World production by area (10 categories)
17. Direct imports by consumers, industry and government
18. Exogenous imports, e.g. coal, gas, electricity, etc.
19. Exogenous exports, e.g. natural oil, gems, etc.
20. North Sea oil and gas production
21. North Sea oil tax allowance
22. Petroleum revenue tax
23. Royalty tax on North Sea oil and gas production
24. Foreign tourists' expenditure
25. Direct income tax rates (standard and other rates)
26. Corporation tax
27. Direct tax allowances -- personal
28. Investment incentives -- building and works
29. Investment incentives -- plant, machinery and vehicles
30. National Insurance contributions
31. Rate contributions
32. Specific tax duties -- consumers and industries
33. Ad valorem tax duties -- consumers and industries
34. VAT -- standard and differential rates
35. Subsidies -- consumers and industries
36. Current transfers by government to persons
37. Current transfers by government abroad
38. Private transfers
39. Rent and property income of local authorities and public corporations
40. Capital transfers
41. Net lending

217

Table A.3

MAJOR ENDOGENOUS VARIABLES (1)

1. Consumers' expenditure (42 commodities)
2. Exports of goods (by 20 areas and 16 commodities)
3. Industry outputs (40 industries) -- gross and net
4. Gross investment (3 assets and 40 industries)
5. Stockbuilding
6. Employment (40 industries plus 9 other activities including government)
7. Employment -- whole economy
8. Unemployment -- whole economy
9. Industry taxes -- (40 industries and 6 categories of tax)
10. Imports (57 commodities)
11. Industrial demands for commodities (40 industries)
12. Total incomes by institutional sector (28 incomes, 7 institutional sectors)
13. Total expenditure by institutional sectors (23 expenditures, 7 institutional sectors)
14. Value of industrial inputs (40 industries, 9 inputs)
15. Industry prices and average wage bills (40 industries)
16. Export and import prices
17. Commodity demands and supplies (57 commodities)
18. Gross domestic product and its main components
19. The balance of trade
20. Personal disposable income
21. Average wage
22. Exchange rate
23. Interest rate

1) This list of endogenous variables is not exhaustive.

BIBLIOGRAPHY

Arnold. "The Impact of Office Automation Skills", in N. Swords-Isherwood and P. Senker (eds.), Chapter 16, 1980.

Association of Professional Executive, Clerical Computer Staff (APEX), "Word Processing Working Party, First Report", Office Technology, The Trade Union Response, APEX, London, 1979.

Association of Scientific, Technical, and Managerial Staffs (ASTMS), Technological Change and Collective Bargaining, ASTMS, London, 1979.

Barker T.S. (ed.), Economic Structure and Policy, Cambridge Studies in Applied Econometrics 2, Chapman and Hall, London, 1976.

Barker T.S. "Projecting Economic Structure with a Large-Scale Econometric Model", Futures, 13, no. 6, 1981, pp.458-467.

Barker T.S., Borooah V., van der Ploeg R. and Winters A., "The Cambridge Multisectoral Dynamic Model: An Instrument for National Economic Policy Analysis, Journal of Policy Modelling, 2, no. 3, 1980, pp.319-344.

Barras R., "Information Technology and Economic Perspectives: The Case of Office Based Services", Paper prepared for the DSTI/ICCP Workshop, OECD, Paris, 27th-28th June, 1984.

Barron I. and Curnow R., The Future with Microelectronics: Forecasting the Effects of Information Technology, Frances Pinter, London, 1979.

Beenstock M., "Do UK Labour Markets Work", Economic Outlook, June/July, 1979, pp.21-31.

Freeman C., "Technical Change and Unemployment", Paper presented to Conference on "Science Technology and Public Policy: An International Perspective", University of New South Wales, 1st-2nd December 1977, 1978a.

Freeman C., Technical Change and Employment", Six Countries Programme on Aspects of Government Policies Towards Technological Innovation in Industry, 1978b, (mimeographed).

Gershuny J.I. (1984), "The Future of Service Employment", IIM Berlin, Working Paper IIM/LMP 84-7.

Green K., Coombs R. and Holroyd K., The Effects of Micro-electronic Technologies on Employment Prospects: A Case Study of Tameside, Tameside Metropolitan Borough Council, Gower Publishing Company, Westmead, England, 1980.

Hazledine T., "New Specifications for Employment and Hours Functions", Economica, 45, May 1978, pp.179-193.

Hunt H.A. and Hunt T.L., Human Resource Implications of Robotics, W.E. Upjohn Institute for Employment Research, Kalamazoo, 1982.

Institute for Employment Research, Review of the Economy and Employment, Institute for Employment Research, University of Warwick, 1985.

Jenkins C. and Sherman B., The Collapse of Work, Eyre Methuen, London, 1979.

Johns B.L., "The Economics of New Technology", Bureau of Industry Economics, ACT, Canberra, Working Paper 6, 1979 (mimeographed).

Landesmann M. "Relative Competitive Performance and Market Share Determination", Cambridge Growth Project Paper GPP 565, 1984 (mimeographed).

Lindley R.M. (ed.), Economic Change and Employment Policy, MacMillan, London 1980.

Malinvaud E., The Theory of Unemployment Reconsidered, Basil Blackwell, Oxford, 1977.

Northcott J. and Rogers P., Microelectronics in British Industry: The Pattern of Change, Policy Studies Institute, London, 1984.

Peterson W., "Employment", Economic Structure and Policy, T.S. Barker (ed.), Chapman and Hall, London, 1976, pp.177-193.

Rush H. and Hoffman K., "Microelectronics and the Clothing Industry", Paper prepared for the DSTI/ICCP Workshop, OECD, Paris, 27th-28th June 1984.

Senker P., Swords-Isherwood N. and Arnold E., Skill Requirements Arising from Microelectronics, in N. Swords-Isherwood and P. Senker (eds.), Chapter 17, 1980.

Sleigh J., Boatwright B., Irwin P., and Stanyon R., The Manpower Implications of Microelectronic Technology, HMSO, London, 1979.

Swords-Isherwood N. and Senker P. (eds.), Micro-electronics and the Engineering Industry: The Need for Skills, Frances Pinter, London, 1980.

Whitley J.D., Wilson R.A. and Smith D.J.E., Industrial and Occupational Change, Chapter 4, Lindley R.M. (ed.), 1980, pp.68-140.

Whitley J.D., Wilson R.A., "Quantifying the Employment Effects of Micro-electronics", Futures, Vol.14, No. 6, 1982, pp.486-495.

Wigley K.J., "Production Models and Time Trends of Input-Output Coefficients", Input-Output in the United Kingdom, E.F. Gossling (ed.), Frank Cass, London, 1970, pp.89-118.

Wilson R.A., "Comparative Forecasting Performance of Disaggregated Employment Models", Applied Economics, 12, No. 1, 1980, pp.85-101.

ANNEX

LIST OF CASE STUDIES*

1. Information Technology in the Engineering Industry
   by R.A. Wilson (United Kingdom) -- Summary ....

2. Microelectronics in the Clothing Industry
   by Howard Rush and Kurt Hoffman (United Kingdom) -- Summary.

3. Automation of Services: The Case of the Banking Sector
   by Pascal Petit (France) ....

   Summary ....

   Introduction ....

   I. Automation and Employment: A Wider Issue in Services than Industry ....
   II. Production and Productivity in the Banking Section: What Measures and Why? ....
   III. Automation Strategies ....
   IV. Towards a Micro-Economic Identification of the Determinants of Employment in the Banking Sector ..
   V. General Perspectives of the Movement of Automation in Banking Services ....

   Notes and References ....
   Bibliography ....

4. The Case of Office Based Services
   by Richard Barras (United Kingdom) -- Summary ....

---

*   Available upon request from the OECD Secretariat.

OECD SALES AGENTS
DÉPOSITAIRES DES PUBLICATIONS DE L'OCDE

ARGENTINA - ARGENTINE
Carlos Hirsch S.R.L.,
Florida 165, 4° Piso,
(Galeria Guemes) 1333 Buenos Aires
Tel. 33.1787.2391 y 30.7122

AUSTRALIA-AUSTRALIE
D.A. Book (Aust.) Pty. Ltd.
11-13 Station Street (P.O. Box 163)
Mitcham, Vic. 3132   Tel. (03) 873 4411

AUSTRIA - AUTRICHE
OECD Publications and Information Centre,
4 Simrockstrasse,
5300 Bonn (Germany)   Tel. (0228) 21.60.45
Local Agent:
Gerold & Co., Graben 31, Wien 1 Tel. 52.22.35

BELGIUM - BELGIQUE
Jean de Lannoy, Service Publications OCDE,
avenue du Roi 202
B-1060 Bruxelles   Tel. (02) 538.51.69

CANADA
Renouf Publishing Company Ltd/
Éditions Renouf Ltée,
1294 Algoma Road, Ottawa, Ont. K1B 3W8
Tel: (613) 741-4333
Toll Free/Sans Frais:
Ontario, Quebec, Maritimes:
1-800-267-1805
Western Canada, Newfoundland:
1-800-267-1826
Stores/Magasins:
61 rue Sparks St., Ottawa, Ont. K1P 5A6
Tel: (613) 238-8985
211 rue Yonge St., Toronto, Ont. M5B 1M4
Tel: (416) 363-3171
Sales Office/Bureau des Ventes:
7575 Trans Canada Hwy, Suite 305,
St. Laurent, Quebec H4T 1V6
Tel: (514) 335-9274

DENMARK - DANEMARK
Munksgaard Export and Subscription Service
35, Nørre Søgade, DK-1370 København K
Tel. +45.1.12.85.70

FINLAND - FINLANDE
Akateeminen Kirjakauppa,
Keskuskatu 1, 00100 Helsinki 10 Tel. 0.12141

FRANCE
OCDE/OECD
Mail Orders/Commandes par correspondance :
2, rue André-Pascal,
75775 Paris Cedex 16
Tel. (1) 45.24.82.00
Bookshop/Librairie : 33, rue Octave-Feuillet
75016 Paris
Tel. (1) 45.24.81.67 or/ou (1) 45.24.81.81
Principal correspondant :
Librairie de l'Université,
12a, rue Nazareth,
13602 Aix-en-Provence   Tel. 42.26.18.08

GERMANY - ALLEMAGNE
OECD Publications and Information Centre,
4 Simrockstrasse,
5300 Bonn   Tel. (0228) 21.60.45

GREECE - GRÈCE
Librairie Kauffmann,
28, rue du Stade, 105 64 Athens Tel. 322.21.60

HONG KONG
Government Information Services,
Publications (Sales) Office,
Beaconsfield House, 4/F.,
Queen's Road Central

ICELAND - ISLANDE
Snæbjörn Jónsson & Co., h.f.,
Hafnarstræti 4 & 9,
P.O.B. 1131 - Reykjavik
Tel. 13133/14281/11936

INDIA - INDE
Oxford Book and Stationery Co.,
Scindia House, New Delhi 1   Tel. 45896
17 Park St., Calcutta 700016   Tel. 240832

INDONESIA - INDONÉSIE
Pdii-Lipi, P.O. Box 3065/JKT.Jakarta
Tel. 583467

IRELAND - IRLANDE
TDC Publishers - Library Suppliers,
12 North Frederick Street, Dublin 1.
Tel. 744835-749677

ITALY - ITALIE
Libreria Commissionaria Sansoni,
Via Lamarmora 45, 50121 Firenze
Tel. 579751/584468
Via Bartolini 29, 20155 Milano   Tel. 365083
Sub-depositari :
Editrice e Libreria Herder,
Piazza Montecitorio 120, 00186 Roma
Tel. 6794628
Libreria Hœpli,
Via Hœpli 5, 20121 Milano   Tel. 865446
Libreria Scientifica
Dott. Lucio de Biasio "Aeiou"
Via Meravigli 16, 20123 Milano   Tel. 807679
Libreria Lattes,
Via Garibaldi 3, 10122 Torino   Tel. 519274
La diffusione delle edizioni OCSE è inoltre
assicurata dalle migliori librerie nelle città più
importanti.

JAPAN - JAPON
OECD Publications and Information Centre,
Landic Akasaka Bldg., 2-3-4 Akasaka,
Minato-ku, Tokyo 107   Tel. 586.2016

KOREA - CORÉE
Kyobo Book Centre Co. Ltd.
P.O.Box: Kwang Hwa Moon 1658,
Seoul   Tel. (REP) 730.78.91

LEBANON - LIBAN
Documenta Scientifica/Redico,
Edison Building, Bliss St.,
P.O.B. 5641, Beirut   Tel. 354429-344425

MALAYSIA - MALAISIE
University of Malaya Co-operative Bookshop
Ltd.,
P.O.Box 1127, Jalan Pantai Baru,
Kuala Lumpur   Tel. 577701/577072

NETHERLANDS - PAYS-BAS
Staatsuitgeverij
Chr. Plantijnstraat, 2 Postbus 20014
2500 EA S-Gravenhage   Tel. 070-789911
Voor bestellingen: Tel. 070-789880

NEW ZEALAND - NOUVELLE-ZÉLANDE
Government Printing Office Bookshops:
Auckland: Retail Bookshop, 25 Rutland Street,
Mail Orders, 85 Beach Road
Private Bag C.P.O.
Hamilton: Retail: Ward Street,
Mail Orders, P.O. Box 857
Wellington: Retail, Mulgrave Street, (Head
Office)
Cubacade World Trade Centre,
Mail Orders, Private Bag
Christchurch: Retail, 159 Hereford Street,
Mail Orders, Private Bag
Dunedin: Retail, Princes Street,
Mail Orders, P.O. Box 1104

NORWAY - NORVÈGE
Tanum-Karl Johan
Karl Johans gate 43, Oslo 1
PB 1177 Sentrum, 0107 Oslo 1Tel. (02) 42.93.10

PAKISTAN
Mirza Book Agency
65 Shahrah Quaid-E-Azam, Lahore 3 Tel. 66839

PORTUGAL
Livraria Portugal,
Rua do Carmo 70-74, 1117 Lisboa Codex.
Tel. 360582/3

SINGAPORE - SINGAPOUR
Information Publications Pte Ltd
Pei-Fu Industrial Building,
24 New Industrial Road No. 02-06
Singapore 1953   Tel. 2831786, 2831798

SPAIN - ESPAGNE
Mundi-Prensa Libros, S.A.,
Castelló 37. Apartado 1223, Madrid-28001
Tel. 431.33.99
Libreria Bosch, Ronda Universidad 11,
Barcelona 7   Tel. 317.53.08/317.53.58

SWEDEN - SUÈDE
AB CE Fritzes Kungl. Hovbokhandel,
Box 16356, S 103 27 STH,
Regeringsgatan 12,
DS Stockholm   Tel. (08) 23.89.00
Subscription Agency/Abonnements:
Wennergren-Williams AB,
Box 30004, S104 25 Stockholm.
Tel. (08)54.12.00

SWITZERLAND - SUISSE
OECD Publications and Information Centre,
4 Simrockstrasse,
5300 Bonn (Germany)   Tel. (0228) 21.60.45
Local Agent:
Librairie Payot,
6 rue Grenus, 1211 Genève 11
Tel. (022) 31.89.50

TAIWAN - FORMOSE
Good Faith Worldwide Int'l Co., Ltd.
9th floor, No. 118, Sec.2
Chung Hsiao E. Road
Taipei   Tel. 391.7396/391.7397

THAILAND - THAILANDE
Suksit Siam Co., Ltd.,
1715 Rama IV Rd.,
Samyam Bangkok 5   Tel. 2511630

TURKEY - TURQUIE
Kültur Yayinlari Is-Türk Ltd. Sti.
Atatürk Bulvari No: 191/Kat. 21
Kavaklidere/Ankara   Tel. 25.07.60
Dolmabahce Cad. No: 29
Besiktas/Istanbul   Tel. 160.71.88

UNITED KINGDOM - ROYAUME-UNI
H.M. Stationery Office,
Postal orders only:
P.O.B. 276, London SW8 5DT
Telephone orders: (01) 622.3316, or
Personal callers:
49 High Holborn, London WC1V 6HB
Branches at: Belfast, Birmingham,
Bristol, Edinburgh, Manchester

UNITED STATES - ÉTATS-UNIS
OECD Publications and Information Centre,
2001 L Street, N.W., Suite 700,
Washington, D.C. 20036 - 4095
Tel. (202) 785.6323

VENEZUELA
Libreria del Este,
Avda F. Miranda 52, Aptdo. 60337,
Edificio Galipan, Caracas 106
Tel. 32.23.01/33.26.04/31.58.38

YUGOSLAVIA - YOUGOSLAVIE
Jugoslovenska Knjiga, Knez Mihajlova 2,
P.O.B. 36, Beograd   Tel. 621.992

Orders and inquiries from countries where Sales
Agents have not yet been appointed should be sent
to:
OECD, Publications Service, Sales and
Distribution Division, 2, rue André-Pascal, 75775
PARIS CEDEX 16.

Les commandes provenant de pays où l'OCDE n'a
pas encore désigné de dépositaire peuvent être
adressées à :
OCDE, Service des Publications. Division des
Ventes et Distribution. 2. rue André-Pascal. 75775
PARIS CEDEX 16.

70595-03-1987

OECD PUBLICATIONS, 2, rue André-Pascal, 75775 PARIS CEDEX 16 - No. 43963 1987
PRINTED IN FRANCE
(93 87 01 1) ISBN 92-64-12927-8